SKIP
NOVAK
ON SAILING

'Skip Novak takes us to the high seas providing technical wisdom, wonderful adventure stories, appreciation of nature and a philosophical narrative about the special joys of visiting remote regions. Novak's writing is easy to read and his prose makes you feel like you are on board with him on his voyages. This extraordinary collection of articles is an important treasure for every sailor's library.'

Gary Jobson, editor-at-large of Sailing World *and* Cruising World, *former President of US Sailing*

'In all of maritime history, there is no one like Skip Novak. In more than 50 years of nonstop ocean racing and high latitude voyaging, he has surely sailed more miles than any mariner living or dead. Skip's writing is like the man: disarmingly modest, wryly funny; written from an unrivalled empirical knowledge not only of the sea and sailing, but also of the literature of the sea. Stories you might have heard if you'd been lucky enough to meet Captain Cook in a pub.'

Peter Nichols, author of Sea Change, *and* A Voyage for Madmen

'Skip Novak is the ultimate sailing adventurer – a modern day Magellan, an Obi-Wan Kenobi/Dumbledore-like character whose opinions, wisdom and insights will glow like flaming coals in the imagination of any sailor. Perusing this compendium is like being given a key to the ultimate hall of sailing knowledge – with deep links to centuries of nautical tradition with a modern day twist – the world where Skip sails.'

Peter Isler, Chairman of American Sailing, navigator of the winning yacht in two America's Cups, author of Sailing for Dummies

SKIP NOVAK
ON SAILING

WORDS OF WISDOM FROM 50 YEARS AFLOAT

WITH A FOREWORD BY
SIR ROBIN KNOX-JOHNSTON

ILLUSTRATED BY DAVIDE BESANA

ADLARD COLES

LONDON · OXFORD · NEW YORK · NEW DELHI · SYDNEY

ADLARD COLES
Bloomsbury Publishing Plc
50 Bedford Square, London, WC1B 3DP, UK
29 Earlsfort Terrace, Dublin 2, Ireland

BLOOMSBURY, ADLARD COLES and the Adlard Coles logo are trademarks of
Bloomsbury Publishing Plc

First published in Great Britain 2024

These columns were originally published in *Yachting World* magazine between
2014 and 2023

Extract from *N by E* by Rockwell Kent on page 6 reproduced with permission of
Wesleyan University Press

A catalogue record for this book is available from the British Library

Library of Congress Cataloguing-in-Publication data has been applied for

ISBN: PB: 978-1-3994-1474-6; ePub: 978-1-3994-1475-3; ePDF: 978-1-3994-1476-0

2 4 6 8 10 9 7 5 3 1

Typeset in Brother 1816 by Deanta Global Publishing Services, Chennai, India
Printed and bound in Great Britain by CPI

To find out more about our authors and books visit www.bloomsbury.com
and sign up for our newsletters

For Lara and Luca, who have turned out to be great shipmates

'And if an author in recording what has interested himself differs from editors – so everlastingly concerned with what may interest others, he may no less, knowing himself the only worthwhile thing for him to be, hope that a hundred thousand souls will see him as the mirror of themselves – and buy his book.'

Rockwell Kent
N by E

CONTENTS

FOREWORD

BY SIR ROBIN KNOX-JOHNSTON

Skip and I first met during the 1977/8 Whitbread Race around the World. Skip was navigating a Swan 65 *King's Legend* and I was skippering the 77 foot long *Condor* for the second and fourth legs. Inevitably we were rivals, but as I had the longer boat, I was the faster. So we achieved Line Honours on those two legs but did not win on handicap. During the second leg I can remember the report from *King's Legend* that their rudder post had shifted and they were taking on water, but the crew managed to control the ingress and finished safely, if somewhat delayed.

Skip went on to complete four further Whitbread Races including skippering *Drum*, owned by Simon Le Bon, and a rather weird Russian entry in the following race where he held the crew together. During this time he built up a vast experience of crew management and sailing in the Roaring Forties and the Screaming Fifties of the Southern Ocean where you can be a thousand miles from any land or assistance if you have a problem. You had to be self-sufficient in those days before satellites when navigation was by sextant and chronometer, just as Cook had used 200 years before. If something went wrong you had to deal with it yourselves as there was no immediate satellite contact to attract assistance in an emergency.

The Southern Ocean is the extreme classroom for sailing and seamanship and Skip earned a Double First. But he had been seduced by the Antarctic and in 1987 he built *Pelagic* and started adventure sailing to the most isolated continent on the planet. This is where we met again when we sailed *Pelagic* through the Beagle Channel and around Cape Horn when we were filming the *3 Dogs* programme with Sir Ranulph Fiennes and John Simpson. It may have been run of the mill to Skip after so many years sailing around the great Cape, but it was exciting for me after sailing past and never seeing what lay behind Cape Horn. It was a wonderful trip, even if the wind seldom descended below 30 knots. It was a great adventure for me, and gave me a huge respect for Skip's ability.

Seamanship is not just about using the sails to make a boat move, nor is it just about how the boat is handled in a variety of conditions, calms, storms, or manoeuvring in tight places. Seamanship is about the knowledge of the boat itself, how it works and how to deal with repairs and the almost certain emergencies that will happen on a long voyage far from assistance. Skip is sharing his vast experience in this book. Yes, seamanship is learned through your hands, but you can learn much from reading the views and experience of those who have spent so many years at sea.

INTRODUCTION

Over eight and a half years I have been filing what has resulted in 101 column pieces for *Yachting World* magazine. When roping me in, the editor said, 'Write whatever you want.' I proceeded to weigh in on many subjects, all things marine, gathered from over 60 years of a nautical life that began while sailing dinghies age seven in a yacht club in Chicago and then graduating into a 'Harbor Rat' with my mates during our long American high school summers.

On the strength and inspiration of reading Conrad, Melville, Hemingway, Stevenson and others in that genre of high adventure to distant lands, I left the Midwest as soon as I could 'fly' and fetched up on the west coast of Florida, struggling to finish a university degree while working as a rigger in a boatyard. I first tasted salt water on an ocean race from Miami to Montego Bay, Jamaica, aged 18 and then on a Transatlantic Race from Bermuda to Spain when I was 20, when I learned celestial navigation en route from our indulgent navigator.

These early deep water experiences stood me in good stead with what was to come. I was otherwise 'at sea' in terms of a career path, confused and conflicted within the zeitgeist of a post-Vietnam War world and chaos of the social upheaval of the early seventies. With poor steerage I took a path that was ordained and just kept sailing, living for many years out of a seabag, able to make a decision to up and go within minutes for the next ocean race, the next delivery, the next voyage to anywhere. To wit, I was clueless about how to go about building a future, pushed only by wind and tide from place to place – and I loved every day of it.

In 1976 at the age of 24 I skippered the German Admiral's Cup yacht *Pinta* on a delivery from Bermuda (we had just competed in the Onion Patch Series) to Brittany and then made my way to the Solent for Cowes Week. I put an anchor down in the Hamble River that has not dragged nor been raised since. Only eight months later, after a 10-minute conversation with the skipper in the Fountain Hotel in Cowes, I landed a berth on the British Cutter *King's Legend* and navigated her to a second place in the 1977/78 Whitbread Race. In succession three more Whitbread Races would follow as skipper – *Alaska Eagle* in 1981, Simon Le Bon's *Drum* in 1985/86 and the Soviet entry *Fazisi* in 1989/90. My ocean racing career culminated in a final circumnavigation on the 110-foot Maxi multihull *Innovation Explorer* in 'The Race' in 2001, 64 days non-stop around the world.

In parallel with all the sea miles I launched a quasi-writing career after the 1977 Whitbread Race when asked by the editor of *Seahorse Magazine* (still today the pre-eminent technical magazine for the serious racing sailor) to write a series on the navigational aspects of that circumnavigation. Today, you are lucky to ever meet your magazine or book editor in person, but back then when discussing the next instalment it was a de rigueur amusing alcoholic lunch in London with the charming Anthony Churchill, founder and publisher of that journal.

After having read my race diary from the 1981/82 Whitbread Race on *Alaska Eagle*, the deputy editor of *Nautical Quarterly*, Michael Levitt, realizing I could string a few words together, commissioned two back-to-back issues with my entire diary verbatim – a raw, no holds barred 10,000-word (*New Yorker* style but with pictures) exposé of that troubled American project. This put me on the map with that magisterial publication of the day (now the set of 50 is a collector's item) and article commissions followed from them and from a variety of global yachting magazines. For my subsequent articles with *Nautical Quarterly*, Mike's advice was always, 'Write like you think and speak; you can't go wrong.'

In a curious overlap and transition, in 1987 with two partners I built the 54-foot steel sailing vessel *Pelagic*, which launched a second life of expedition voyaging in high latitudes that is ongoing, 36 years later. What started out as a passion in seeking remote areas accessed by sail to go mountaineering, became a business model in a particular adventure charter market.

Having written about many of these sailing experiences and adventures, both racing and cruising, on craft from dinghies to behemoth catamarans, the editor of *Yachting World* figured I was a good choice to take over from Robin Knox-Johnston's long standing column, as she knew I could do so with minimal editing, had the discipline to stick to the maximum of 800 words and could be relied on to produce comment on a wide range of issues, if not hands on, then as a pundit.

Recently having retired from the column having felt I had exhausted my repertoire, or at least not wishing to wind up as an old fool banging on forever, (and I flatly refuse to write about anchoring techniques *ad nauseam*), this book came to mind; to gather what are simply my thoughts, opinions and anecdotes under one cover, as a record for myself to close a loop on one hand, but mainly to offer an entertaining compendium to those who had read some of my columns, but like most people would not have seen them all.

Rather than put them in chronological order as published (other than the first and last, which significantly 'book end' these texts), I decided to group them in general subjects, (many overlapping) for readers to dip into as a focus. The pieces are dated as published, which is important to note and I have added comment as a postscript to some in italics as indeed, my opinion on some subjects has changed with time, circumstance or my age. Trends that are beyond debate and have become unstoppable also deserve further comment and there are others where an opinion I had was dead wrong at the time.

To be clear this is not a book to be read cover to cover. The appropriate place is having it to hand is on your night stand when bored with Proust, in that basket next to the loo and certainly on your bookshelf on board in the pilot house (if you have one) for those long watches.

Devon Island
Arctic Canada
August 2023

MY ANCHOR DOWN IN THE HAMBLE RIVER

'Skip Novak takes a trip down the Hamble River and memory lane'

Skip's first column for Yachting World, *October 2014*

On a June Sunday a sailing friend suggested we take our families for a spin on the Hamble River on his motor boat (sailing friend converted). With 440HP on the back, once out of the Itchen River we went at speed down Southampton Water passing by various racer/cruisers ambling up and down the channel under sail. I felt slightly traitorous with the dirty looks. But I see my friend's point if you want to get from A to do something at B. The kids of course loved it, but the fun part for the oldies really began at the entrance to the Hamble River as we throttled back to the required six knots. Gee, we passed the very spot where we embarrassingly ran the Whitbread Maxi *Drum* aground on the south bank in 1985...

It was one of those magic sunny days on the river, with little or no breeze, but enough zephyrs for fleets of dinghies to make way colouring the Warsash and Hamble village riverbanks in kaleidoscopes of different hues. My kids have been to the Hamble on previous visits but it was their first time there afloat, if you didn't count the public jetty where crabbing was the activity. I reflected that the last time I was actually on the river (and not in a pub by the river) was more than 20 years ago. The memories came alive with each passing feature.

The Royal Southern Yacht Club; Simon Le Bon caught with a barmaid from the King and Queen in his room – a tabloid field day. The jetty at Port Hamble; I brought *Drum* alongside the Maxi *Cote d'Or* under sail after we blew off our propeller in the Solent. Skipper Eric Tabarly, a man of few words at the best of times, gave his nod of approval as we glided to a halt safely alongside. One of those grand moments...

Hamble Yacht Services was the sailing base for *Drum* in the Whitbread 1985, and then *Fazisi* in 1989. Our engaging Soviet crew became a focal point of amusement and bemusement for the 'locals.' I will never forget paying off all our creditors from a suitcase full of cash in the PortaKabin on the hard, just prior to the start.

I used to kayak up and down the river to work at Moody's. On this sunny day kayaks were out in force, along with all manner of floating objects; old and new, in repair and disrepair; rowed, paddled, sailed and motored, all with contented folk picnicking away... Of course, the fairway is much narrower than 20 years ago as marinas have gobbled up riverbank space so the flotilla jockeyed for position while working up and down tide. It was right out of Jerome K Jerome's *Three Men in a Boat*, 2014 edition.

At the bend in the river I could just make out the Old Ship, our local pub for the *Drum* crew. Rick Tomlinson and I once jumped out of the second storey window as the morning work whistle blew. It had been a mega 'lock in', even outlasting the publican. Not much accomplished by either of us that day.

Look to port, The Jolly Sailor, now renovated for family lunch; hard by the celebrated Elephant Boatyard, now, as then and hopefully in the future, left unchanged. We passed under the A27 and lo and behold even more marinas! The iconic Aladdin's Cave chandlery barge still exists, though, where I regularly trawled through for old parts and fittings when building *Pelagic* in 1987.

Finally, north of the M27 we find open river and some solitude. We took high water at the creek that leads to Curbridge and the Horse and Jockey. After kayaking up on a rising tide on one of those misty winter mornings long ago, a pub lunch ended in a desperate struggle covered in mud trying to get back afloat late that afternoon – tide down and several pints accounted for.

Postscript

And so it continues. In the spring of 2021 we had Vinson of Antarctica *on the dock at Hamble Yacht Services, finishing the fit-out (the chandlery did well out of us) and prepping for the maiden voyage to Svalbard. Of course, the days of high jinks are long gone and we all behaved ourselves impeccably.*

1 LEARNING TO SAIL

I had the luxury of growing up in a sailing family, spending all of our summers on the Chicago lakefront and cruising the vast expanse of Lake Michigan. It was easy to learn to sail, like riding a bike, as I spent all my free time doing it from an early age. It was a time of few if any distractions and my parents felt no need to introduce me to other activities. In the summers we sailed, period, because that was what my parents liked to do.

Times have changed for young people, at least from families of some means and education where sailing might be a possibility for little Johnny or his sister Emily depending on how they are doing with the other half dozen activities (oh, how I hate that word!) they are being continually exposed to, outside of their many other core activities as part of a school programme. You get the picture? It is hard to now carve out the time to get really good at something like sailing in all its manifestations.

Speaking from the point of view of an outdoors person, I consider sailing as one of those life skills that if it is on offer needs to be nurtured. Skiing or snowboarding, scuba or free diving, kiteboarding or wing foiling and rigorous trekking are for me the core skills that you can travel on, and if relatively competent, fit into almost any social situation with active people. Of all those activities (sorry, that word again!) sailing is no doubt the most complex, which is one reason that many young people do not stick with it from the dinghy sailing on up.

Adults on the other hand, with no prior sailing experience but who want to learn, are fast-tracked into bigger boats and usually miss out on the dinghy aspect where it should all begin, no matter the age.

Then there are the other skills needed of making a boat get from A to B. Read on.

THE FEEL OF SMALL BOATS

'"The feel" is what separates a good sailor from a so-so one, and you'll never get it unless you've had a good soaking in a tippy dinghy'

February 2015

I started my sailing career as a fresh water pirate in Belmont Harbor in Chicago. As part of the junior programme at the Chicago Yacht Club we started in Lehman 10 dinghies, a round bottomed contraption with little form stability. Patched up with fibreglass over many years, some of these must have been double the weight of others, I suspect. The set up was a simple mainsail, mainsheet and rudder. They were two-man boats but the crew only provided ballast sliding port to starboard on the thwart. The winds in Chicago were never constant either, whistling through the high rise apartment buildings in a westerly or rebounding off same in an easterly veering or backing by several points on the compass in an instant. In the blink of an eye you went from a calm to fighting to stay upright, expletives part of the experience.

Given the boats and the conditions capsizes were common. This certainly sharpened your skills if not your wits and sense of survival, especially when 'frostbiting' in the fall and spring. Adults as well as juniors sailed on Sundays until the ice formed near the end of November and we started again on the break up in March. It was a lot of laughs, thrills and spills. Looking back on it now, it was that training that set me up with the ability to competently sail just about any floating object big or small. Over a life-time these have included a variety of dinghies, windsurfers, Great Lake's racer/cruisers, premier ocean racers including the Whitbread Maxis, ice boats, Thames Barges, dhows, Maxi multihulls and a few superyachts thrown in. It is all the same in a way, if you have 'the feel' – inculcated long ago by the fear of getting a good soaking.

Acquiring 'the feel' is difficult, nigh on impossible while learning to sail on the midsize boats used by the proliferation of instructional programmes for adults which certainly include the corporate entertainment phenomenon that hit the Solent some years ago.

All these training agendas, along with the events they feed into, are desirable to get people on the water of course, but this dinghy stage for aspiring adults has been grossly neglected in what should ideally be a natural progression of learning to sail. Start small and go bigger seems so obvious. I understand, though, that being repeatedly thrown out of a Laser can be less than glamorous while you 'get the hang of it.' The ultimate risk in not having 'fun' is probably a change back to the golf course.

What I am talking about is learning to sail by 'cookbook' methods, which are the default in mid-life when most people require some scale, space and comfort. Also boat handling, under sail and power, is another example that is difficult to master on a full blown yacht if you have never mucked around on small craft. It all boils down to 'the feel.'

No matter what size of boat, the seasoned sailor having been brought up through the ranks will instinctively shift his weight to windward, be alert to easing the mainsheet or traveller and just as instantly snap back into the former aspect when the wind subsides. You can recognize the lack of feel in someone at once when the wind strengthens, as often it will produce little reaction. Sailing continually overpowered is also a classic indicator of someone with the lack of feel which in the extreme case leads to control issues (wipe outs) and possible damage to the boat and its gear.

However, it is never too late! To address this fundamental aspect of learning to sail in the truest sense of the word, we should encourage sail training organizations to run parallel programmes on 'tippy' dinghies for debutante sailors to realize the importance in coordinating the fundamentals of wind direction/strength, helming and body weight. It will make them much better sailors for every kind of floating object going forward.

SAILING IS THE EASY PART

'The wind-in-the-hair sailing bit is only the icing on the cake of this experience we call yachting. First, you've got to get down and dirty'

May 2015

Many years ago, a woman friend joined us on *Pelagic* for a cruise down the coast of Argentina. Full of unbridled enthusiasm she was keen to, as she described it, 'learn how to sail.' We were still in the midst of our annual refit, high and dry in a filthy shipyard in Buenos Aires. I thought it appropriate to copy Sir Richard Branson's technique, but only figuratively, turning her upside down head first into the starboard fuel tank – to muck out the sludge.

This did not put her off and after several days of testing her resolve with a list of unpleasant jobs in the bowels of the vessel, most of which resulted in painting herself in black epoxy tar, she hung in there cheerfully and eventually enjoyed the post refit liberation due to her. I can picture her now on the first day offshore – staring out to sea over a clear horizon, her hair blowing in the wind and without words it was clear she was revelling in utter contentment. The image was like we see in magazine adverts that use sailing as a metaphor. What had she learned, though? Well, the complete layout of the bilge including the position and function of every seacock and valve, which is not an insignificant piece of knowledge. Course 001, in Sailing 101, *Pelagic* Syllabus, was complete.

The point is folks, 'sailing' is often the easy part of the equation (though it is a complex one) of 'going sailing.' The art and science of navigation, helming and working the deck – in essence making the boat go from Port A to Port B – are the enjoyable parts. This icing on the cake of a successful voyage is only possible when underpinned by a sound vessel which requires a whole host of manual skills in order to keep that vessel running smoothly – tradesman's type stuff – *enabling* it to sail from Port A to Port B. The short list? Diesel mechanics, plumbing, basic electrical, sail repair, rigging, fibreglass repairs, scuba diving for under the water repairs, simple fabricating (out of whatever is available) and the ability of installing same, not to mention a strong stomach to deal with things like diesel leaks and, frankly, raw sewage. And you *gotta* enjoy it, if not the latter two, then certainly all of the former.

I remember the story years ago of the fast-track RYA students who were having a practical exam afloat and the engine suddenly quit going out of Portsmouth Harbour. It was reported in *Yachting World* that they did not have a clue about what to do next in getting it back up and running. It was a prime example of how fast-track methods fail by their own definition. Of course, if you are going for a career in superyachting working up through the ranks from deck officer to captain, fine, as professionally trained engineers who keep all things running on these yachts, which are really ships in disguise, are a given. Sailing your own small yacht away from marina services, though, requires the Full Monty of knowhow. To cruise successfully is an exercise in endless problem-solving.

Well, if we are all not New Zealanders (who seem to have these trades up their sleeves as part of their overall education), it bears thinking about before we go to sea. Are all the bases covered to some extent? Therein lies the conundrum. How do we train up for all these trades, with time at a premium, especially the younger generation who will never benefit from fiddling with repairing their own cars (now quite impossible) or making their own skateboards or go-karts, or building their own Optimist dinghy (how the class started). Sadly, there are now too many things laid on, bought off the shelf, or too sophisticated to replicate in some fashion or another, in DIY.

All I can suggest is arm yourself with the 'how to' books, make sure you have plenty of spares, parts, materials and tools; then put to sea and get on with it.

SAILING IN ALL ITS FORMS

'There is no activity more varied, with more opportunities to inspire young people to a lifetime's interest, than sailing'

October 2015

The debate which at times seems *ad nauseam* regarding keeping young people involved in sailing as a lifetime activity is certainly well warranted. Unless you suffer from severe, life-threatening hydrophobia it is hard to imagine not taking on board some form of watersports under sail whether racing or cruising from naught in arms to the end game, assuming a 'well-rounded' lifestyle is desirable.

When I have the time to peruse the sailing web forums, which is not that often, I am always amazed at the diversity of competitive yacht racing genres, as well as what goes on in the cruising world. It is enough to make one's head spin how much is out there.

Let's start at the bottom of the scale. We have youth racing starting in the controversial Optimist class, often described as the solution or the cause of the failure in the continuity of sailing as lifetime activity. Then regard the various dinghy classes worldwide – does anyone know how many? Take a guess and probably double or triple it. Now, go collegiate racing, Olympic campaigns male and female, skiff sailing, scow sailing, windsurfing and kiteboarding, club racing in one-design keel boats and racer/cruisers, match racing, premier offshore events; Fastnet, Sydney Hobart, Transatlantic, Transpac to name a few. There are the elite classes such as TP 52s, Melges 32s and many more. You can single-hand, double-hand, go fully crewed inshore, offshore and around the world (sometimes in the 'wrong' direction!) on either multihull or monohull.

Traditional yachts are further divided into original restorations and others classed by age or compromised by the addition of modern materials. Even Thames Barges go racing. Maxi yacht regattas continue to proliferate on both sides of the Atlantic. What about sailing record attempts? There are a plenty: 24 hours, Transatlantic, Jules Verne around the world and clipper ship routes. Builders and designers now weigh in; Swan regattas, Dubois regattas, Southern Wind regattas et al, exist for a rarified social Mediterranean experience. Let's not forget Tall Ships Rallies. Stadium exhibition racing like The Extreme Sailing Series provides a spectacle for a live audience. Did I mention ice boating when the water goes hard? And arguably the pinnacles of the fully crewed game; offshore the Volvo Ocean Race and inshore the America's Cup. And it is predicted we will be foiling on all things eventually. There is something for everyone either to participate in, aspire to, follow, or dream about.

Back to the life's activity argument, or let's call it a lifestyle. Then compare sailing to other sports which can also be considered a lifestyle activity for some and a burning, all consuming passion for others. Tennis? Same court with a few variations of surface, same ball, same racquet, same game. Golf,? OK, changes of courses, but same game. Equestrian sports? Variations exist, but horses all have four legs last time I looked. Ditto cycling with two wheels. As far as I know these and especially the ball sports have had almost none or only incremental changes over the years.

Dare I say it, motorsport might come close; cars (karting to Formula 1), motorbikes – track and motocross, jet skis, monster trucks, snow mobiles… Before I am hoist by my own petard, I'd better stop there and just say for now motorsports might be a far second in range and diversity, but don't hold me to it!

When I started sailing over a half century ago (yep, that's right!) most of these boats and events didn't exist. I have been lucky to have participated on many platforms as things evolved and I enjoyed them all. Conclusion: when it comes to being on the water on anything that floats and is propelled by the wind, there is no parallel. Advice to keep young people interested: beware of a single approach and expose them to what is now an inexhaustible raft of choices. Surely they will find one.

Postscript

I was dead right about the prediction that we will all be on foils soon, or at least some of us.

FOOLING AROUND FIXING BOATS IS HOW I GOT STARTED

'Working on yachts as a teenager set the scene for Skip's adventures worldwide, but times for youngsters have changed'

September 2019

If any readers are tired of my 'back in the day' stories please send a letter to the editor. Possibly my advanced age is to blame, and realizing I might never get a chance 'to foil.'

What brought this reminisce on was a recent experience putting my 15-year-old son Luca to work during the annual *Pelagic Australis* refit in Cape Town. Having lost his monthly allowance through a catalogue of misdemeanours he was hard up for cash. I told him it is about time to realize what a proper day's work is like and he would get paid the minimum wage in South Africa (which is not a lot). His first job was to chip off galvanizing slag on 115 metres of our anchor chain on the hard. Sitting on the concrete in the hot sun with hammer and cold chisel he reminded me of those pictures of Nelson Mandela on Robben Island breaking rocks, which was not appreciated when I told him. Plus, he was missing a day in the surf, his passion that has taken over his life. This was somewhat of a reluctant trial for him.

I remember my early days in Chicago working with my dad (definitely unpaid) in the boatyard on the north branch of the Chicago River on spring weekends. I must have been eight or nine when this routine began. He would hand me a piece of sandpaper and point to a hatch cover from our 40-foot racer/cruiser and remind me again to, 'sand with the grain.' With a real job to hand I felt very important. At lunchtime we would sit on the old wooden pier eating our Swiss cheese and salami sandwiches on rye, talking about the sailing season to come. I cannot recall that I had any other 'activities' that conflicted. This is all that we did on spring weekends.

By the time I was 14 I was spending the entire three month American summer holiday as a liveaboard in Belmont Harbor on Chicago's north side. There was a gang of us – we called ourselves the Harbor Rats. We only saw our parents at weekends and to this day we still wonder what exactly they thought we were doing during the week, much of which is unrepeatable to this audience. However, on the positive side we each had a stable of boats that we worked on during the week and prepped for the weekend's racing – washing the decks and topsides (the soot was horrendous, well before the Clean Air Act) with a bucket and lanyard. The interior also needed a pull through. Putting ice on board on Saturday morning and often bringing the boats off the hook and on to the dock was the best part of the job. We even shared a 'hooka rig' for cleaning the bottoms. It was entrepreneurial – sort of a modern day boat valeting service without the crisp white uniforms, the fancy branded van and pressure washers.

On our own time we fooled around repairing old outboards, fixed sails and rigging, messed around with dodgy petrol engines in deep bilges (luckily no one was asphyxiated or emolliated) and generally enjoyed being a 'Harbor Rat' ready to lend a hand to whatever needed doing. We were tolerated by the club members and I suppose at the same time feared for what we might get up to next. This freedom and self-reliance at a relatively young age set the scene for my future wanderings worldwide, without question.

It seems quite improbable what was an idyllic set of circumstances for a teenager could ever be repeated in modern times. Firstly, 'live-aboards' are hardly allowed in marinas, let alone minors on their own. In any event, they wouldn't be able to free roam given the security systems in place. And work ad hoc on boats as a 14- or 15-year-old? The legalities of child labour laws would make what we enjoyed a non-starter, not to mention letting a kid loose with a variety of power tools? Health and safety would certainly have something to say about that. And insurance issues – oh gawd!

The fact is, though, the argument here is somewhat moot as young people today have little or no free time to even contemplate such a situation. The standards and stresses of education today underpinned by organized recreational programmes have all but scuppered any form of underage entrepreneurship, let alone an engagement in a part time job to earn a crust.

As I write there is still six weeks to go before *Pelagic Australis* sets sail back to the Falklands. Plenty of Saturdays and Sundays for Luca to get stuck in and earn the money for that new surfboard he is dreaming about. At least he has the incentive.

Postscript

Having sailed on the original Pelagic *in Tierra del Fuego on family holidays and a project on the Antarctic Peninsula 2014, Luca was still 'along for the ride.' In the summer of 2023 he and a surfing buddy from South Africa, both age 19, worked under Tor Bovim, age 24, and fully prepped* Pelagic *in Maine for our Arctic summer, with little or no intervention from me. They had to figure things out for themselves. I would have been a negative directing this show. We went on to have three months in high Arctic and this set the scene for what could be a career in sailing. The message is it is never too late to start.*

SAILING SHOULD BE A VOYAGE

'To inspire a love of sailing, even the youngest dinghy sailors need the thrill of a voyage'

October 2020

Like many of us who read this magazine sailing is not only a life skill, but a way of life. This is certainly the case for me. I grew up at a yacht club in Chicago and the usual format for young sailors was the classic sailing school geared for racing. This was fine at the time and I enjoyed it and I would continue to race 'around the cans' worldwide thereafter.

The ongoing chronology, when you were big enough to be of some use, was crewing on the racer/cruisers of the day, not only on course races, but racing up and down to small port towns on the Michigan or Wisconsin shore, with the highlight being the annual Chicago Mackinac Race, all of 330 miles. For a teenager from the suburbs this was high adventure indeed. From early on, if I had the choice of racing endless triangle windward leeward courses or going somewhere, it was always the voyage. Besides the sailing, what I had learned and realized pretty early on was this was a great way to see the world, and there followed an ocean racing career and on to the expeditioning in high latitudes.

Having retired from ocean racing about the same time the children came along (sort of related) I looked forward to the time when we would without question start the dinghy programme with them. How else do you teach your children to sail competently? It is very true that without a sound racing background it is almost impossible to pick up the many nuances you need to know to be considered an expert.

We started with the usual Optimist solution as being the only class for that age group in Cape Town. We didn't get any farther. I attribute part of this sad story to the Optimist itself, a boat conceived on the back of the Soapbox Derby. For the non-cognoscenti, a soapbox is a DIY wooden car that you race down a hill, which most of us in America had built and tried at some point, managed by a long suffering father. The nautical equivalent was invented by Clarky Mills over 70 years ago in Clearwater, Florida – a clever invention built cheaply with 'three sheets of plywood' and got kids afloat. The class became and still is the world's standard starter boat, allowed to exist by the sheer weight of numbers. The downsides are that it is painfully slow, it pushes through the water like a bathtub and needs bailing often. If you fill her up in a failed manoeuvre you are out of the race (in spite of the coaches and parents yelling from the safety boat, 'keep bailing!'). The point is... the concept is 70 years old. The French have invented the Open Bic, my starter boat of choice if and when I ever have grandchildren.

On the other hand, the Optimist is a highly technical boat to rig and tune, so therefore the kids who really buy into the competition side of things thrive where the type of boat becomes almost irrelevant. I defy any parent whose child has won a tough 'Opti' race not to have Olympic thoughts running through their brains. My son, although gifted with natural talent, was turned off simply because he was bored and discovered surfing and this was a no-brainer for a young thrill seeker. My daughter got slam dunked too many times by aggressive older kids and threw in the towel and turned to mountain activities. Also, sailing in confined spaces like small lakes and dams there was nowhere to go for a 'voyage' and have some non-racing fun. For me, I suffered the fate of many of my sailing contemporaries with children who never had or had lost all interest in sailing. And we were not alone; the attrition rate of the families who started about the same time was staggering. It is a subject that continues to be discussed and agonized over by many sailing parents, namely 'how did it all go wrong?'

Although the kids, when still small, were happy to sit beside me on my Laser and bomb around at speed, it wasn't until recently when they were both heavy and strong enough to handle a Laser on their own in a breeze that the spark was re-lit. We now have two Lasers where they can 'match race' each other or I can sail side by side and coach one of them. We don't do any fleet racing, but we have a ball exploring a pristine estuary north of Cape Town with abundant wildlife, and deserted beaches for picnics among stunning geographical surroundings. Being tidal and open to the ocean there are currents strong enough to get you into trouble so seamanship all comes into the equation. How to get out of tricky situations like breakdowns and more comes into the curriculum, without a safety boat to bail you out.

I am now confident we have gotten over the hump where so many young people try sailing and for one reason or the other drop it and never return. I am told that youth programmes in the UK have realized this and at least for the beginners there is more on offer than just racing.

I can't think of anything more satisfying than sailing up the Hamble River on a dinghy, playing the tide, just to get an ice cream for the children at the Jolly Sailor. Make that a pint for me. To keep sailing alive throughout life, you need to sail, but to sail somewhere.

FIXING THINGS THE RIGHT WAY

'Practical skills are still key for those who want to work in the marine industry, but these days formal training is necessary too'

January 2022

My son Luca took his final high school matric exams in November 2021. He is not university material, at least not yet. 'I hate sitting in a classroom,' he says, which is a chip off the old block.

When asked what he wants to do in life he has often told me that he would like to take over my Pelagic business. Well, I was one of those boat bums from the seventies, winging it all the way with no plan whatsoever. One thing led to another and here we are. And I explain to him, often, that 'times have changed, my boy...'

I have had many similar conversations with young people, who would like to 'get into yachting', where they think they can take their STCW (International Convention on Standards of Training, Certification and Watchkeeping for Seafarers), maybe even do some RYA courses to start off, but otherwise can offer no manual skills at all. Yes, you might get a job on a superyacht on that basis, but you will be doing plenty of hosing down, cleaning, polishing, making beds, napkin folding and serving drinks and canapes, for a long time, or forever.

Anyone who has skippered what I consider to be real sailing yachts – I mean, those of say 100 feet or less – will know full well that the sailing side, providing you have a small boat background, is the easiest part, ditto the piloting and navigation which is the hinge pin for getting your licenses. But when it comes to the engineering on board – meaning fixing engines, pumps, hydraulics, electrics, electronics and more, all of which are becoming increasingly complex – there is no substitute for a solid polytechnic education or deep manual skills training before going to sea. Then you need the sea miles, away from marina services, to experience all the failures with this technology, and learn how to bodge it all temporarily. If you can come to the table with that background you will be immediately of value and climb the career ladder quickly.

This discussion always reminds me of the wave of immigrants into the American 'corinthian' yachting scene in the late 60s and early 70s. Most had sailed up from New Zealand, Australia or South Africa, or across the pond from the UK. I met a few in the Great Lakes when an impressionable teenager and many of the rest during the 1972 Transatlantic from Bermuda to Bayona, Spain, when I was 20. They had colourful nicknames; The Fat Rabbit, The Flying Nun, The Wharf Rat, Thirsty, Bruce the Goose, Jocko, Tom the Pom and Frizzle to name a few that are printable here.

I was enamoured with their continuous and amusing repartee; they could all sing a song, tell stories, drink hard, and to the point could fix things. The young Americans of that era who were in that genre, and there were a few, were mainly from well-to-do set ups, destined eventually for the family business, disappearing into the 'big smoke' when they eventually threw in the professional sailing towel. The immigrants by contrast were, I say with the utmost respect, 'working class.' They were returning colonists (at least when in Europe) who took over by storm and facilitated what was an exceptional travelling roadshow.

In that era of ocean racing it was a continuous circuit on boats that were liveable and went everywhere on their own bottoms. In 1973 I took a job as a rigger and fitter at Ross Yacht Service in Clearwater, Florida. This was a focal point for many IOR (International Offshore Rule) yachts prepping for the annual Southern Ocean Racing Conference (SORC). After a six week series ending in Nassau, next stop was Miami for the race to Montego Bay. And then, like migratory birds we sailed north for the Annapolis Newport Race, then the Bermuda Race (biannually) ending with the Marblehead Halifax Race. It was only a skip across the Atlantic and you could be there by Cowes Week, with or without a Fastnet. The Skagen Race out of Scandinavia was then possible, with this whole circus finishing with the Middle Sea Race starting in Malta before it was time to head back to Florida, post hurricane season. The Sydney Hobart, the Cape Town to Rio Race and the Transpac to Hawaii were occasional side shows.

To explain how clever these foreigners were, it must have been in 1974 when one of them took up with a local lady (no surprise) who wanted to build a house. Before building regulations existed (or were ignored) in that part of Florida, a half dozen of these sailing blokes volunteered to get on with it and build it. Almost interchangeably they decided then and there who would be in charge of the foundation, the framing, the electrics and plumbing, as if this random methodology was second nature.

It was a long time ago. Some of these immigrants returned 'down under', but many stayed and were by and large absorbed into the marine industry, in the worst case. In the best case a few married boat owners' daughters, and never looked back.

Take note, all would be careerists, these successes can still hold true today, but formal training in manual skills will give you a leg up. All food for thought when choosing a life at sea.

FINDING AN ISLAND

'Navigating the South Atlantic using celestial techniques becomes a true test when the ship goes "dark"'

July 2022

Vinson of Antarctica has now docked in Cape Town, concluding what has been, if I do say so myself, an extremely successful first year for a new custom vessel. More often than not a new build's first few months, let alone the first year of operation, is spent de-bugging all the systems. And this is the point I belabour to my audience of admirers or detractors (*ad nauseam*, I am told) that we have here an example of how to design and engineer a sailing vessel that works 'out of the box', which also implies by definition that ongoing issues years down the road are kept to a minimum. Less is more – my favourite aphorism!

Our schedule has been full on from the launch in March 2021. We first went north to Svalbard in July and August supporting a German government geological survey collecting one and half tonnes of rocks for analysis. The north/south transit of the Atlantic followed in October with scientists on board from the University of Florida and the Russian Academy of Science collecting plankton along the way. In January we hosted a penguin biology team from the Field Museum in Chicago along with Cornell and Bath Universities – a project in South Georgia and the Antarctica Peninsula was all about collecting samples for DNA analysis. Then after a short break in Port Stanley off again to the Peninsula with a UK film team in February.

Our last voyage might be the most interesting. This is our end-of-season programme that includes the RYA Ocean Yachtmaster shorebased course in Puerto Williams followed by a cruise in the Beagle Channel, then a short passage around Cape Horn before heading across the pond to Cape Town – a 42 day commitment all in all.

Before I sold *Pelagic Australis*, this was her routine for many years and had been one of our most popular trips on offer and to be frank the best value for our clients on a cost per day basis. Passage planning and global weather considerations are features of this course, which are valid no matter how you navigate, but the main challenges are mastering celestial navigation.

I wrote about the questionable value of doing celestial in *Yachting World* back in April 2015. I posited that learning celestial was more of a hobby and prophesized (with some evidence) that at some point it would drop off the RYA requirements for an Ocean Yachtmaster. Well, I was wrong on that account as it is still very much with us today. And it seems it is even more in demand as a learning experience from otherwise experienced sailors of a certain vintage.

Although our classroom instruction was a given, the real test was to put this into practice at sea. Although we did encourage our 'students' to practice celestial en route it was sort of a half-hearted affair. If you don't have to do it, most people won't with GPS data staring you in the face from the instrument array. Like many things the bare minimum was enough to get you through the exam after the voyage by simply showing an examiner your sight reduction workings and chart work from a few days running.

Our *Vinson* crew have taken this a big step further and immediately after departure from Cape Horn blanked out the GPS readouts. Our eight students, including two young aspiring Chilean trainees from Puerto Williams who we sponsor, had to get stuck into this seriously and peer pressure was brought to bear. The sextants were out in force and the goal was to 'find' and make landfall on Tristan da Cunha in the South Atlantic. For those of you claiming this might be irresponsible, hang on – they did have the AIS (automatic identification system) functioning without the GPS display visible and a radar watch at night. There is not much traffic along this route.

Sailing to and landing on Tristan, on an otherwise delivery passage to Cape Town, is a gamble. If the wind and swell are onshore it makes landing impossible, and if along the way you have to struggle on the wind to get there, it makes sense to give it a miss and slide off on a comfortable reach well below it. This is exactly what happened.

Luckily, though, Gough Island, 225 miles to the south-south-east of Tristan and more or less along their course to Cape Town, became a surrogate objective. On 28th April after two days of overcast skies making dead reckoning critical, they made landfall and sailed close aboard the island's south coast. What a way to realize that all the hard work of taking those sights and grinding down pencil leads, has paid off after 15 days at sea. A memory has been created that will stick. I must remember to raise those charter prices in future...

2 OCEAN RACING

The truth is the last time I did an ocean race (around the world non-stop on a Maxi catamaran in 64 days) was in 2001. This category, then, has more opinion pieces on the state of the art, than practical experience of relevance today. Yes, this is punditry and it can be ugly at times. Of course, my benchmark was 30 years of doing pretty much nothing but. And the ocean hasn't changed – or has it?

We of that era will often default into the point of view that the boats we sailed, heavy displacement hulls with heavy gear in sails and rigging, were physically tougher to sail than the sleds and now foil-borne craft that seem all pervading. I think this is true to some extent and delusional in others. Yes, the gear was heavy, the boats were hard to control at times, and we were passed over by the weather rather than riding with the systems as planing craft do today, meaning many more sail changes. The difference today in top level and elite ocean racing is that it is now highly professional and the crews much more focused and seriously minded than most of the crews on the ocean races that were done say, prior to the early 90s. Today's racing sailors are in no doubt fitter, stronger, trained up and single-minded, implying they might possibly be less eclectic and amusing than my shipmates of yore.

The Whitbread organization, which evolved into the Volvo Race and now is the Ocean Race, by way of example, has finally stopped asking me to comment on comparisons of how it all was then and how it is today, to be on a fully-crewed race around the world. The fact is that today comparisons of any value no longer exist.

THE VOLVO GENDER BENDER

'Taking a deep breath and donning a hard hat, Skip launches into the Volvo gender question: why do all-female crews do so badly?'

June 2015

Never one to avoid what will inevitably put people's noses out of joint, let's now talk about Team SCA's less than impressive performance in the Volvo Ocean Race. We know that the organizers had decided to grant the female team three extra crew which I would assume was a concession to strength and endurance issues. So this is a clear acknowledgement of a disparity between the genders. Then we know for a fact that Team SCA's boat was the first off the blocks and the team has had the most time on the water training. We must also assume that this team has the best female sailors money can buy. Indeed, their inshore sailing skills are beyond question from stellar results in the in-port races. On the Volvo PR material it is stated, 'The entry of the all-female team is no coincidence given that the new boat design puts less of a premium on physical strength and means an all-female team can be just as competitive as any other professional team.'

If all three of these facts hold water, then there is no harm in asking the question 'what is happening?' If a level playing field was created by the organizers and no expense spared in the crew selection and the training, one wonders if there is more at play here. Dare I offer the conclusion that women are inferior to men offshore? How can this be when we have seen the likes of Ellen MacArthur and Florence Arthaud, you say. Indeed, there have been many female singlehanders, mainly French and British, that have impressed.

Is singlehanding as intense as a fully crewed race where there is no respite from your shipmates? It is no secret that peer pressure on board can be dramatic. It must also be accepted that going 100% all of the time while singlehanding is impossible and throttling back at times to recoup is all part of that equation. Catching your breath is not the case in today's Volvo. If you are female and feeling indignant by this stage note that there is not one female crew member in any of the other entries. Does that tell you something?

Well, carrying on in this discussion will only land me in hotter water than I am already in for bringing up the subject in the first place. So I will let the reader ponder these things over while they cool down.

In the meantime I will offer a solution that can possibly eliminate any further discussion, and one which I am sure many people have contemplated and even suggested to the organizers if they haven't thought of it themselves. Simply, crews comprised of 50% guys and 50% girls, which is a good ratio when you consider world population demographics and a lot else, including procreation for that matter. It takes two to tangle right? This simple and elegant solution will once and for all quench these awkward comparisons between the genders in fully crewed offshore racing. It's a 'we're all in it together' concept. There is another benefit here in that having more female sailors involved by a simple rule requirement will bring more female sailors up to speed in offshore sailing. And, from the human point of view, imagine the great stories that would unfold both on and off the water! Boys will be boys and girls will be girls.

It has been a long passage for women making their mark offshore. I am thinking of Clare Francis skippering *ADC Accutrac* in the 1977/78 Whitbread, Tracy Edward's groundbreaking all-female crew in the Whitbread of 1989/90, but then we see the all-female team of *Heineken* in 1993/94 9th out of a 10 boat fleet, *EF Education* in 1997/98 last, and in 2001/02 *Amer Sports Too* also last. Might persisting in the all-female crew concept for this pre-eminent event be a step backwards? If you see me on the dock at the finish I will be the one wearing a hard hat and body armour.

Postscript

The Ocean Race, aka the Volvo Ocean Race going back to at least the 2014/2015 edition referred to here, has made some progress in addressing the gender imbalance. In that edition females made up 18% of the total sailors involved (obviously because of SCA's all-female team). In the 2017/2018 race this creeped up to 21% mainly due to the organizers mandate of one female member minimum on board each boat. In the 2022/2023 this rose to 28%; the increase, although minimal, is attributed to meritocracy rather than regulation. This is an ongoing subject and I suspect it will be a long time coming before we see a 50/50 gender balance. And having said all this the present fog of gender identity will also play a part one day.

OLYMPIC SAILING IN AN OPEN SEWER

'Pollution in Rio compromising the sailing Olympics? A clean-up is not going to happen. This is Brazil; just enjoy the carnival'

September 2015

I know Rio well enough. We stopped there in the Whitbread Race in 1978. That was the year many of the competitors (and the security guards along with the lawn furniture) wound up in the swimming pool in the middle of the awards ceremony at the Rio Yacht Club. It took tear gas to clear the crowd. The story has been retold so many times it is now Whitbread legend verging on Whitbread myth. You had to be there.

I also remember how filthy Guanabara Bay was – a first-hand experience as I dove to the bottom of *King's Legend* before the start to give her a clean. It was not until we were well offshore after the start on the way back home that the sea turned from brown to blue. It is estimated that 15 million people inhabit Rio's greater metropolitan area which forms a human and industrial ring around Guanabara Bay, which is basically an enclosed arm of the sea. It is therefore no surprise to me that it was still a virtual cesspool of human and industrial waste in 2015. In fact, I drove around the bay the previous January with a friend as we were extricating ourselves from the traffic on our way out of town on the road to Sao Paulo. I noticed the changes since 1978 alright – more people, more congestion and more industry.

And let's be frank, this is not America decades after it passed the Clean Water Act in 1972 – which is a revelation to one who knew the Great Lakes in the 60s – it is Brazil, a first world country for a few, but a third world country for the majority of the population who have few amenities and lack much of an environmental view. Worrying about pollution for humankind and the negative consequences for industry who use the bay as a dumping ground has historically been way down the government's list of priorities, in spite of political posturing to the contrary.

How the International Olympic Committee were led to believe that the powers that be in Rio would miraculously clean up the bay turning it into a sailing paradise of sorts by removing 80% of the pollution is beyond the definition of naivety. The present dilemma of pollution (micro and macro) that will compromise results in the 2016 Olympics, now continually in the sailing news forums, is not the fault of Rio in having sold this promise to be unfulfilled. Rather the reality the sailors will face next summer is clearly the fault of the IOC for believing them in the first place. We, the public, are led to believe that the members of the IOC who decide these things are global citizens who would immediately recognize that this promise by local and federal government would never be viable.

There's no point to make a meal out of it, though, digested or not. Regattas take place on a regular basis there. People swim in it. People scuba dive in it. To my knowledge, no sailors have died because of it. Granted the Brazilian crews might have a distinct advantage having built up an immunity to the bacteria. There will be compromises and complaints. Rudders and boards will catch plastic bags and hulls will collide with other debris, unless of course the organizers along with government can conjure up a hydro hoover yet to be invented that can anticipate tidal flow and quickly clear the race course before each race of large solid objects. That will be a tall order in itself, but somehow doable. Sickness brought on by bacterial infection will be more controversial and more difficult to assess in view of results compromised. Precautions will have to be taken.

But hey! This is Brazil and if there is one thing the Brazilians can do is create a carnival atmosphere out of a controversial situation. As usual with all things Brazilian it will somehow be right on the day.

Postscript

As expected the sailing teams got through it all, but one can't help to continually wonder how and why these decisions about selecting major sporting venues are made. Conclusions are usually obvious, the latest football world cup in Qatar being an obvious example. Money decides it all.

THE AMERICA'S CUP GOES THROUGH YET ANOTHER ITERATION

'The new America's Cup show is spectacular, but I have to admit to missing some of the shenanigans of the old-style game'

December 2015

I recently became aware of the new rules in the America's Cup whereby the challengers are subject to fines if they publicly criticize the Cup organization; $25,000 for the first offence (small beer), $100,000 for the second (makes one think now) and $250,000 for any subsequent offence (lose your job time).

This really signals the end of the America's Cup as we knew it, well, for those of a certain vintage, pre-foiling at least. I mean, lest we forget the espionage, subterfuge and at times plain mendacity resulting in vitriolic exchanges that were without doubt a feature of all America's Cups heretofore and were certainly entertaining. Some of these shenanigans inevitably led to litigation followed by a media storm, most of which had little to do with the actual sailing. To be honest, this is what always interested me about the America's Cup; how the captains of industry and finance apparently relished these battles via their floating proxies.

Voyeuristically, we love the tycoons and their eccentricities. Millions squandered to win a boat race (remember 'there is no second') and when things went pear-shaped or didn't work out according to plan, they'd launch the legal team to find a breach in the opposition's defences, taking it all the way to appellate courts in New York City. (Surely those courts had more important things to do?) It has always been a 'hard ball' game for sure. With the new format are they now a dying breed? I think yes, at least in the sense of supporting a Cup campaign as sponsorship takes over those much heralded reduced budgets. Already, one well-known yachting gentleman has thrown his baby out with the bathwater because of the new regime and it is likely more might follow as the Cup moves ever closer to a one design competition.

There is no point whining on about this, though, as this is a simple and predictable evolution. It has happened in the Volvo Ocean Race and the Cup boats are not far behind. Pre-eminence in sailing skills will be the theme rather than a financial competition in hiring the best hydro-dynamists and aero-dynamists – and of course the best lawyers. In one respect it is a pity for the America's Cup to be now so similar to most other events with that simple to understand formula of 'the best sailors will win.' So we must all sit back and enjoy the show because it is nothing short of spectacular to see. I challenge any racing sailor, male or female, not to be stimulated when these AC45 catamarans rise up erect out of the water and take off at blistering speeds, the crew helmeted and body-armoured, performing gymnastics that most of us are long since past, or never had the ability to do in the first place.

What is lost, though, is that vicarious experience the average sailor could enjoy when watching the grass grow on the 12-metres' course (and to a lesser extent the AC 72s), with plenty of time to mull over the tactician's failures and fortunes. You could actually imagine yourself on the helm or in the grinder pits. All of this was vaguely familiar to the sailing we have always known. Unless you really are a seagoing Walter Mitty, it is quite unreasonable to imagine yourself alight on the foiling AC45s. It is a sport in the strict physical definition of the word.

The America's Cup today suits our time in history perfectly, though. Let's face it, the appreciation of an old Turner Classic Movie with long contemplative scenes, complex dialogue and the camera resting on nothing more thought provoking than a landscape is going by the board. Action films with scenes measured in milliseconds and YouTube clips are now where it's at, to suit our mooted attenuating attention spans. The America's Cup is a perfect fit.

Postscript

Well, I was wrong about where the America's Cup was heading. Although the boats, now foiling monohulls, resemble a box rule of sorts, the same millions (measured in the hundreds) are being spent on these campaigns for indeed the best of the best boffin designers. And although sponsorship exists, it is a thin veil cast over the real money coming from captains of industry and finance. Not much has changed since 1851 in fact.

CITY RACING HAS ITS RISKS FOR CREWS AND SPECTATORS ALIKE

'Thrilled though he was about the ACWS visiting his hometown of Chicago, Skip is not a fan of big city racing'

September 2016

When I read about Ben Ainslie's frustration in sailing underneath New York City (literally) in the Louis Vuitton America's Cup World Series in May 2016, and knowing that Chicago was coming up next in June, I thought there was a real chance of him throwing the baby out with the bath-water – in this case Lake Michigan, which is sort of bathtub shaped.

I hale from Chicago – Captain Haddock's 'fresh water pirate.' Having grown up sailing dinghies in Belmont Harbor on the near northside shore I remember the frustration of offshore winds whistling through high rise buildings catching you off guard – worse when we sometimes capsized in those non-rightable boats during frostbite series in early March when the lake ice was still on the way out. This was well before sailors used wet- or drysuits or any specialized sailing clothing so these painful experiences surely sharpened your senses for abrupt wind changes in view of staying dry. Those semi-survival lessons have stood me well for a lifetime of all sorts of changing conditions on the 'far side of the world.'

What must have been more of a concern for the organizers of the Louis Vuitton Series than variable winds whistling through skyscrapers – now two and half times as tall as what I suffered – is Chicago's notorious light to non-existent winds in summer. While still a teenager racing keel boats, I can remember countless hours becalmed in front of that city. This always provided a ready excuse to sit on the pushpit looking for zephyrs off the end of a cigarette. This urban vacuum proved to be the case on Saturday, day one of the two-day Louis Vuitton event. Luckily, a northerly kicked in for the Sunday, creating the spectacle needed for the punters on Navy Pier which is arguably one of the best venues for a big city public to hold witness. Let's face it, though, a motorboat race would be more of a sure bet to satisfy the media and the crowds than a sailboat race with all the usual unpredictables that make sailboat races so interesting, at least for those of us who do them. In spite of half the event being a washout what turned in to a one day race event was a resounding success which is great news for the 'Windy City.' Organizers take note: the sobriquet 'Windy City' does not relate to wind alone, check Wikipedia.

Holding this event successfully was a fitting accolade for fresh water, Great Lakes sailors who if truth be known have always punched way above their weight when it comes to many international sailing events both on fresh and salt. Buddy Melges comes to mind, as do the Harken brothers, launching their careers from tiny lakes in Wisconsin. At a young age I was lucky enough to have been press-ganged into several Corinthian sailed yachts from Chicago that had stellar ocean racing careers. The owners needed foredeck fodder and I was the one to sort out the tangles up the rig and also jump over the side to put rubber bands on the folding propellers. Those privileges (going over the side in Lake Superior in May focused my mind to become a navigator as soon as possible), were my one-way ticket out for a life traversing the world's oceans, but I have never forgotten my Midwestern roots. I was overjoyed to hear that Chicago is firmly on the America's Cup map.

Although this stadium racing is all the go, it must be said that the risks for both organizers and sailors are substantial in these big city, urban environments where so much heat – both real and 'hot air' – is generated that any breeze at all often goes straight up. Coupled with too few days that are locked into live media slots it seems like a crap shoot to me, and in the end the casino always wins. Next stop Las Vegas?

THE VOLVO RACE RETURNS TO THE SOUTHERN OCEAN

'As the Volvo Ocean Race returns to its roots, Skip is glad to see the Southern Ocean leg returned to its proper place'

October 2016

I was very pleased to see the new course for the 2017 Volvo Ocean Race. Looking at the map graphic, the course line is more or less a logical circumnavigation. In previous editions the line that defined the course was a pretty unseamanlike piece of rope – thrown haphazardly across the deck of the world. It has now been re-run and straightened out, with only a single bight north to Hong Kong on the 'far side of the world.' This should appease the diehard traditionalists of the Whitbread era. Having said that they might gulp in their beer as the new course is a staggering 45,000 nautical miles. The Whitbread Races were a mere 27,000.

The classic stops are accounted for. Cape Town, 'Tavern of Seas', is always a given. Frankly there is no practical alternative. Known to the Dutch East India Company as a 'refreshment stop', that description is as true today as it was then when their ships took on wood, water and provisions. I will never forget Table Mountain looming above a clear horizon when 50 miles out on Leg I in the 1977 Whitbread.

Auckland is in and would be a tragedy to ignore given the Kiwis' enthusiasm and support for the event during all these years. I love the place so much I became a New Zealand resident after the 1989 race on *Fazisi* – but then lost it when I focused on my charter business in Tierra del Fuego. And of course Brazil (if not Rio this time) to recover from the cold and have some fun in the sun is a must. We were bust in Rio in 1977 on *King's Legend*, but no matter with the carnival in full swing. And now there is the mandatory stop in America at Newport before the finale. After that the rope's end gets frayed and messy, tangled up in European ports to satisfy various commercial interests that evidently cannot be ignored.

Yes, the ports still have leverage. Such was the paucity of entries on all previous recent editions that any semblance to an 'around the world race' had gone by the board. It was more of a regatta that happened to take in the entire planet. Abu Dhabi's decision not to take part in the coming edition and no other takers from the Middle East certainly made the impetus to simplify the course that much easier.

More continuity is certainly evident, largely due to the legacy CEO Knut Frostad left behind. He is largely credited with saving the show. The decision to finally go for a one-design was clear thinking and represented a watershed. Recycling the former fleet into the next event was the guarantee. If anyone can build on this situation it is the new CEO Mark Turner, the Svengali of ocean racing management – and he is off to a great start.

What is exciting for everyone, though, is the return to some serious Southern Ocean sailing. This is what always attracted those of us during the Whitbread era. We looked forward to diving south and enduring the thrills and spills. And equally we were very glad when it was all over when we turned that corner at Cape Horn into the relative calm of the South Atlantic. Note that we never had limits on how far south we could go. This will be interesting to address given event management paranoia about routing the course through ice zones.

And while offshore our races were private affairs. It is fun to imagine if we had been wired up with cameras semi live to race control, the media and the public, how it would have been received. Well, I can't really. Much of it would have been censored for one reason or another and so many beeps for strong and inappropriate language the narrative would have been meaningless. I'm sure there will be a few beeps here and there on the internet feeds for 2017, if the Southern Ocean lives up to reputation – well, at least I hope so.

Postscript

Mark Turner's plans to revolutionize that event were too radical for 2017 and he was forced out of the driver's seat. He was two events too early and largely what he was planning did happen for the 2022/2023 Ocean Race (yet another moniker) with foiling IMOCA Boats, although with a paucity of entries. But the event continues to struggle to get a field of 10 starters, which is always the goal of the organizers. It lumbers on but how long this format survives is anyone's guess.

THE VOLVO OCEAN RACE STILL STRUGGLING WITH EQUITY

'The Volvo Ocean Race's system to encourage female crew is confusing. There is only one good solution'

December 2017

And they're off! Another Volvo Ocean Race (VOR) is underway – the toughest fully crewed race around the world. And how it has evolved over the years with all sorts of permutations of boats (some weird and wonderful during the Whitbread days) at last culminating in the current one-design. The idea of a circumnavigation also has seen major changes through the event's history. Most were marketing-led course detours away from that original simple string pulled tight around Cape Agulhas, Cape Leeuwin and Cape Horn – with the necessary hockle in the block of Auckland. You can't have a Volvo without it. The race had to evolve in various ways to survive, no doubt about it.

Yacht racing's impresario Mark Turner, the briefly crowned CEO of the Volvo who resigned on the eve of the start (and who took over from Knut Frostad, who is credited with saving the event after some tricky moments), breathed yet more life and dynamism into the Volvo, but possibly went too far in his plans for a two-year cycle in foiling mono-hulls along with foiling cats for the inshore series. At the time of writing this column it is not clear what the future holds for the VOR.

This current edition is noteworthy for the obvious attempt to get more female participation. Remember my column in *Yachting World* in June 2015 (see page 37) that caused such a storm of controversy and not a few letters to the editor during the final stages of the last race? I had to keep my head down after suggesting that a succession of all-female crews since Tracy Edwards' groundbreaking all-female team in the 1989 Whitbread, for various reasons mooted, were not capable of getting past a last place. I suggested an elegant solution – 50% female and 50% male for the next event – as the only way to solve this dilemma of gender equality let alone participation. Arguably, though, there is a case that has been made that there is a dearth of female sailors of the calibre required for the Volvo. That argument is specious judging by the number of female applicants that could have easily supported a 50/50 split.

Then, you have the former Volvo Race winning skipper Paul Cayard making the point that why, for the world's premier offshore event, should there be any compromises at all with regards crew selection? Good point made. But today gender equality often trumps expediency. And we cannot imagine a separate Volvo Race or equivalent for females only. This is not tennis or golf.

So now we have a confusing system (for everyone, not least of all the general public) verging on an algorithm for crew combinations to 'even it all out.' To wit, you can have seven men; or seven men and one or two females; or seven women and one or two males; or five men, five females (my suggestion!); or eleven females. This minor absurdity masks the bare fact that men, just as women, come in a variety of shapes, sizes, strengths and weaknesses. It is a contrived invention at best.

Looking at the current crew lists at going to press it appears that save for Dee Caffari's *Turning the Tide for Plastic* at 50/50, all the other campaigns have gone with the two female, seven male option. Of course, this can change leg on leg, but it is an indication that an all-male crew is a non-starter for the obvious reasons of lack of pure person power with only seven all up, but maybe more to the point is politically incorrect. Even with seven superheroes, it would be a brave campaign indeed not to have some female participation.

Thanks to *Turning the Tide for Plastic* bumping up the numbers, this means we have roughly 35% of the Volvo crew list female. This is not as good as the percentage of females in the British parliament, but generally more favourable than a basket of global companies where females are on the boards and a lot more favourable compared to women in senior positions in those companies. Sweden, by the way, home of the Volvo is a front runner in this regard. So we are making progress if gender equality is what we are after in the Volvo. The only way to ultimately solve this quest is to simplify the equation to 50/50. It is the only logical option.

We should all wish Dee Caffari and *Turning the Tide on Plastic* the best of luck for a good result to drive that point home.

Postscript

For various reasons the actual figure for female participation in this event turned out to be only 21%. No doubt due to leg by leg crew changes.

LOOKING BACK IN TIME HAS REACHED ITS LIMITS

'There is little comparison between the Whitbread Race of old and the Volvo Ocean Race of today. These days it's for experts only'

March 2018

The last time I did the Whitbread Around the World Race was decades ago, but the Volvo Ocean Race organizers have never failed to resurrect me as a race 'Legend' (their word, not mine!) for enhancing subsequent editions. This has been one of the strengths of the Volvo Ocean Race in that they have never forgotten the contribution made by the pioneers and adventurers who set the scene for the magnificent spectacle we see today. The Legends Regatta in Alicante in 2011 was an example, followed by an invitation to the veteran yachts (some now almost museum pieces) to compete in a special last leg race to the Hague in June to coincide with the Volvo finish. I suppose there is something special about a circumnavigation of the planet under sail that keeps the history alive and this goes right back to Magellan and Drake, through Slocum, Chichester, Knox-Johnston and all those that followed whether singlehanded or fully crewed, racing or cruising.

During the Whitbread era the race course was a logical route around the world, which in order to survive into the future, not least in times of economic uncertainties, evolved into a marketing campaign of 'taking flyers' and 'overstanding lay lines' to accommodate entries from somewhat non-traditional locations. This has provided controversy and soul-searching for the organizers and the competitors alike. I am told there is now a strong move, even among the current Volvo *commercialistas,* to get the race back to approximating the original route and with fewer stopovers. This might be possible as even more on-board media technology brings the race ever more 'virtual' thereby decreasing the leverage of far-flung, off-the-trade-route ports. It will be interesting to see how the recent change of guard grapples with these options in defining the way forward whether the next edition be in 2019 or 2020.

Early on in the 1990s I was often asked to write articles for the pre-race brochures followed by the official race books comparing what it was like back then to now. This was interesting during that period of transition, but 27 years later the comparisons are arguably irrelevant. Stories of navigating around the world and finding Cape Horn with a sextant and timepiece I'm afraid are, by and large, generationally lost. And comparing the boats – well, there is no useful comparison other than to say the Volvo boats are in my view easier to sail as the gear is infinitely lighter and more reliable because of modern materials coupled with innovative sail control systems a plenty. The level of risk, though, due to the speeds and the amount of green water routinely coming aboard the Volvo 65s, is not to be taken lightly. It is now a very dangerous game only for expert crews.

During the events in 2011 and in 2014 during the Cape Town stopover I was asked to call the inshore race and the start from hospitality vessels for Volvo guests and the media but admittedly I knew very few of the competitors and had to wing my way through the narrative a bit by smoke and mirrors

For this Volvo I was convinced the connection had finally faded, but before the start they invited me as a VIP to participate at one of the stopovers 'of my choice.' I thought to myself, 'Here's a lark!' But where to go? I figured there were 'Legends' aplenty in Auckland so I put my hand up for China, as I had never been there. Alas, they realized I still lived in Cape Town so no air ticket was forthcoming! I was invited on board *Turning the Tide on Plastic* for the inshore race in Cape Town, which was an eye opener. Upwind on the chine at 25 degrees of heel I felt my age – and my knees.

This was a unique experience for me. I was told I was not allowed to do anything on board, nor tell anyone else to do anything! An awkward first! Dee Caffari and her crack young crew (including four Olympians no less) were relaxed and handled the boat with aplomb including making two out of three 'bang on' gennaker sets at the top mark. And you know what? The mix of 50/50 guys and girls looked and felt right. (Organizers, take note). Alas, we came 5th. When I watched the fleet after the Sunday restart beating along the coast into a cold southerly, as always and as you do, I momentarily imagined myself out there with them. You never quite lose that around-the-world race feeling.

GOLDEN GLOBE RACE COMPROMISES

'The Golden Globe Race is a simple concept but, like all recreations of events past, is also full of compromises by necessity'

January 2019

I have taken a new interest in the Golden Globe Race. How can we not? Peter Nichols, the author who wrote the acclaimed *A Voyage for Madmen* chronicling the 1968 epic might be already contemplating the sequel: *A Voyage for Madmen and One Woman* could be a title, or maybe *A Voyage for Mad Persons* would be more politically correct. Out of 18 starters the attrition rate is impressive at halfway around the world and there is a lot of stormy ocean left for the eight remainers to negotiate. Best of luck to them!

The concept of looking back in time to celebrate achievements of our past heroes is always worthwhile. The 'test voyages' of Tim Severin including the leather boat *Brendan* that sailed from Ireland to North America and Thor Heyerdahl's *Kon-Tiki* both come to mind , but they were academic endeavours using traditional vessels built with traditional materials in order to prove a hypothesis. And there was a lot of real adventure into the mix – well before the age of satellite phones and rescues on tap.

There have also been many journeys following the classic exploratory polar treks. For decades this has been a regular feature for adventurers – to follow in the footsteps of Scott, Amundsen, Shackleton and others. The idea is to emulate their achievements by pitting yourself against the same conditions in weather and terrain. A nice thing to do for sure, and that is about the extent of the value – a very personal journey with publicity attached or not. Of course, some of these projects get all blown out of proportion and ludicrous comparisons are made between then and now. To set off on a polar journey using anything but the most modern equipment and using current techniques would be foolhardy, so any comparisons of like for like are very debatable if not specious.

However, Tim Jarvis in 2007 went one step further with an attempt in re-creating Douglas Mawson's survival story in the Antarctic using traditional equipment and supplies. In 2013, he attempted to follow the famous Shackleton boat journey by using a replica *James Caird*, the crew dressed in traditional clothing, and using navigation equipment from the day. When people asked me what I thought about it all, my stock reply was, 'Impressive, but they did not eat the penguins...' – meaning that however you try to recreate a piece of history it can never be 100% authentic – so you have to be careful what you intend and later claim. These projects can never be more than attempts, as to emulate the original version is quite impossible for all sorts of reasons, not least of all as it doesn't have to be attempted in the first place. Mawson, and Shackleton's men, had no choice in order to survive. Having said all this, Tim's project from an educational perspective was a job superbly done, having reached a wide audience about all things Shackleton.

The Golden Globe Race has sort of found itself in the same boat. For being a back to basics project by definition it should be reasonably simple, but the Notice of Race is very complex indeed. It is full of compromises by necessity, both for safety and legal reasons. It remains a great adventure for the participants but many people will question the concept of setting off on a sea voyage, let alone a race around the world (with media pressures to boot as they are being tracked and interviewed along the way) without modern, standard, seafaring equipment and this implies the design of the boat itself. I'm not a nut on safety but I can very much appreciate that having a boat rigged and equipped from the 1960s compared to what is available now would inherently put people at some risk. I think we are seeing the evidence of this in the dropout rate. And let's be frank, Robin's *Suhaili* was anything but 'state of the art' in 1968. A convenient analogy in re-visiting a famous yachting competition would be the mighty J Class. They are full of carbon fibre, titanium and modern sail control systems. Doing it in the original way as they were built and equipped was a non-starter.

For myself, who knows only too well how much time it takes to do a 'day's work' of celestial navigation, I can imagine the participant's time is indeed short for many other daily urgencies assuming they are doing their calcs on a blank sheet of paper. The temptation to have smuggled on a $300 dollar Garmin GPS must have been huge – a piece of equipment that can easily be thrown overboard before the finish. Too harsh an assessment? Well, let's not forget Donald Crowhurst!

Postscript

The only female entry, Suzie Goodall, pitchpoled 2,000 miles west of Cape Horn and had to be rescued, dismasted. Of the 18 entries only five finished the race.

In the event in 2022/2023, the only female entry, Kirsten Neuschafer, won the race, and only three of the 16 starters finished. Two more, who made repair stops, were demoted into the Chichester Class and made it to the finish.

This continues to be a popular event and there are no shortage of entries for the next one.

CAPE TOWN IS ON THE MAP

'Cape Town has, of necessity, always been a vital stop for sailors. Now they're making a point of paying a visit'

February 2020

At the bottom of Africa it is a long way from traditional yacht racing venues other than for scheduled stops or for emergencies repairs on the various globetrotting races that are yearly in one form or another. The Tavern of the Seas has lately been in focus for several headline projects. Cape Town is firmly on the map.

Superyachts on a world cruise occasionally pop in, but the likes of the 86m ketch *Aquijo* was a show stopper. Arriving in mid-October for a quick refit her 92m rigs dominated the city skyline for three weeks. She came up from the Indian Ocean and was bound for Europe with a stop in St Helena. I had the privilege of piloting her in Tierra del Fuego and around Cape Horn in 2018.

Some weeks after *Aquijo* departed, the Clipper fleet arrived on a very short pit stop before continuing on to Fremantle, Australia. I ran into Robin Knox-Johnston at the Royal Cape Yacht Club and caught up on news. We had sailed together around the Horn in 2008 for the BBC's *Top Dogs* programme and immediately the talk turned to sailing expeditions. He tells me he is off to East Greenland next summer... Robin is now 80 but hands on as usual. After I distracted him with various other ideas, he excused himself and rushed off to help repair a rudder on one of the Clipper boats.

Sadly, at the restart of Leg 4 of the Clipper Race the yachts *Visit Sanya, China* and *Punta del Este* had a port/starboard incident just before a turning buoy in Table Bay. After adjudication and extensive repairs to both boats, this disqualified *Visit Sanya, China* from Leg 4. This was a 'bear away' gone wrong, which I suspect was a fouled mainsheet – something a non-professional crew member might easily do. It is one thing to foul a winch offshore in the middle of nowhere, another when at close quarters at the beginning of an ocean race with 4,000 miles to Fremantle. *Visit Sanya, China* (on port) drove their bow sprit right into the cockpit of *Punta del Este*. Luckily no one was injured – or worse. The intensity of racing on the Clipper, which started out many years ago as a rally cum race, is noteworthy. It is now no rally. Let's not forget how in the last edition of the Clipper when *Greenings* ran aground by getting too close to the beach near the Cape of Good Hope she was unsalvageable and was written off.

No sooner had the Clipper fleet left than we had Giovanni Soldini's Multi70 trimaran *Mazerati* pull in, fresh from breaking various clipper ship records. They are entered for the Cape to Rio Race that begins early January. They claim they can make Rio in six days, in what has become a staggered start event.

Then on 21st November two of the four 'Ultime' trimarans – arguably more aircraft than sailboat – in the Brest Atlantiques (race) made unscheduled stops. Starting and ending in Brest, Mandela's Robben Island was a mark of this ocean triangle along with an island turning mark off Brazil. Trimaran *Macif* drifted outside of Cape Town Harbour for a few hours to effect repairs on their steering system, while *Sodebo* was obliged to enter the port after breaking her starboard rudder and stripping off the back end of that float. Service teams from both boats had flown in and were logistically supported by Manuel Mendez and his boatyard in the V&A Waterfront – who seems to be involved with every visiting yachtsman that comes to Cape Town.

Sadly, while *Macif* took off at speed, skipper Thomas Coville on *Sodebo* was forced to retire after discovering more structural damage in the starboard foil case.

Although Cape Town lends itself by simple geography as an obvious stopover, planned or otherwise, note that the TP52 fleet arrived in February 2020 as deck cargo for a regatta in early March followed by the TP52 Worlds at the end of that month. Clearly, this pre-eminent owner driver's event chose Cape Town for its exotic location, not to mention extra curriculars for the crews including the Cape of Good

Hope, the Cape winelands and many other tourist attractions. Shark cage diving, anyone?

It was all very exciting to see so many ocean going greyhounds in port and such pre-eminent events scheduled in. This is a boon for Cape Town and for its sailors. Long may it last.

BACKING OFF TO WIN

'How hard should you push in a race as competitive as the Vendée Globe? There must come a point when it's time to back off'

March 2021

I am a lousy fan – of any sport. If I can't actually do it, I am ambivalent. However, I do tune in to the FIFA World Cup and Rugby World Cup finals and of course as a Yank, the Super Bowl, for no other reason than to arm myself for the 'Monday morning' conversations downstream. Best not to be totally ignorant of any important world event, whether that be famine, war, an election or sport.

Same goes for yacht racing. The amount of sailing news on various forums is overwhelming. I am wondering how people have the time to take this all in and still function with a job and family to support. However, in the same vein I will watch the actual America's Cup, but to follow the whole story from the end of the last one is too time consuming. And the Volvo Ocean Race is also too long and drawn out to keep me interested. Not so the Vendée Globe, though, as it is short enough to capture even my attenuated attention span. And being based in Cape Town was reason enough to stay tuned in. We had three Vendée 'visitors.'

This post by Charlie Dalin certainly caught my eye on 3rd December 2020. At the time he was the race leader:

'I am discovering something I have never had to do before,' said Dalin. 'I have to un-trim, detune my boat. I feel now 50% of the time I am trying to trim the sails and the foils and keel to go faster, and 50% of the time I am de-tuning the boat. I find myself looking for the brake pedal. The sea state in the Indian Ocean is really what is limiting my speed. Sometimes the boat accelerates in the surf and we go to 28–30kts and you don't know how it is going to end. It is a really weird to way to think, "I have this wind strength, this wind angle is this and I have these sails up, and I have the foil set like this, but if I change all these setting I should slow the boat down, and slow the boat down." I never had to do this before in my racing career.'

This was a shocker for yours truly, who during his antediluvian ocean racing career always accepted that you cannot push 100% all of the time. I thought anyone doing something like the Vendée would take this as a given. But apparently not, and although the attrition rate in retirees is nothing out of the usual, could this be the reason we saw those first structural failures in the Atlantic more or less at the start of this ocean racing marathon? Was it pedal to the metal and come what may? I do get the impression that especially the younger pilots, fresh off the Figaro circuit (and maybe those who have been around the block and should know better), just wind these fragile machines up and then hope for the best. With the speeds having increased dramatically with the new generation of foiled IMOCA 60s, hitting 'square waves' surely has to be avoided. In the heat of the moment when there was all to play for by dropping first into the Southern Ocean and possibly gaining an enormous advantage on a weather system you can appreciate the reasons for being a bit over zealous, and consequently the loss of the bigger picture.

Even when sailing those painful IOR medium displacement boats back in the day, it was impossible to keep pushing 100% and you had to finesse your way through certain wind, and especially sea, conditions. On the wind, pounding in a head sea would spell some sort of serious breakage, if not sails exploding and bow sections delaminating, then possibly the whole rig going over the side. Off the wind, pushing too hard for too long meant a broach or a Chinese gybe – and you rarely escaped those two fiascos unscathed. With a full crew, there were also psychological considerations. I can very well remember when I was pushing things a bit in the Whitbreads, grumbling and strange looks from the rogue's gallery on the weather rail made me take a pull. And I imagine while singlehanded, if I may say so having no experience myself, going full tilt all of the time must be poor judgement in the first place which leads to dodgy decisions downstream simply due to the stress factor.

Short course racing is a different story where to win does require a 100% flat out approach – I suppose you can include a transatlantic in that category where total time at sea is measured in days, not the months which are still required for any circumnavigation. There has to be some down time calculated as needed in the mix. I remember in the 1997/98

Volvo Ocean Race when that short course racing supremo Paul Cayard on *EF Language* would later admit that when they pushed too hard at the start of Leg 2 out of Cape Town they got their comeuppance in the Southern Ocean and scared themselves into a different *modus operandi.* He got smart quick and went on to win the race.

I suspect the previous winners of the Vendée at some time or another would also have had that epiphany, before it was too late.

KIRSTEN ENTERS THE
GOLDEN GLOBE

'Dwelling on the past is not in Skip's nature, but the next edition of the nostalgic Golden Globe Race has piqued his interest'

April 2021

During the 'time of the Covid', while recounting my past sailing history on webinars, podcasts, Zooms and other online forums, of which I have done far too many for my own ego, I had to re-visit the fact that I really don't like dwelling on past events. To wit, I have never re-read my two books, *One Watch at a Time*, or *Fazisi – the Joint Venture*. I will do so someday, to amuse myself, but must wait for complete immobilization when my number is up. No, I like to look ahead to the next project and luckily have always kept something on the boil to plan for and execute.

However, that's not to say I can't vicariously become involved in the most famous of retro sailing events, the Golden Globe Race (GGR). Sceptical of the whole idea during the first edition, I could not help but follow the second, which began on 4th September 2022. Why? One of my *Pelagic* skippers, Kirsten Neuschafer, was entered – the only female entry in the field of 31.

Kirsten, a gem from South Africa, landed up in the *Pelagic* world in about 2016. I can't even recall how she got on board, but after sailing with her on an expedition to South Georgia I was sold. She has crewed on *Pelagic*, then *Pelagic Australis* on many voyages to the Antarctic Peninsula and South Georgia and logically took over running *Pelagic* in 2018. She is one of those increasingly rare individuals in the yachting game who as we used to say, 'just gets on with things.' She is in the game for the doing. Not that I don't pay a fair wage, but wages, holiday times, rest periods and insurances just don't come into the equation for Kirsten. She is happy with simply a challenge. And she took on a big one.

An inveterate singlehander, the Golden Globe must have been in the back of her mind for some time. Of course, dreaming is one thing and putting a plan together and following through is another. How many of these sailor's dreams must have washed ashore on the rocks of despair or gathered dust on the shelves of what might have been?

During the spring of 2019, after delivering *Pelagic* non-stop from the Falklands to Bermuda (stopping there only to apply for a US visa), she eventually fetched up in mid coast Maine where I had friends scheduled to help her prepare for what was to be an Arctic sailing season. For a variety of reasons our refit was delayed and what was left of the summer was a friend's cruise circumnavigating Newfoundland, by all accounts a very satisfying experience. Not needing too much encouragement, over saloon table conversations Kirsten bought into the idea of the Golden Globe. She did some research and located a Cape George 36 for sale, coincidentally on the north coast of Newfoundland. The boat was surveyed later in the fall and purchased with help from her Newfoundland crew.

When Covid struck in March 2020 and shut down all things everywhere, the adventure of getting back to the boat had begun. Back in Maine we optimistically relaunched *Pelagic* hoping that charters we had in August (once the curve had 'flattened out') could continue. The plan then was for Kirsten to bring her Cape George 36 *Minnehaha* back to Maine in early fall to begin the refit for the GGR.

Of course, she never got there – until December. Sailing from Newfoundland to Maine in mid-winter might seem cavalier, and many of us advised against it, but she was determined to get south. The real challenge was getting herself across the border into Canada, which, after so many attempts and false starts, where most of us would have thrown in the towel, she pulled off by some bureaucratic loophole. In short order the boat was launched and she set off cautiously down the Newfoundland coast in one snow storm after another. After crossing the Cabot Strait, she called a halt at Summerside, Prince Edward Island, at the onset of the winter freeze up. The locals took her in and a heated shed on private land was offered her, so she could get to work. This is 'on the hoof', come what may, from the school of 'one thing leads to another.'

Within days the teak deck was ripped up, hatches dismantled and a dicky engine and drive train seriously looked into. The plan was to continue to Maine in April, re-rig with a new mast and begin the sea trials – and continue to raise money to make this dream a reality. From that point she had a year and a half to prepare for the start of the race.

Getting this project together was a tall order, but I was very confident she would pull this off and get to the starting line and beyond to the finish. I speak for all my charter clients who have sailed with Kirsten who have without exception have been more than impressed with her abilities and more importantly in just being an excellent shipmate – not, however, that the latter is critical in the Golden Globe! As any single-hander knows, you have to be comfortable in your own skin. Kirsten surely has the 'right stuff.'

Postscript

As it turned out, and is usually the case when you are in a place with enthusiastic helpers, the refit became more extensive and continued right through the summer at Prince Edward Island (PEI) and into the fall. As a sea trial she left PEI and sailed non-stop all the way to Cape Town, arriving there in late January 2022. She then sailed non-stop all the way back to Europe for the pre-start commitments.

Note that for the dreamers – the 31 paid up entries – only 18 made it to the start with three dropouts soon after the fleet left France.

GOLDEN GLOBE COMPROMISES

'Are "retro" race competitors better off being left to battle the elements undisturbed?'

December 2021

With the start of the Golden Globe Race less than a year away, the media machine kicked in. There were now 27 competitors including my race favourite, Kirsten Neuschafer, the only female entry and our beloved *Pelagic* veteran of many years.

As I have said and alluded to in this column previously I am not a huge fan of these retro events. They attempt to recreate something that is not possible to achieve in the truest sense of the objective. They start out with an ideology and along the way many compromises are made to address safety and the realities of this day and age. Having said that the interest of many would be circumnavigators (armchair ones included) has taken hold and the event is a winning formula. Hats off to Don Macintyre.

One of those compromises is the media. As an organizer you cannot run an event like this as it was in 1968. The whole show depends on getting those stories from the skippers out to the wider public. Everyone's budget depends on it to a greater or lesser extent. There is no turning the clock back on this necessity, but a dilemma exists.

In spite of passing by Cape Town himself in 1968, I can't help wonder what Bernard Moitessier would have made of the required media gates along the way where competitors essentially drop off film cannisters and do an interview while coming in contact with points of land during what should be a no holds barred race around the world. I think he would be rolling around in his grave in fits of Gallic laughter.

The fleet is required to pass close to Cape Town harbour, which took not only me, but also many of my deep water cronies aback. For a logical safe passage, yachts on any non-stop around the world race should be, by the time they are at the longitude of Cape Town, at least 400 miles south and well stuck into the following winds of the Southern Ocean. Arriving into Cape Town can be problematic, battling the storm force southeasters coming off the land which is a regular feature during the summer season. Leaving can be trickier. Not only the southeaster can bring you up short in trying to make southing, but more serious can be the temptation to cut the corner across the Agulhas Bank rather than dip straight south to avoid it.

There are two good reasons for giving it a miss. First, this is ship-breaking country, where the west-going Agulhas Current pushes into the prevailing westerlies at two to three knots creating big and confused seas, not to mention volatility of a warm current meeting colder oncoming conditions.

Second, if you follow the shortest course coming off a stop in Cape Town, there is a zone where the bank at 200m dives down to over 3,000m over a distance of 20 nautical miles. On the way back from Marion Island on a charter in April 2021 we jumped up and over this ledge and had to drop all sails in a panic when tossed and twisted around like a cork from rail to rail and bow down to stern down. It didn't last but a half hour, but it was dramatic. *Pelagic Australis* is 74 feet. This condition could easily capsize a 36 footer.

Another media stop in Storm Bay Tasmania is also a circumnavigator's *bête noire*, as it takes you out of the rhythm of the Southern Ocean into variable conditions and up an estuary! Not only can this be frustrating but it introduces unwelcome unknown scenarios for the competitors. Some will get lucky with a quick in and out, while others will be becalmed and languish for days, depending on when they arrive. That interview could produce a disappointing outcome.

The fact is, deviating from a logical route introduces situations where these small boats might be obliged to beat their guts out to an interview when they could be sliding off on a reach, safely along the course. This also holds true for all the Southern Ocean 'marks of the course' whether they be islands or virtual buoys defining a maximum southern latitude. I am reminded of Josh Hall's Class 40 Global Ocean Race in 2011/12 where he had a virtual buoy to round in the South Pacific to keep the fleet out of the ice. They found themselves on a gruelling windward leg in the Southern Ocean. Two boats retired due to damage or lack of will. That was in open ocean. What is worse is trying to weather a sub-Antarctic island to avoid a time penalty which if you get it wrong can put a boat on a lee shore.

Unlike the Vendée IMOCA 60s travelling at speed that can run from weather, I would like to offer the opinion, as unwelcome as it might be, that the GGR boats with tortoise-like speeds at mercy of the weather are in comparison more at risk in fighting big seas and winds while trying to round marks, than they are at risk of hitting ice. I think the southern max limit should be abolished as today we all know going too far south is too risky not only for ice, but also for possible headwinds. These natural limits should be implied and understood rather than regulated for.

Back to the media addiction, surely there must be a way to satiate the public with simple text only stories via say the Garmin InReach and let the sailors get on with their challenge, in solitude, safer. After all, wasn't that the point of entering? And for us, the fans, let's leave something to our imagination, and maybe the anticipation of a book or two at the end.

Solution? How about some industrial action? Let the sailors decide by a super majority vote (not making the mistake of the Brexit simple majority) whether they want these media gates, virtual buoys and marks of the course – or not. Remember it is their race.

Postscript

Although many others expressed this opinion as well as several of the competitors, the media as advertised had to be sated. No changes were made prior to the start, but it will be interesting to see what will change, if anything, for the next event.

Regarding the ice limits, I am told that what can be an arbitrary line of latitude is dictated by how far out the various 'search and rescue' services are willing to go for a rescue and this mainly concerns Australia as they have been involved in quite a few Southern Ocean operations. However, it was painful to watch some of the competitors struggling to just keep out of the penalty zone – they must have been cursing these rules.

Of course, this is all history now. Kirsten won the race, the first female sailor (although she would never make this distinction) to have ever won an around the world race event. Her level of preparedness and what was a more than extensive test sail were some of the many contributing factors that led to her success in winning the Golden Globe Race. Finally, like Moitessier and Knox-Johnston in 1969, she was obviously, out of all the entries, the most comfortable and happy just being at sea.

3 DESIGN AND MAINTENANCE

The Pelagic 77 *Vinson of Antarctica* launched in the spring of 2021 and soon to be joined by a sister ship for expedition charters, are the culmination of everything I have learned about what it means to sail efficiently in high latitude environments. They are all about form following function with little compromise. Rather than the same old lines, more or less of every boat in a given marina, these vessels do catch the eye right off the bat. Insofar as design issues then, every awkward looking shape and profile or unusual feature has a reason, which only becomes apparent when you are truly at sea. None of my boats were ever meant to be hanging around the docks for very long.

Then there are the details. In spite of trying to stick to my mantra of keeping things simple, these boats are certainly more complicated in systems than the original *Pelagic* (1987) and *Pelagic Australis* (2003), mainly due to coding and frankly failing to find those simpler solutions that are no longer available. Nevertheless, my thoughts on the minutiae required in maintenance always holds true.

I am also continually amazed at the amount of equipment that is on offer in yacht chandleries and online – much of which is low quality, junk if I be so bold. Out of some necessity when I do visit a well-appointed chandlery I begin to feel ill, as I do in a shopping mall when I can't help but to ponder if all that is for sale there really adds anything to one's wellbeing and happiness.

The mountaineer/sailor Bill Tilman said in his book *Mischief in Greenland*, written in 1962, 'What a lot of money owners of small boats waste on mechanical devices that cannot always be depended upon and which anyway save only a few minutes' labour!'

THE ILLUSION OF WEAR AND TEAR

'"Well used" is surely a compliment for a yacht cruising off the beaten track, where keeping things "just so" is an exercise in futility'

August 2015

When superyachts began coming to Tierra del Fuego and the Antarctic Peninsula in the mid-90s, I gave some professional advice and provided a pilot/guide to a well-known German owner of a 45-metre sloop. When they dropped anchor in the bay of Ushuaia, this impeccably maintained luxury yacht certainly stood out while the motley crews of the motley cruising fleet took high notice.

During the pre-departure preparations and discussions on board I invited the owner and his guests for a drink on my *Pelagic*. This was a risky gambit on my part. The owner was, as you would expect, a serious, no-nonsense gentleman. He sat down in our main saloon, taking his time to look around, and eventually curled out his lower lip, a habit that many German's have when in thought or about to make a judgment call. He simply said, 'Well used...' I'm sure he noticed the worn and abraded edges on the interior furniture (we didn't have a dog on board, but it looked like we had). Ditto the smoke stains on the overhead from the diesel heater. The saloon table sported enough dings, scratches and burn marks that if they could be translated would fill a short story. I served him an aperitif in our chipped tumblers, and on and on.

'Well used...' I like to think it was an accolade and not a criticism. If so it implied a vessel fit for purpose and looking like it. That encounter sticks in my mind every time another precious yacht rocks up in the far south, and can of course be applied to any location off the beaten path with no marinas and marine services. Superyachts of course are a different kettle of fish. High end maintenance by professional crews lends itself to perfect appearance always and that spirit is ingrained in the culture. Trying to maintain your small to midsize cruiser on your own with that same level of perfection is an exercise in futility. The French cruisers, famous for venturing further afield than most, discovered the joys of bare aluminium hulls and decks long ago for this very reason. If your priority is cruising to see the world, then at a minimum the sailing and mechanical systems must function and the aesthetics be damned.

Even keeping a certain level of cleanliness can be challenging. Rafting up with other yachts less pernickety can be a source of amusement, especially in the far south. When a new, pristine arrival makes alongside the rickety jetty it is always worth hanging around if the locals begin to stack up outboard (usually unannounced). Crises occur and tempers flare as it is impossible to take off shoes (invariably muddy) in this climate when crossing a nice teak deck. Filthy fenders, lifelines stepped on, water hoses and electrical cables dragged across the coach roof without notice and heaven forbid – trooping through the cockpit and not around in front of the mast.

Beyond simple appearances where paint jobs having 'gone south', the leather on the steering wheel is now patched with tape and there are scuff marks on the topsides, there is also the consideration of wear and tear on standing and running rigging, sails, shackles and other fundamentally important parts and pieces. This requires some knowledge of safety factors and loads and what can last the distance before replacement is necessary. A 'D' shackle 30% worn through might be OK for one application but dangerous for another. A certain amount of wear and tear in these cases should be acceptable. It is impossible to maintain a cruising yacht 'like new' all the time. I have seen this mindset compromise many a cruise and in fact make for an unhappy ship in the attempt. Best to kick back a bit, do as the Romans do and enjoy it while it lasts, as you will be back in marina land soon enough.

CAPE TOWN REFIT – NOT TO BE MISSED

'Cape Town is an ocean away from my base in the Falklands, but it's worth the trip to get a proper refit done. The scenery's nice too'

February 2017

Sailing to Cape Town is a long haul from just about everywhere. Rather, it is more of a logistical break en route to somewhere else. The Dutch East India Company was the first to realize this in the mid-seventeenth century. Initially they stopped to take on wood and water and thereafter established farms and livestock to augment fresh provisions for their ships sailing on to Batavia. After several skirmishes, by the close of the Napoleonic Wars in 1814 the British finally affirmed possession via the Anglo-Dutch Treaty. And so the Cape Colony evolved, known to seafarers down through the ages, right through the present as a *de facto* stop for the Volvo Ocean Race.

Right off the trade wind cruising map South Africa also suffered sailing sanctions in the late 80s during the death throes of Apartheid. In fact the Whitbread Race skipped it and went to Uruguay in 1989. Recently we are seeing an increase in traffic coming through Cape Town. Super and mega yachts both sail and power have been stopping here for lengthy periods staging themselves for their next cruises going west to the Caribbean or east about into the Indian Ocean. And for the small to medium size cruisers the Royal Cape Yacht Club is always welcoming – situated right in the middle of the port's ship repair facilities with the most extraordinary commercial vessels to marvel at.

For one who has spent a fair amount of time in refits living in less than salubrious shipyard environments, the port of Cape Town is a dream scenario. We do an annual service on *Pelagic Australis* from June to September which is our off-season. It is worth sailing across the breadth of the South Atlantic – albeit with charter clients on the way there and dead heading on the way back – to avoid South American ports (I have tried them all) having to negotiate bureaucratic hoops and ladders and dealing with a less than efficient workforce.

Although there is a lack of hauling out facilities for small craft in Cape Town and little or no hard space to linger on, 'in the water' refits benefit from a well-represented marine industry. A large portion of the world's catamaran charter fleets are built here with Robertson and Caine leading the field. Southern Wind Shipyards build three 30m+ super sailing yachts per year to European standards. Mast makers and sailmakers are on hand and for parts (yacht spares or hardware items) or raw materials these are easily accessed in either of two industrial parks within a ten or fifteen minute drive. It is all so easy when compared to chasing bits and pieces across town where the shops with the O rings are on one side of the city and the alternator repair shops are on the other. We have all been there, done that, spending our days in taxis.

But what I really enjoy, if doing a refit can ever be that enjoyable, is the atmosphere in the V&A Waterfront Marina. For those of a certain age who remember what developers did to Newport, Rhode Island, in the 70s and 80s stripping out all the commercial wharfage, shipyards and fishing boats to accommodate condominiums, restaurants and knick-knack shops the V&A stands out as perfect blend of a waterfront shopping mall that co-exists seamlessly with a real working port. The artisanal fishing boats are still there, as are cold storage facilities. A dry dock serving medium size ships is an attraction for the tourists, while the syncrolift which we come up on is next to a five star hotel. Granted that is not for luxury yachts – we spend a fair amount of time when up on the syncro side slipping away from shot blasting operations and dodging overspray from work done on commercial rust buckets from all nations. However, with the winelands close by, beautiful beaches up and down the coast and the wilderness of Table Mountain overlooking the city there are plenty of distractions when the inevitable frustrations of a refit gets to be too much to bear.

Postscript

All the above is still true, but we can say since I wrote that piece there has been a lack of evolution in Cape Town for yacht services. A superyacht complex was mooted within a revamp of the waterfront at

Granger Bay, and then scrapped when funding from Dubai was pulled out. More plans to modify the dry dock to create hard space is the latest idea, but I am not anticipating it. The wheels of government decision-making turn almost imperceptibly in South Africa. Yachts are not a priority, whereas hard space for container distribution and ship repair is. The Royal Cape Yacht Club is under continuous threat of losing their lease in the port with nowhere else to go. There is a 100-tonne travel lift in Saldanha Bay Yacht Port, but it is a two hour drive to Cape Town in case you need a 10/24 machine screw easily found in Paarden Eiland. Not so viable for refits other than a haul out.

Having said all of this, and not neglecting the fact that Cape Town, as all other parts of South Africa, suffers at times up to 12 hours a day without mains electricity, it is always an inspiring and dynamic place to cast your lines ashore for a time.

A WORKING FOREPEAK
SHOULD BE DESIRED

'A yacht with no stowage in the forepeak and beds instead of berths forward of the mast is only fit for day sailing between marinas'

September 2017

Where have all the forepeaks gone? After perusing the websites of some of the best known yacht builders, I am struggling to see a design with an adequate forepeak, at least one suited for cruising beyond 'marina land.' I'm talking about a walk in, full head height forward space where you can 'swing a cat.'

I mean, if you buy a yacht billed as a 'world cruiser', a 'go anywhere concept' and a 'blue water dream', at least for me this implies load carrying capacity for 'stuff.' Here is a short list of a few big, should have items for a midsize boat planning to cruise the mid latitudes and the tropics : spare anchor and rode, inflatable dinghy and one spare, spare outboard, some spare running rigging and cordage, snorkelling and diving gear, fishing gear, paddles, oars, awnings, a gennaker and more. Then there are the optional toys – SUPs (inflatable), surfboards, kiteboarding gear, folding bicycles and the rest according to your interests and fancy. Go high latitudes and you can add camping gear and skis.

Unless you plan to voyage as a floating boat jumble with most of this gear lashed all over the deck and some of it suspended from gantries and bimini tops, which is pretty unseaworthy, all this equipment must somehow disappear into the lazarette and cockpit lockers when offshore, which by definition even on the best designs are small, horrendously uncomfortable spaces accessed by deck hatches. All possible of course, but when it comes time to get out the fins and masks quickly to jump over the side and watch that sea turtle, the turtle will have long since disappeared by the time you have dug down through multiple layers of other kit, like a Houdini, bruised knuckles and all. Sound familiar?

When renting or buying a house the price is largely determined by the number of bedrooms, and so it seems this has transcended into yacht sales. Often, cramming the maximum number of berths in is the key marketing tool. Maybe I'm getting old and intolerant, but the idea of 8 to 9 people cruising on a 55 footer? This is what catamarans are for.

Not only the number of berths, but a certain configuration has also become a standard. Almost invariably, the owner's bunk is now in the forepeak and resembles a five star hotel suite with a free standing double bed, not a 'berth.' And of course, like a five star suite would be, it is absolutely useless at sea for sleeping. This forward space on any yacht is really only fit for inanimate objects, lashed down. Even with some clever dividers and lee cloths suspended from pad eyes on the designer ceiling, can a berth with no bulkhead surrounds ever be comfortable at sea? I realize for Mediterranean mooring this is very desirable and for marina bound charter fleets operating in sheltered waters it is now a standard feature. But to market this concept as an owner's cabin for a yacht capable of world cruising is stretching credibility in truth in advertising.

An alternative layout, especially on larger yachts is the hotel suite aft, with the professional crew, if you have any, or possibly your guests, wedged into tiny forward berths hard by the crash bulkhead. They will have to migrate aft when at sea, taking up space in the main saloon.

On my boat I sleep in the foremost cabin just forward of the mast – and it is a wild ride enough. Forward of that any sleeping accommodation would be exquisite torture of levitation and then impact. Even downwind it is a pretty unpleasant sensation. I suspect quite a few owners have realized when it is all too late that they will have to move aft into a guest cabin offshore. Probably not what they had in mind, when signing the contract.

To have a real working forepeak seems fundamental for any serious cruising design. Back in the days of the IOR racing fleet, with yachts that doubled as cruisers between regattas, this was a practical necessity. Sail bins for an enormous sail inventory encouraged by that rule shared that space with cordage and all manner of racing hardware. It was also a great place when in port to have a bit of fun in the folds of the 2.2 oz. spinnaker... I suspect even the current designers when in their youth might have indulged. Maybe that's where the concept of sleeping up there in the first place got started.

Postscript

Six years on any effect that this column might have had has been ignored. We still get, however, nods of approval and envy by anyone visiting the Pelagic yachts, right up to Vinson of Antarctica, when they peruse the forepeak space. The problem is designers and builders, custom or production, are so ingrained with this concept of 'bums on berths' that to do otherwise is a hard sell to a market generally ignorant of what is really necessary to build a fit for purpose 'world cruiser.'

ARE THEY REALLY EXPEDITION YACHTS?

'Expedition yacht designs have proliferated, but are they really fit for true expedition sailing?'

May 2018

In adventure travel today it appears everyone is on an 'expedition' in one form or another. It is to a great extent an overused word usually out of context, but it is sexy sounding – unlike being on a 'tour.'

I use 'expedition' liberally in my charter business and I hope we can claim some semblance of veritas, although I am obliged to admit that those of us who sail to the high Arctic or deep south or anywhere else in between for that matter are all tourists in the end. The days of geographically exploring 'blanks on the map' are really over, unless you leave your laptop with Google Earth behind on purpose.

The accepted definition of 'expedition' gleaned and distilled from various sources on the web goes something like this: 'An organized journey or voyage for a specific purpose, especially for exploration or for a scientific or military purpose.' To be honest, the purpose can simply be a pleasure cruise however adventurous.

My own caveats to the above are 'a journey that is extended, one that goes into a relatively remote area and where one is self-sufficient.'

These are the parameters that dictated the build of my two expedition sailing vessels *Pelagic* and *Pelagic Australis*. Both were overbuilt for all the knocks, groundings and general wear and tear that expedition sailing implies. Both can be autonomous for two months with respect to fuel and provisions. More to the point they are relatively simple in their systems so that our crews can keep them going in the field and make any running repairs needed – the purpose being to finish the voyage without the need to bail out because of mechanical failures. I can say with hand on my wooden heart that things work all of the time. The secret is simply to have less equipment and less elaboration.

I am continually amused and bemused when I see the proliferation of production 'expedition yachts' advertised and in build. Not a month goes by when one of these is not featured in *Yachting World*. They are marketing success stories in most cases so you can't gainsay the business model, but, without exception when you look beyond the bare aluminium hulls which are *de rigueur*, there is not much difference from the fleets of normal blue water cruisers which in fact suffer from many of the same drawbacks for extended sailing at any latitude.

Take the interior layouts. I have yet to see any of these designs that have adequate stowage for provisions to last for several months in the field. Open any locker and rather than finding a storage space, the locker is an inspection port for runs of pipes and wires and/or a transformer or two. It is noteworthy that many of these expedition yachts have more conveniences and gadgetry than the average well-appointed home. None, it appears, have any way to store fresh provisions of fruit and vegetables. Eating out of tins for months was something Robin Knox-Johnston in the Golden Globe Race was obliged to do, or maybe he just loved his tins. To drive the point home if you can't store at the very least potatoes, carrots, apples and oranges for six weeks in a cool climate you have not thought about the requirement.

I have yet to see any of these designs with forepeaks big enough with convenient access for stowage of equipment and necessary spares (anchors, dinghies, outboards, cordage, toys to name a few). Rather there are berths and head compartments that are useless at sea. Like all cruising boats they are marketed for the number of berths – like pricing homes by the number of bedrooms, however small.

Engines are generally light on power and fuel capacities are insufficient by what I estimate to be on average 60 to 70%. Two good examples of expedition cruises that need extended autonomy are the Northwest Passage and the coast of the Chilean fjords. Figure 2,000nm on the former and 1,050nm on the latter between fuel stops that don't need pre-arranging, if arranging is possible at all. And much of both of those are motoring passages.

The dilemma is that to market a design with less gadgetry and conveniences in lieu of more space for storage and capacity for fuel is akin to justifying a certain cost for what are void spaces. No designer or yacht builder in their right mind wearing their commercial hats would ever risk attempting to pull off what could be a clever conjuring trick of designing a true fit for purpose expedition yacht that in fact would be to the benefit of a buyer in the long run. That might be a tough call.

THROUGH-HULL FITTINGS AND KEEPING THE BOAT AFLOAT

'It's time to get down to basics. How much do you think about your yacht's skin fittings, and how often?'

August 2018

Enough philosophizing and dishing out opinion pieces. Let's get down to some basics for a change. There is no better place to start than with plumbing, and fundamental to keeping your boat afloat is integrity of your through-hull fittings. Skin fittings we call them.

This topic came to mind while reading yet another sad story of a yacht now sailing in Davy Jones' fleet after mysteriously and uncontrollably filling with seawater so quickly that the crew were overwhelmed without finding the source. By the time the floorboards were awash it was deemed too late and too difficult to investigate so there was nothing for it but to deploy the liferaft. They had not hit anything. They suspected it could have been the bow thruster housing. It can only be assumed that something had given way below the waterline and the most likely culprits are skin fittings, if not the shaft log or the rudder bearing.

All of us who go to sea and have worked on boats have had the catalogue of frights with plumbing below the waterline. Dangerous corrosion, frozen valves, hose clamps missing and soft hoses brittle with age – fittings falling apart when looked at the wrong way. Boats continually try to sink themselves given half a chance. It is our job as crew to be vigilant and prevent one potential disaster after another.

The mode of failure for skin fittings and valves can be incompatible materials – the classic is bronze fittings on an aluminium hull. Aluminium valves are hard to come by, so better stainless steel, but there is also galvanic potential as well over time and the bigger the mass of the stainless fitting, the more vulnerable the alloy hull will be as its foundation. Composite materials are available, but may not be coded for purpose, especially in the engine room where metal pipework and fittings are required.

Another issue is a lack of maintenance. Skin fittings need to be inspected and the valves attached to them exercised often. Hose clamps need to be replaced when any corrosion is present – some are all stainless steel and last longer than the cheaper combination of steel and stainless steel. We use double stainless steel exhaust hose clamps on anything bigger than one and a half inch fittings. Vibration and improperly fixed hose runs can also cause chafe and splitting, especially at the nipple ends where a hard interface is created.

And all of the above is compounded by accessibility issues. Every through-hull fitting and valve must be readily accessible, not buried under fixed floorboards where only a Houdini would be capable of seeing, let alone inspecting them. This goes back to the design phase for any yacht and should be prioritized. Alas, that is easier said than done. Another good idea is to minimize the number of skin fittings by combining them into manifolds for various services. The fewer the fittings, the less risk. Every working crew member on board should know where every skin fitting is located with a posted A4 laminated sheet to hand for reference.

In flooding scenarios when underway (flat water is the worst, as no sloshing will occur, and especially when motoring where noise levels mask the sound of rushing water, accompanied by likely failures of bilge alarms which should never be trusted), by the time the floorboards start floating it is very difficult to locate the source. Some skin fittings might be in deep bilges, buried under stowage modules. At this point the priorities become safety for the crew in getting liferafts deployed rather than last ditch efforts to find the problem. This is more of an issue with yachts which have no watertight bulkheads which are the vast majority. Where do you start to look? With watertight bulkheads there is at least a chance of containment and the compromised compartment is more than obvious, but having said that, show me a watertight bulkhead on a small yacht that is truly watertight and I will be impressed.

If you do manage to bung the hole or stop the flow by whatever means, then there is the issue of pumping it all out, or at least keeping pace with the rising tide. A lesson learned from the folks on the yacht described above who quickly realized their variety of pumps could not keep pace. As a prophylactic measure flood your bilges every so often and have a go – just to remind yourself what you might be up against – and therefore go to sea better prepared.

Postscript

It is true that on most small to medium size yachts the bilge pumping systems (manual or electric) will not be able to keep pace with a major flood scenario. The most efficient system is a high capacity pump running off the power take-off off the engine, which can through a manifold double as a deck wash, anchor wash and firefighting pump. But when the engine also fails/floods? The Cruising Club of America in their safety at sea seminars advocated a portable gasoline/petrol pump to have at the ready. I have not tried this, but it is certainly something to consider – especially when making what is a risky run through the Orca fleet when entering the Mediterranean.

A GALLEY YOU CAN COOK IN AT SEA

'A well-designed galley is a fundamental asset for serious offshore sailing'

January 2020

We know that an army marches on its stomach. This is also true of any yacht crew. All is possible at the dock, but in rough weather you should be able to carry on in the galley and not default to cheese, biscuits and Mars bars. When I peruse galley layouts in the medium range (50 to 80 feet) of blue water cruisers I am often perplexed on how it was all conceived taking into consideration 15 degrees of heel and the occasional roll to 30.

Many, if not most of these interior features in the competitive sailboat market are style driven, otherwise there is a risk of not selling these vessels where deals are closed at boat shows on the hard or in the water at the marina. If you display something functional that will work at sea, it will be by definition all too agricultural looking.

As you might expect, I have some unconventional solutions that might not lend themselves to facilitate *cordon bleu* preparation but they do work for assembling 'gut luggage' of high quality, and quantity – just what you need offshore, and especially if you are dealing with big numbers of crew. Events like the ARC come to mind.

It is a given that a galley must be on one side or the other. A floating island in the centre (like in a house) would not do as the hull is needed to ground lockers above counter height, as this storage space is always needed. Something hard to achieve the smaller the boat, but the cooker as the fundamental piece of galley equipment should be facing fore or aft, not athwartships. This means you can lean against the counter space and cabinets below on both sides. This is not only more comfortable but safer – being trapped into a galley strap in front of an athwartships cooker is a recipe for an accident as you are in the firing line of anything taking flight in a big roll. The negative, though, is that a gimballing cooker of hob and oven facing fore or aft takes up an inordinate amount of space. But read on.

Another fundamental is that the sinks also should be as near the centre line of the boat as possible so they can drain by gravity on both tacks. Non return valves get stuck, and although you can have a Y valve and switch to a hand pump, a sink on the lee side is more often than not likely to be continually flooded below the waterline. The inboard side of the sinks (if near centre line) should have a high splash-back, say 300mm to keep things neat.

Now to some details. We all have cooked on yacht cookers with three or sometimes four burners where it is impossible to have pots or pans of any size on the centre of the burners. They just don't fit. Regarding the hob, our solution – rather than starting with the cooker, we began with two primary pots and made a custom hob with high fiddles to fit exactly those two pots aligned fore and aft. For our capacity (up to 13 people) we have two 12-litre Lagostina pressure cookers. The regime is one pot of stew or sauce and the other for the pasta, rice or potatoes. The oven is an electric domestic fixed installation. This has some limitations at sea, but certainly works for baking bread, baked potatoes and anything more or less dry, using wedges to level the pans.

Many people are afraid of pressure cookers but even if you don't use the pressure function, they are ultimately safe because they are deeper than a normal pot and you can close the lids positively if need be. Back to the sinks which should be double – again we started with those pots and have made custom sinks integral to the countertop, which are deeper than off the shelf models and big enough to get these big pots in the sink and comfortably under the tap.

Lastly, I am amazed to see galley countertops without substantial fiddles. Ours are 75mm high on all sides. Seems high, but that is what it takes to rest a jar or cup against it without tripping up and capsizing. The counter top is best in stainless steel and fiddles the same, with nicely welded and grounded corners for cleaning. The counter tops need to contain major spills which will occur – often. Best to keep the sauce off your shoes and the walls.

The downside is there are costs to bear as most of this fundament equipment is bespoke. But there is no better way to spend the money.

It all goes down to whether you will be spending more time offshore or at the dock.

Postscript

Of course, we have incorporated all of these features into our new expedition vessel, the Pelagic 77 Vinson of Antarctica. Three people can work efficiently and comfortably in this functional galley. It is more a commercial rather than a designer kitchen. I have yet to see anything comparable on any of the prominent production or custom blue water cruisers that I come across, most of which have decidedly absurd features, obviously with little or no thought to being at sea.

CUSTOM-BUILD BLUES

'While building a new expedition yacht, Skip's extreme utilitarian philosophies are being tested'

September 2020

Yet another consequence of the Covid lockdown which is very much still in force in South Africa is that I cannot, in person, follow the construction of the new Pelagic 77 in the Netherlands. This vessel is for a private owner, but will eventually be chartering at times under the Pelagic brand. Launch date is after the first of the year. The Dutch builders never really stopped during their lockdown and they continue to forge ahead. The last time I saw her was in mid-March, as a bare aluminium shell and deck.

Sadly, I am now missing being at the builder on a regular basis to monitor the machinery, systems and interior that are going in at pace. This is when, no matter how experienced the builder – and KM Yachts is top of the line for expedition style vessels – it always pays to have someone with hands-on boat operation and maintenance on site to tweak this and that. We have been doing it as efficiently as possible on email but it is not the same.

Having said that, long gone are the days at a custom builder, unless you go the painful artisanal route and take years, where things are decided ad hoc as you go along. Back in 2002 on *Pelagic Australis* we were in a big shipyard environment and although we had the design finalized, much of the decision-making with regards installation was done on the job, and I was at the yard four days out of a four and a half day work week in Durban. They had the capacity to react to my desires and whims, often having to unravel an installation and start again with little loss of time.

Today, that approach is anathema to a builder. On the Pelagic 77, designed by Tony Castro, everything was 'drawn' in 3D down to every locker space, shelf and fiddle, likewise every bit of machinery in the engine room and throughout the bilges. Once you start the construction to make any changes implies substantial delays and substantial cost increases. You have to have your ducks in a row.

However, being on site during the build, there is still much a sailor can contribute. Practical matters like placing equipment in the interior can impact how easy it is to access and also how people will move round it. In the engine room, you must ask yourself and demonstrate things like; can you swing a normal spanner to get that bolt off to remove such and such – or is it buried with other pieces of equipment compromising the access? Shifting something a few centimetres this way or that might make all the difference instead of having to hire a double-jointed 12 year old as a crew member. Years back, I remember having a look at a well-known production build where they had the genset mounted above the main engine in an otherwise impossible space where you could not pull the injectors without removing the genset. This was extreme, but similar situations must sound familiar to many of you.

Bilges are also a minefield of problems. Can all hose connections be accessed? Are through-hulls easily got at without removing interior fittings? Can strum boxes be lifted? Can bilge pumps be serviced in double quick time? It is an endless list if you study these problems, all in aid of not only making life easier, but the implications of safety and sea-worthiness, especially when it comes to plumbing, cannot be ignored.

And that brings this discussion to my *bête noire* – the plumbing in the head compartments. In my somewhat extreme utilitarian philosophies this ranks at the top. Firstly, you must ask the most fundamental question about what you will be doing in that compartment, and how long do you want to linger in there. For me, it is 'get it done' and get out.

Then there is the all-important question of maintenance, and especially in a charter situation. Blockages, which there will be, have to be dealt with in quick time. On *Pelagic Australis* we achieved a system where-by some, but not all, of the head (toilet, sink and shower hoses, valves, pumps and fittings) are easily accessible. I had a dream. It was to make the Pelagic 77's head compartments an example of plumbing, if not art then a pleasing feature of practicality – shiny stainless steel fittings, all hoses well clipped in, visible on the bulkheads and discharges down into standpipes with a valve above sink counter top level.

Alas, various forces where brought to bear on my radical ways and although we have now a properly fitted out head module as is the norm, we have tried to give access to all the important fixtures. I do not envy the skipper and crew however, when those blockages occur. Oh, those bruised knuckles!

I had a dream...

Postscript

When this construction was finished we realized many of the critical plumbing features like valves, Y connections and siphon breaks were 'buried' in the polyurethane foam insulation behind the attractive joinerwork. A lot of heartache went into making these accessible when the boat returned to the shipyard after the first summer up north for the 'snag list.' If someone knowledgeable (and the one that would have to fix things) had been on site during the construction the chopping and changing of the built-in interior could have been avoided.

TRY NOT TO SAIL A BOAT JUMBLE

'When does being prepared become hoarding? Skippers should avoid the temptation of "just in case"'

November 2020

How many times have you heard or have said, 'You never know when you might need...' It is true that when cruising on the 'far side of the world' with few or no marine services to hand self-sufficiency is the key. You need spare parts galore, a full range of tools and basic materials to make things for the unpredictable gear failures.

This philosophy can be taken to extremes however. I always had an annual routine purging of the contents of the original *Pelagic* back in the 90s. This was a time when, based from Ushuaia in Tierra del Fuego, there were no spare parts available whatsoever, hardly any useful tools on offer and materials like stainless steel and aluminium were 'rare earth metals.' We carried lengths of spare standing rigging of every size and the terminals; timber, cut to length to fit odd spaces in the bilges, we always had plenty of wooden wedges on board, too much rope always, metres of plumbing hose, boxes of bolts and screws, a huge selection of stainless steel and galvanized shackles with no purpose or justification other than the usual refrain, 'It might come in handy...'

Added to this were small sheets of stainless steel, aluminium and plywood plus threaded rods of several sizes (the latter two used in earnest to fashion an emergency rudder) and in addition to a very comprehensive tool kit we had many hardware items e.g. sledge hammer, shovel, woodsman's saw, ratchet straps... But when all this and more was loaded off the boat on to the dock on a random pile it was shocking. How did it all fit in? We would then pick through it debating thumbs up or down and then proceeded to reload most of it with not much going in the trash bin.

The fact was we were hoarders. If we found an orange fishing float on a rugged shore we always made an effort to get it, even taking some risks, as that was a useful fender. Any piece of cast away cordage from another yacht was assessed and gobbled up, ditto pieces of plumbing that might, 'with a bit of modification, be useful.' When one of my charter colleagues took his cast offs to the dump, the rest of us headed him off for an inspection.

There was also the 'leave behinds' of our charter clients. Often, we would discover we had piles of sea boots and Wellies, tangles of ski poles, various pieces of clothing donated or forgotten, and with a certain nationality if you looked hard enough in the bilge spaces, empty vodka bottles. Most of this stuff was indeed, given away or dumped.

I recently went through this exercise in Cape Town on *Pelagic Australis*. In spite of the charter season in the South American sector looking to be a total washout due to the Covid hurdles that are too high to jump over, we managed to land a unique project taking a five-person UK film team down to Marion Island in the South Indian Ocean, along with a seven-person science team that needed to get there for their term of duty manning the meteorological and biological research base maintained by the South African government. With our three crew that meant a full boat of 15. And film teams don't travel light – we loaded 60 boxes of technical equipment.

In order to accommodate this 'cargo' we had to be ruthless about creating space that is otherwise taken up. I thought we would be able to purge many debatable items and gain some ground. But because we were much better organized than in the pioneering days, we were paired down to the essentials. Everything had a purpose. Only a few things were offloaded and stayed ashore: a 40 kg bag of rock salt that was lost to memory after our icing up experience in 2014, was prised out of a corner of the lazarette. Fender boards could stay behind and so too all the dock lines – where we were going there was nowhere to tie up alongside. Same for the fenders. We gained a locker space by offloading all my climbing equipment under my bunk. All this dunnage went into our storage container.

We keep what we think are very meticulous parts and maintain an equipment list, often updated. What should be on board; what is actually on board; and what is needed are the entries. But still it is never

100% accurate. I was sure we had a 10m piece of anchor chain for our backup nylon anchor rode in case we had to 'lose' our main anchor and chain. It was not there no matter how hard we looked. I had to buy another at the last minute. Not a biggy costwise, but a critical piece of equipment. My advice is to offload and reload often and keep your spreadsheet updated. 'You never know…'

TUMBLEHOME HAS ITS USES

'In praise of tumblehome: why rounded topsides can be a saving grace'

December 2020

More often than not when *Pelagic Australis* is in Cape Town for her annual refit, we are docked at right angles to one of those elegant locally built Southern Wind Shipyard yachts. They share the same pontoon berth for their commissioning. This September it was with the impressive Farr-designed *Southern Wind 96*.

Southern Wind and *Pelagic* know each other well and I like to refer to this mating of opposites as the 'beauty and the beast.' Each to his own and no comparisons worth making. But we often like to stare at each other in wonderment.

We comment politely on the attributes of these two chalk and cheese yachts; one a belt and braces practical workhorse, the other a cutting edge technological emporium and *objet d'art*. Always interested in our somewhat unusual features, many of which ain't all that pretty, the *Southern Wind* commissioning skipper commented on the tumblehome we have in the hull, which might be considered generous, but not excessive compared to some of today's designs of smaller yachts. Meanwhile his crew was trying to figure out how to keep their fender lines from chafing on the sheer of their vertical topsides, something the Farr office most surely would not have considered. To think this article is all about fenders may not be obvious yet, but it is correct.

By strict definition in naval architecture tumblehome is where the maximum beam is at or just above the waterline and then the beam measurement diminishes in the uppermost portion of the hull. It's that pregnant guppy look if seen from astern or ahead, and in extreme examples looks like the hull was inflated by an air compressor.

Adding in tumblehome was, in the days of the International Offshore Rule, a method for fiddling with the rating, or rather taking advantage of a beam measurement in the formula. In fact, on *Bea Bay*, a Sparkman and Stephens 50-foot design from the late 60s I sailed on as a young lad, Pat Haggerty from Texas Instruments was one of the first owners to radically tinker with and find loopholes in the IOR. He added substantial tumblehome to the original design by using ping pong balls in amongst the filler (to reduce weight) on the outside of the aluminium hull. A great dock talk story that went from legend to myth but was in fact reality – I helped fair that hull in Sturgeon Bay Wisconsin.

But the story of tumblehome is also historical and goes back to ships of the line in the days of sail, motives being gun deck placement with respect to weight and being able to fire when at heel. Taking on incoming shell fire, possibly as a deflective measure with the sloping side to sheer above the gun deck, was also a possible factor for designing in tumblehome. The debate of tumblehome's pros and cons is alive and well, and never more so in modern yacht design. Some designers just like the look of tumblehome.

In our utilitarian world of *Pelagic* it has nothing to do with aesthetics. It is merely a solid fender – the hull itself. Because we spend the majority of our time alongside walls and jetties that are often rough as guts, having that 'pregnant look' gives us a margin of security for our stanchions and shrouds. Quite often we are caught out and being blown on to these jetties with an alarming angle of heel. The extra gap that tumblehome provides makes this if not a pleasant experience, at least a survivable one. With a vertical hull side or worse one with a flare, this would be untenable.

The other feature of note is a continuous toerail with holes at least on 200mm centres – useful for not only unlimited outboard sheet leads, but also for hanging fenders – again, a design feature rarely thought about but not to be underestimated as important. First of all, when going foreign you never know what situation you will be in at the dock and being able to hang a fender *anywhere* on the hull is a must. But this must be attached to something solid, not on lifelines and stanchions. If this is your only option you will need plenty of spares stanchions when fenders get caught on odd shaped jetties and bend stanchions or even pull them right over.

A horrendous night in Port Stanley in the Falklands comes to mind to demonstrate this argument. We were inside a raft of four smaller yachts on the East Jetty which has protection from the prevailing westerly. Maybe it was the pub session that precipitated a panic, but we all got caught out when a nasty easterly filled without notice making it impossible for the rafted boats to peel off and go to anchor. The carnage was substantial. Broken stanchions, bent chain plates and dented hulls – them not us. We were riding to a Yokohama fender and took it all on the chin, in spite of being heeled over 10 degrees.

If you are designing a world cruiser and the designer starts wincing when tumblehome is mentioned, insist on giving it heaps. You won't regret it.

THE AGE-OLD QUESTION

'Asking the unaskable question: when is it time to give up sail in favour of power?'

November 2021

After 30 days on charter in Svalbard with little or no wind, where the sailing vessel *Vinson of Antarctica* motored everywhere we had to go, the old question of sail versus power, at least for a working vessel, again loomed large. After an experience like that, discussing the pros and cons with the crew, and with the charter clients, becomes inevitable.

Several of my colleagues in the south have evolved (or devolved depending on how you look at it), from sail to power and a few are contemplating making that move. For a working platform a motor vessel of the same length does have several advantages over sail. More internal volume is obvious, but things like more deck space and more cargo carrying capacity are all positives for film teams, science projects and the like, who always bring on board inordinate amounts of equipment including unwieldly gadgets that can be difficult to accommodate and handle on a sailing vessel. When on-site, usually along the coast and within an archipelago, there is no doubt a motor vessel trumps sail, as often it is either not possible due to ice, or practical for detailed navigation, or just not worth the effort, to make sail. You end up carrying around those poles in the air while tripping over running rigging lying idle on the deck... and you begin to wonder.

The caveat, though, is for reasons of perception and aesthetics sail is 'environmentally friendly.' And wildlife films often now include the mode of transport in the 'how we made the film' add on, which lends itself to favour sail. Frankly, some of these belt and braces motor-driven support vessels can be downright smelly and ugly.

Fuel consumption aside, the major negative, though, for anyone experimenting with a motorboat solution is that the ride offshore to get to these points of interest can be a horrendous experience rolling your guts out along the way, with not much else to do except survive in some level of if not misery then for sure boredom. We find this in super and mega yachting for the Antarctic in that most owners' and charter' parties prefer to fly in and join the vessel there, rather than 'suffer the Drake Passage.' Pity they never get to see the albatross...

There is also a question of age. Not the boat's, but the owner's, which points to a motorized pre-Valhalla, certainly in the recreational genre. This seems to be a logical progression, in spite of all the push button sail control systems on offer in mitigation of one's physical ability going south over time. It is hard to gainsay this ultimate solution in staying afloat by any means fair or foul. But it is a watershed decision and can be an agonizing one for many – if and when to lower the sails for the last time and throw in the towel. When this takes place, the reaction among peers can be one of polite surprise, possibly empathy, maybe pity, and in the worst case grounds for treason.

It is worth being philosophical about this choice of sail or power at any time in one's maritime career whether that be your baptism in the sea, or for those final voyages. It requires serious thought and clear thinking.

By coincidence while up north I was reading Joseph Conrad's memoir The *Mirror of the Sea*, which are his reflections on his career in the merchant navy. He mused on the comparisons between sail and steam during that transition in the late nineteenth century. It was relevant then and is relevant today when he said, 'It (steam/power) is less personal and a more exact calling; less arduous, but also less gratifying in the lack of close communion between the artist and the medium of his art. It is, in short, less a matter of love. Its effects are measured exactly in time and space as no effect of an art can be... Punctuality is its watchword. The incertitude which attends closely every artistic endeavour is absent from its regulated enterprise. It has no great moments of self-confidence, or moments not less great of doubt and heart-searching.'

On our way back around the north coast of Spitsbergen, the breeze filled enough for the first time in a month to put out full sail on a beam reach just as we were approaching Moffen island, an outlier at 80 degrees north. Thick-a-fog, in the half light of a waning Arctic summer we ghosted along in welcome silence close aboard what is nothing more than a sand spit with a lagoon well offshore in the Arctic Ocean. We slipped along in 10 metres of water keeping distance off with the radar and all of a sudden we were surrounded by a melee of spy hoping walrus in their hundreds. An unforgettable moment, and I thought how different it would have been if we had been under engine.

Therefore, the question must be asked yet again. Sail or power? I still say sail – every time. If that day comes when I don't want to hoist those rags at every opportunity, that is the day I will turn around and march my way inland with that symbolic oar over my shoulder.

THE BOAT MANUAL IS THE BIBLE

'Why every yacht's user manual is a vital and ever-evolving project'

February 2022

I've written about 'manual' skills training for aspirant sailors. Now I'm referring to another 'manual' – the boat manual. My research on Wikipedia tells me we have here a homograph.

My experience with perusing boat manuals written by the manufacturers of production boats is that they are wholly inadequate. They are more of an operator's manual, the sort you get with your car in that A5 pamphlet, and full of advice that tells you if such and such fails, contact your dealer.

With custom builds they are by nature much more elaborate in general but it depends on the shipyard how far they go into detail. And again, these are operator's manuals used with the assumption that everything as designed and built will function, simply by pressing the right button. If something fails on your sailing holiday and you are in a marina environment all is not lost as help is at hand. If you are at sea you are on your own. You need all the 'what if' scenarios imagined and elaborated on in a good place to hand.

On my boats we have filed away the shipyard operator's manual and have written our own. It is an axiom that as soon as you take your first sail, the shipyard's manual will be out of date. The variables that immediately surface when operating a vessel are inevitable and many procedures on how not only to use the equipment but also standard operating procedures are dictated by the style of how the boat is run.

The homegrown boat manual should be a living document, always on the desktop of the computer and added to continually over time, all changes dated and signed off on who made that change, and of course a hard copy print out generated as needed. This is especially important for skipper and crew change overs in the case of a professionally run yacht, and not least of all as a fundamental report for a new owner if the boat is sold.

In a Word document it is easy to drop in photos and technical drawings, cut and paste important routine service protocols from equipment manuals, and it should also include a detailed stowage plan, routine maintenance schedules and trouble-shooting procedures for every piece of equipment. On *Pelagic Australis*, when the boat was sold, it ran to over 100 pages. Procedures are as important as the technical details of the equipment. We have standard operating procedures (SOPs) as annexes for things like making sail, reefing, launching and recovering tenders, hoisting people aloft and anchoring – and how to lift the anchor when the windlass fails, which it will do eventually. You can't have enough SOPs. The point is in trying to instill routines to avoid confusion and possible chaos.

The introduction to our manual briefly says it all. 'The intention of this Manual is to provide a "cookbook" guide for a new skipper and crew coming on board completely "green" with no one on board to brief them. This means no operational procedure should be neglected nor implied. Full explanations of how this boat is run (not in a general sense) must be listed. Particular attention should be paid to quirky systems, special tools required to affect a repair or adjustment, etc., which are not evident at first glance.'

Although the exercise in getting this all down is a major work, it is not onerous as the content will grow over time as things go wrong and new ways of doing things become apparent. It is an evolution of mistakes made and lessons learned. Take the simple case of starting the engine. How many steps do you normally observe? In our manual it is 12. And it finishes with the heads-up safety message redlined 'It is essential that when you are working in the engine room you take out the ignition key from the start panel!'

You can make it an amusing read. Here is a gem for changing the propeller in the water. It starts off, 'How to change a prop at anchor in South Georgia – as done by Miles, November 2010. If you have to do this, you are a poor miserable @#!*#@$, and should be more careful of ice in future.'

This job description is several pages long, meticulously documenting the procedure, beginning with this bit of advice: 'If it is bent, motor slowly, or sail, to a secure anchorage before attempting to change it. It's best if the anchorage is not prone to glacial meltwater as this makes visibility much worse, and the job more difficult.' It finishes with among others these two tongue-in-cheek 'Top Tips', post a successful operation: 'Go to Antarctica without a spare prop to give yourself more incentive to be careful around ice', and 'While doing this send any charter clients away on a very long walk (without a Zodiac ashore) so they can't give you any helpful advice.'

LET'S GET ANAL

'Details count, right down to the size of a split pin'

June 2022

And now for something completely different. Soon after the launching of *Vinson of Antarctica* I had to instruct the shipyard to pull out and reinsert all the split pins in the masts. This might have been construed as an over the top obsession with a detail, but I had to insist, to be 'true to my school.'

All the split pins were too long and bent over into 'curlicues' back around the clevis pin. We have all seen this and I believe it is an aircraft specification and understandably so for things that could fall out of the sky.

How many times have we all been through a monumental struggle to extract split pins installed in this fashion? You start out with a pair of pliers and soon you have been down and back up from the workshop a half dozen times and are surrounded on deck by vice grips, plumber's pliers, screwdrivers, eventually resorting to the hacksaw and a punch set with a hammer, all resulting in bruised knuckles and at the same time shocking bystanders with your expletives. It is a much harder job doing this aloft, say when taking down headstays to service furlers. At least the crew on deck and any bystanders are spared the rhetoric.

For those of you of a certain age you will know who Olin Stephens is, arguably the most famous yacht designer of the last century. Only a few, though, might remember his brother Rod who I had the pleasure to meet back in the 1970s. Rod was also a designer but more of an engineer and one of his jobs for the US design firm Sparkman & Stephens was to do a final inspection of the thousands of S&S designs built around the world. He came on board the *Dora IV*, a beautiful 61-foot sloop, before the 1972 Bermuda Race and nosed around dishing out advice to our young crew. His passion was rigs and inherently wiry and strong he loved to go aloft, even into his 70s. On *Dora IV* in Newport he soon focused on the split pins, a ritual he became famous for. He was not impressed with our set up and gave us a good lecture on it.

He told us in no uncertain terms the length of a split pin had to be one and half the diameter of the clevis pin. If they are too long you need to cut them down to size. The ends need to be rounded off with a file so as not to snag on ropes and sails. The split pin should face down along the fork or toggle and not stick out beyond it. When opening the split pins each leg should spread by 10 degrees, giving 20 degrees symmetrically. The idea being if you have to pull that split pin out in a hurry, say on a dismasting, you only need to slightly close the legs and give the eye a pull. Rest assured readers, with a 20 degree spread it is not going to work itself out.

Although his lecture might have seemed anal to some, it was not to me, as I already had my share of badly set up rigs in my boatyard days as a rigger in Clearwater, Florida, and the split pin problem was endemic. Split pins are usually put in in a hurry and that's that. This is one of my many pet peeves and that is an understatement.

Rod had more to say of course about all sorts of things in the rigs he inspected and I had the pleasure of having him on board on other yachts I was on where the split pins were 'just so' and I loved to watch him give me the nod when we got to the base of the shrouds.

I think we can take Rod's obsession with split pins as a metaphor for the detail that is required when not only setting up rigs, but everything else on board a yacht that is critical. One badly set up piece of equipment eventually will lead to another problem and in quick time you have a serious set of circumstances on your hands.

Sticking to rigs, how often do you go aloft and do a thorough inspection? Before each voyage, after a voyage or both? Do you search out cracks in the welds of masthead cranes and spreaders? If you have simple 1/19 stainless steel wire for standing rigging do you closely check each terminal whether they be compression fittings or swaged? (You need a magnifying glass to check for cracks on swages.)

Are your shroud rollers easily lifted to inspect rigging terminals, turnbuckles, toggles and chainplates? If you have to unscrew them from collars they are not. Any evidence of loose screws on mast tracks and pole car tracks?

Question: does a rig inspection take 5 minutes or 30? I know the right answer.

4 TECHNOLOGY – PROS AND CONS

I think it is true to say that when designers, yacht builders and equipment suppliers in the marine industry hear my name mentioned they cringe... because they consider me a Luddite of sorts and bad for their businesses. Taking the designers, it is their remit to innovate continually and what they draw has to be performance-based, usually meaning optimizing light air performance, not heavy air. Understandably no one wants a dog with his name on it. Aesthetics also come into it, sacrificing practicality in function for the benefit of dock walkers rubbernecking in St Tropez and Porto Cervo.

Boat builders are keen to add as much equipment as possible on the specifications. It is in their financial interest to do so as every piece of equipment has a margin, and more man hours means a more expensive boat and not least of all elaboration is what the client wants or is led to believe he wants by the designers, builders and equipment suppliers. You can't gainsay any of these entities as they are in business after all, but I can't help believe to a large extent an uneducated yachting public is being led down a *cul de sac* of questionable necessities, at least if efficient cruising is what they have in mind. The accepted mindset is, 'Give them what we think they should have, not what they need.'

I am a big fan of the founder of Patagonia, Yvon Chouinard, climber, surfer, innovator and one who with his company spearheaded the concept of setting aside a substantial share of his profits for environmental causes. He once said, and I paraphrase, 'Look at every piece of technology and take what is absolutely necessary – and disregard the rest.'

Food for thought when on your next visit to the Southampton Boat Show.

SAILING NEEDS TO BE PHYSICAL

'Racing and cruising are poles apart these days. While racing has become more extreme, cruising is now arguably too easy'

January 2015

I suppose we can divide 'sailing' into two convenient categories – racing and cruising. Decades ago the two were more or less intertwined activities on board racer/cruisers which still exist to some extent at club level. However, it is a fact that the two taken on their own have significantly diverged with respect to the physical 'work' put into making them 'go.'

When I grew up the racer/cruisers where really the only show in town. We are talking about boats from 30 to 50 feet. You raced them on the weekend, either around the cans, or maybe up to another port town on Lake Michigan, and then cruised them back to base. The family cruised them up and down the lake for extended summer holidays. They were live-aboard boats. There was not much difference in handling them whether racing or cruising as the functions were the same, only the intensity and concentration differed. This status quo continued through the 70s and then stripped out racers made their appearance which were arguably unfit for cruising, largely from a down below comfort point of view.

Racing these boats through various rule and class permutations would become more and more athletic culminating in what we see today in extreme racing genres where body armour along with clever location and rescue devices for safety are *de rigueur.* Likewise, beer can in hand while telling stories on the weather rail has gone by the board. There is not much chance of holding on to anything while your legs and arms as ballast are extended through the lifelines in horrendous contortions. (Not my cup of tea.) To seriously race today, you have to be reasonably fit and able to suffer, if not gladly. This is a logical evolution with no argument.

True cruising boats, now firmly separated from the cruiser/racers of old, need less physical input as function of not only clever rigging systems (welcome) but also powered assist sail control systems (many suspect).

And after all these years I have been living under the impression that sailing, including the cruising kind was if not 'sport', then certainly an active pastime. Otherwise, why leave home? Current trends in design and fit-out seem to argue for taking the home with you via conveniences and amenities.

I admit to a primitive nature. I still enjoy grinding a winch until out of breath. Handing sails, lines and running gear is a joy, not a burden. When it's hot I enjoy sweating it out and when it's cold I enjoy the biting feel. I like to think I sail in the environment which is thrown up at me, rather than altering that experience with unneeded distractions. Now, though, if you are really clever you can make sail and get from port to port with little physical effort, as long as all the buttons function.

Could this be the reason why the committed racing sailors of today rarely go cruising? Is it too tame? I mean, can you imagine the likes of macho Grant Dalton pushing a button to furl up the jib on a 40 footer? Is there something missing now in the cruising formula? Something that many people do not realize they have lost?

In addition to the inevitable march of technological solutions to everything, the argument of course is that as we all get older, and I certainly fall into this category, making it easy keeps us on the water. If you suffer from a physical infirmity these enhancements can be critical to participating at all. But for otherwise fit individuals it is the very nature of staying physically active that keeps us agile, supple and 'young', at least in our own imagination. May I suggest that exertion and an occasional struggle can be positives? Well, I will stick to my guns here – the day I have to push a button to trim the jib, is the day I quit sailing. If you catch me out, shoot me.

Postscript

Of course, since this was written in 2014 we have now even more 'enhancements' to avoid the old struggles. I have nothing against a clever system to make control of sails easier and I do embrace them. But when electrical/hydraulic assists are deemed necessary, there is only one conclusion if you stand by my philosophies articulated above – the boat is too big for you.

HOW WE WERE IN THE MAIN SALOON

'There's nothing like a good debate around the saloon table on a stormy night, but computer access to facts is threatening the fun'

March 2015

I've weathered many a storm down south, offshore, inshore and at anchor. The latter is always the preferred location given a choice. With lines to the rocks or trees, well-secured with wind whistling through the rigging and no need of an anchor watch it should be an enjoyable if not an inspiring experience.

During lengthy periods hunkered down, when not reading from our extensive library or writing in our journals, we defaulted to the art of conversation at the saloon table, usually over a bowl of popcorn and a bottle. Lively debates evolving into full blown arguments were common. Obscure topics left open to conjecture could be the distance from the sun to Neptune; the politics of Nepal or more likely Wales; why and how the National Health Service was failing; or the merits of Shackleton versus Scott. Some questions (when did Captain Allan first make an appearance in the Tintin series?) were easily answered as we had the entire collection on board. Bowditch, *The American Practical Navigator*, was also a mine of information to settle debates about nautical phenomena in question. But many discussions festered on, sometimes for days, argued by half-truths, assumptions or pure bluffing – much to the amusement of the spectators that were loosely involved. Needless to say our game of choice was liar's dice.

This banter fundamentally changed when my mate Hamish, a computer guru still arguing the merits of DOS long after Windows made an appearance, came on board with an *Encyclopaedia Britannica* dongle. It must have been around 1995. I will never forget when Julian and Matt were hotly debating the chemical methodology of distillation – a fine topic indeed – Hamish smugly plugged in the dongle and his professorial tone of voice proceeded to read out nine pages of text to settle the argument of how in fact it all worked. Thrusting his hand into the bowl of popcorn signalled the end of the speech. We had just heard the bald truth, and the truth was ugly. An awkward silence ensued as we all came to realize what had just happened.

From that point forward we tended to stay away from argument that could easily be solved by accessible fact, and instead invented conundrums to ponder over. In spite of this, as the 90s closed out, more and more computers started to come aboard and with them was an inverse proportion of philosophical discussion around the table.

A further devolution of social interaction occurred beginning around 2005 when digital photography became well established. On a once in a lifetime cruise to Antarctica recording the images was paramount and if digital gear was not to be trusted (the oven was used to cook out the moisture from many of the earlier models) theretofore, by then it was the norm. Formerly, with print and slide film, there was nothing to do but reload for tomorrow and clean the lens. Now, after a long day out of doors, we would all retreat to the main saloon for a cocktail, but instead of settling down in conversation, editing pictures had taken over the table, hardly leaving room for the *hors d'oeuvres* and drinks; the settee a tangle of cables, chargers and hard drives, as we all struggled to download, backup and edit out the rubbish (in many cases in the thousands per day).

I am happy to report, however, that technology has finally triumphed and made this digital filing so efficient and generally foolproof that time and space has once again been created and we are slowly relearning the attractions of debate. On our last trip this August, it was back to Scott versus Amundsen to the South Pole and Shackleton came out on top as the supreme leader of men in polar travel. Argued more by emotion rather than the facts (that were to hand), I felt I had come full circle back to the joys of 26 years ago on that first voyage south.

Postscript

Almost ten years later, though, we have arrived in dangerous territory for 'philosophical discussion' as woke issues, gender identity, colonialism and the like are almost inevitable to surface at some point. And the 'discussions' we used to have, although heated, can now with the change of topic become decidedly ugly. You would never have left the main saloon after losing an argument about what Bill Tilman had quoted, but now that same quote (often unacceptable to many) can land you in troubled waters within the confined space of a vessel. Watch out!

CELESTIAL NAVIGATION – PAST, PRESENT AND FUTURE

'Is there any point in learning celestial navigation these days, when nobody is ever likely to use it in anger?'

April 2015

In November 2014 I was asked to participate in a Shackleton symposium at the Scott Polar Institute Cambridge. My topic by their request was Frank Worsley's navigation during the famous boat journey from Elephant Island to South Georgia, and how his methods differed to a voyage today by GPS.

Of course, the differences even to a landlubber are more than evident. So to flesh out the talk beyond revealing that Worsley's methods in 1916 were decades behind 'state of the art' as he was still using the 'time sight method' as opposed to Sumner Lines *a la* Marc St Hilaire, I discussed the future if any for what is surely a dying art and science.

I had the privilege of using celestial for about eight years before Sat Nav, the precursor to GPS, made its appearance in recreational craft in 1978. I nipped in just under this wire having navigated *King's Legend* around the world in the Whitbread Race that ended early that same year. I could bring down five selected stars and make the calculations on a piece of scrap paper and determine my position in less than a half hour. The point is I had done so much celestial out of necessity before it became obsolete almost overnight, it is still ingrained in my DNA and could be brought out of the locker if need be.

Fast forward to anyone becoming an RYA Ocean Yachtmaster, which in the main requires that the licensee have a sound knowledge of celestial navigation and demonstrate his calculations and chart work to an examiner. It's easy enough to learn, but it's sort of like learning a differential equation in the calculus, just to pass an exam. Of course, all the calculations and the almanac are on an app nowadays but the 'art' in taking sights in good weather and bad must be practiced regularly.

The popular counter argument for keeping it all alive is that if all your electrics on board are down, then what? Yes, but a fool would not put to sea today without an inexpensive handheld GPS powered by double-A batteries. Then there is the more insidious theory of the Americans powering down (or at least dumbing down) the system in a global conflict. Possibly the European Galileo system will nullify in part the latter point when it becomes available in 2017, but both of the reasons are pretty specious given that not many people that go to sea recreationally will know one end of a sextant from the other.

UK merchant mariners are still required to study it, but a captain friend says he knows of no company that requires their deck officers to practise it at sea. He adds that most modern commercial ship have enclosed bridges with no side decks so it is nigh on impossible to point anything at the sky.

The RYA's position is clear in that there is no plan to drop celestial from the Ocean syllabus and that is underpinned by requirements from the Marine and Coastguard Agency (MCA) for licences of higher tonnage. However, an insider in the system has told me, 'My personal view is that celestial is interesting, personally satisfying, but when assessing on a risk basis is probably something we could do without these days as far as it being a "requirement".'

My sextant now sits at home (plastic one still on board!), a decoration on a shelf, along with my old SLR manual cameras. Every now and again I take my son Luca down to the rocks off Cape Town and we bring a low sun down to the horizon over the South Atlantic and wait for the stars. Will he learn celestial one day? Possibly as a hobby (there are plenty of hobbyists on web forums), maybe even to please his dad in his dotage? Will he have the satisfaction of shooting the stars through a hole in the clouds, fixing his position and making that critical landfall? Sadly, almost certainly not.

Postscript

Well, a 'knowledge' of celestial navigation is still part of the RYA's Ocean Yachtmaster requirement and that certificate is necessary to skipper a small commercial vessel for Category 0 (open ocean, globally).

Pelagic Expeditions, over 20 years since we first started, is still running our RYA Delivery (now on Vinson of Antarctica) from either Chile or the Falklands across the South Atlantic Ocean to Cape Town. The syllabus is primarily all about celestial, and the programme is hugely popular. Having a solid 20 days offshore with the GPS blanked out is the only way for these techniques to stick. It is all about repetition. However, I sometimes wonder how many Ocean Yachtmasters can pick up a sextant years after passing the exam, and still fix their position?

ELECTRONIC CHARTS STILL HAVE THEIR LIMITS

'Relying solely on electronic charts when you're sailing in remote areas is a mug's game. Keep your paper up to date and "navigate"'

November 2015

I had to upgrade my electronic charts for Tierra del Fuego and Antarctica for this season. It is all so simple, rather than messing around getting paper charts corrected, and then painfully paying a fortune for the ones that are out of date, worn beyond recognition or beyond correcting. However, no matter how laborious it all seems, it is still necessary and we should not be fooled by the realities of navigating electronically anywhere outside of the urban waters which are proven.

The *Vestas* grounding on a reef in the Indian Ocean on Leg II of the Volvo Ocean Race has been analyzed in great detail and in spectacular fashion reopened the subjects of scale, resolution and chart datums. But I venture to say most of us are as usual staring into the chart plotters, lessons learned or not. In Europe you can bring a boat alongside the jetty in utter confidence in full electronic mode – maybe. Further afield, while 'world cruising' it is best to simply adhering to simple protocols regarding the use of both paper and electronic charts, rather than expecting ultimate reliability electronically when there clearly is none.

Certainly in high latitudes and this must also exist in remote tropical areas, suspicion should be a mindset in using electronic charting. Ask yourself: how comprehensive is the hydrographic survey in the first place? Are you 100% sure that the chart datum agrees with your GPS? Those two questions alone, as they both introduce uncertainties, should put any navigator worth his salt on tenterhooks. When I say tenterhooks I mean the feeling we always had inshore prior to GPS where continuous checks and cross checks of range and bearing were axiomatic. It was called 'navigating.'

Electronic charts are definitely a useful convenience when passage-making on small scale and sailing well offshore along coastlines. This is safe enough and it negates the need for any physical plotting (although purists will still put a mark, at least daily or watch per watch on a paper chart). At the minimum it is prudent, though, to at least record the GPS position in your log book hourly for obvious reasons.

As we approach the coast and have visual contact with the shore, the level of complacency must give way to increased due diligence. Start bringing out the larger scale paper charts. Start plotting positions. Start watching the depth sounder. And most important of all when you make contact with the land, get off your butt and go outside and observe. Pre-GPS, at this point we used to take running fixes over the compass on points of land to get our distance off. If you have radar, fire it up and this will give you the same as long as there is adequate elevation. Even if you are following a track on your screen inshore, best to be outside to observe the relationship between the track and what you are seeing. Now make an experiment. When really close inshore, turn off the GPS and plotter and rely on depth sounder, radar if you have one and visual observation. After dropping anchor in your cove, turn the GPS back on. Often, if it is to be believed you will be surprised to find no need of the dinghy – as you are a mile inland.

Of course ships and even yachts, subject to flag state requirements, are now allowed to go completely paperless, given they have two separate electronic systems (power supplied included). But remember ships travel the same known routes without deviation and certainly never go off soundings. On yachts we can never or should never claim this luxury while cruising the 'far side of the world.' Keep the paper on board and keep your pencils sharpened. That is if you have a chart table at all, which also seems to have gone by the board and out of 'fashion' in yacht design. But that is another subject indeed.

Postscript

This sooner or later will be a lost cause as the electronic charts are becoming more accurate to a degree in more remote areas. I admit to relying on them more and more while inshore, but only when at the wheel outside to combine what I see on the screen with what I see in reality. One without the other is not good enough. To wit, this summer in Greenland we were not one mile inland while at anchorage, but often certainly onshore on the screen. An improvement, but not enough to avoid a catastrophe while coming inshore in the fog.

The main argument, though, to have the appropriate paper charts is still and will remain the 'what if' scenario if your electronic system (or the electrical system of the vessel) goes down, which is always possible.

And the UK Hydrographic Office (UKHO), after prematurely planning to phase out all charts in their catalogues including 'thematic charts' by 2026, have now pushed that to 2030 after an enormous outcry, primarily by operators of small vessels and yachtsmen. So, we are facing a situation soon with no backup paper available. The message – don't throw those old outdated charts in your loft away, it might be all that is left to you for that critical backup.

PART TOY, PART TOOL – UAVS

'We used a drone to find our way through ice this season. Finding one safe anchorage would have been doubtful without it, so they are here to stay'

May 2017

Going to the first spreaders up the steps, or to the top of the mast in a bosun's chair to scout a route through shallow water, through the coral or in our case through ice in the Antarctic is common place. The lookout is a yo-yo, up and down at short notice; or you could just leave the poor sod up there and tie off the halyard. That is pleasant enough in the tropics, but could be a desperate business in high latitudes. And in our case on *Pelagic Australis* the masthead only gets you 28 metres off the waterline. Good for what's immediately off the bow and bit further.

Skipper Dave Roberts has had his UAV – or drone in the vernacular – for the second season on *Pelagic Australis* and during our February Antarctic expedition cruise it was the first time I had witnessed it in action. We used it extensively to find our way through brash and last winter's sea ice in Crystal Sound which is at the latitude of the Antarctic Circle. A skilled pilot can have his drone out of the box and up in the air within five minutes. Without this capability it would have been doubtful in finding at least one safe anchorage that had an ice bound approach. On another occasion we faced spending hours navigating through brash ice hoping to find an ice edge in search of a lost emperor penguin said to be in the area. It was obvious from our drone footage it was not worth the effort.

In the Antarctic, like everywhere, UAVs are controversial. Within a short space of time the phenomenon has evolved from hobbyists who built their own into a mass market recreational item, albeit with many commercial applications coming to the fore, some justifiable, others verging on privacy issues. Like a GoPro camera that is a 'must have' item for any teenager who does individual sports, to have a drone on board is fast approaching a 'must have' item for cruising sailors. It's a case of bigger toys for bigger boys and girls.

In sensitive areas like the Antarctic there are two aspects that are of concern. Before the tour ship industry realized what was happening guests were arriving on board with drones in their suitcases, expecting to fly them. The chance of an errant drone out of control through pilot error or suffering a software failure and flying into a crowd on the deck was real. So the industry has agreed there is no recreational drone flying by guests. Only commercial flights are allowed which implies the company can take promotional pictures for their websites, the drone piloted by staff. Commercial film teams are also exempt from the ban. South Georgia has banned them full stop, taking a precautionary approach.

While in the Northwest Passage last August I witnessed the problem first hand. A guest on the 900-passenger *Crystal Serenity* flew a drone near the helicopter deck of the RRS *Shackleton*, the British icebreaker that was in support and anchored close by. When this covert pilot was discovered he was summoned to the bridge to see the captain – and never seen again.

The other concern is disturbance to wildlife. The tourist guidelines for drones now have coastal areas as no fly zones, especially where wildlife is concentrated. But this is vague and the jury is still out just how far away certain species are disturbed if at all. Losing a drone is also a worry. Operator error, software failure or high winds beyond the flight velocity can make a drone owner cry like a baby losing his rattle. Therefore, line of sight during flight is required and a maximum ceiling of 250m. Having said that it always tempting to push beyond those limits for aerial reconnaissance. Floats are also required for ditching into the sea, but pilots don't like them as they affect control and stability which is not great for filming.

In spite of these precautionary guidelines and recommendations, UAV use is continually under review and many opinions are in conflict. My feeling is that for yachts whether for recreational use in image making or as a necessity for reconnaissance, they are here to stay. It is no exaggeration that if you are in a crowded anchorage almost anywhere in the world best to keep a weather eye out. Needless to say, for nude sunbathing on your deck, you are now taking your chances. If you hear that characteristic sound of a giant mosquito, grab a towel quick. At least we don't have to worry about that where we sail.

CRUISING AT SPEED

'The prospect of foiling technology trickling down to the cruising yachts is exciting, but it will have its downsides'

April 2018

Flipping through the pages of the current *Seahorse Magazine*, a specialist yacht racing monthly, you can be left in no doubt on the future, which is here now, of all manner of water craft flying through the air on foils. From the gymnastic Moths to the Olympic class Nacra 17s, Vendée Globers and right through to Maxi multihulls who will attempt to set yet again new records for the Jules Verne Trophy, there is no turning the clock back on this evolution which is nothing short of awe-inspiring. Foiling is not a new idea, but modern materials have made getting airborne or at least partially on all kinds of yachts a reality.

The 2021 America's Cup was sailed in monohulls, harking back to an earlier era. When that was announced by Team New Zealand it was met with enthusiasm by traditionalists – until they read further down the page that these monohulls would dispense with lead ballast entirely and be fully foiled 70-footers able to capsize.

It is all about speed, of course. We have been trying to go faster across the water since Jason went to sea in search of the Golden Fleece. Although not immediately obvious speed on passagemaking enhances safety simply be reducing exposure to heavy or catastrophic weather. During my Whitbread days doing 10 knots was fast sailing, surfing to 15 a wild ride. At those speeds we were vulnerable to weather that was passing over us and therefore encountered much more heavy weather and squalling on the backsides of fronts than the Volvo and Vendée boats do today. They have the ability to ride with weather systems for thousands of miles and if need be run away from a ball buster. On The Race in 2001 for unlimited Maxi multihulls we rode only two weather systems from the South Atlantic to the Cook Straights of New Zealand and then another one that took us to Cape Horn. This was a safe way to sail through the Southern Ocean, no doubt.

Therefore, that old case (in justifying the outlandish costs) can be made for innovations from that pinnacle of yacht design, the America's Cup, trickling down to cruising yachts. It is already happening if not being at least mooted. Cruising concepts with swing keels, foils and sliding stabilizers across the stern are now in vogue at least on paper. Cruising catamarans are getting souped up. Let's face it, the designers could hardly help themselves and the market awaits.

However, there must come a point when cruising – in the implied sense of the word – that the faster you go the more dangerous it will become. Eight to 10 knots on a midsize cruiser is efficient and still relaxing. Objects come up over the horizon, whether on visual or radar, in a time frame that can be anticipated and dealt with. At 15 knots on up you had better be on alert, and at 20 on tenterhooks. And sailing like this in the middle of the ocean is one thing; in congested waters of Europe or inshore pretty much anywhere when at speed you will quickly become a lethal guided, or possibly unguided, missile.

Cruisers have always tried to sail faster, but this reality of speed on tap will have to be squared in the minds of the crew, and judgment calls to slow down will play a big part for safe sailing and passagemaking. In a way this means the level of expertise required to sail these speedy cruisers will need to be at a higher level.

There is another side to what will surely become a debate on all this in that watching the world go by at a leisurely pace is indeed an enjoyable pastime. A good comparison is cycling to hiking. The cycler has to pay attention all of the time, the hiker less so and therefore will take in more of his surroundings. I remember on deliveries we often were content to sail at four to five knots – good trolling speed for those tuna and also good for cooling off by hanging on the end of a rope astern as shark bait. The ocean has a lot to offer but at 20 knots you will miss most of it. For safety sake and also your own enjoyment of simply being on the ocean, jumping on and off the foils at the appropriate time will be critical.

DRIVERLESS DOCKING – A FRIGHTENING PROSPECT

'The advent of self-docking technology threatens to erode a vital and enjoyable sailing skills base'

September 2018

Just when I started to agonize over a topic for this next column with the deadline on the horizon a windfall materialized – a subject that is irresistible. Volvo announced recently that they have developed and tested the technology enabling self-docking of yachts. They proved this by squeezing a motorboat in between two Volvo 65s in Gothenburg during the race stopover – hands off. The idea, so explained the Volvo engineer on YouTube, is to remove the stress of these 'tricky' situations. Another clip then popped up that said something to the effect that you can buy a $9 million dollar yacht but you can't buy the skill to bring it in. What will we, in our collective wisdom, think of next?

Of course marinas around the world are full to bursting point. Space is at a premium and boats seem to get larger not smaller. The technology addresses the need. But I have to remain nervous in my scepticism as I have done with driverless cars where technology is dulling down our skills base. Our senses are being sacrificed to sensors, not to mention that we are sacrificing the pleasure of hands-on control. And safety? We are only just beginning to realize the pitfalls of driverless car technology as the companies roll out these trials.

Software failures are unavoidable in this AI game, even if you fail to question that the human brain can outdo an algorithm. Losing a few UAVs as we have done on the ocean where the software went down and the drone disappeared into the wild blue yonder is one thing – nothing more than a shoulder shrugger. The death of a pedestrian due to a software failure in an Uber driverless trial is of course another matter and those Uber trials had to be suspended. The wider question we are all facing is this unstoppable erosion of basic skills and whether these skills will be desirable to achieve in the first place, let alone enjoyable and satisfying to have. Seems like the answer should be an obvious yes, but technology is creeping in everywhere to compromise this premise.

Of course, the analogy that comes to mind that refutes my paranoia will be that commercial aircraft land and take off almost exclusively on auto. I dare to say, though, that the variables on the runway are far less than in a marina and certainly less than in a town. And more to the point, commercial air travel is a service – yachting is an activity and therein lies a fundamental difference of purpose.

There is also a trickle-down effect. Self-docking technology of big motor yachts will eventually arrive as standard kit on small to medium size sail and power boats. If in doubt witness that bow thrusters (granted necessary on a superyacht) are almost standard equipment on boats as small as 45 foot. The result? A loss of those seamanship skills of bringing a boat into a dock or on to a buoy by gauging the wind and tide and getting the boat tacked down smartly.

Anyone who has been at the St Barths Bucket and watched the captains and crews manoeuvre the fleet of sailing superyachts stern to at the dock, side on, in a fresh Caribbean breeze with centimetres to spare is nothing short of impressive. What a shame to relegate this spectator spectacle to a non-event assuming this technology becomes more or less reliable.

For those onshore the attraction in watching docking manoeuvres is in anticipating the unexpected – a euphemism for the possibility of a right balls up. This is simply human nature – the German's *schadenfreude*. Admiring excellence but admonishing incompetence is as natural as watching any sporting event. Every time a boat is about to dock you naturally drop what you are doing and prop yourself up into a comfortable position to enjoy the show. The explorer Bill Tilman, no stranger to maritime fiascos, described this very well back in 1955 while trying to leave the quay at Punta Arenas with his Bristol Channel Pilot Cutter *Mischief*. They managed to drop a jib over the side, went aground when the engine quit and then were rammed by a Chilean cruiser trying to help. He said, 'It was a Saturday afternoon and one could almost hear the happy sigh of the crowd as they realized how wise they had been to spend it on the jetty.'

On a serious note, if we assume this evolution results in captains, crews and owners getting out of practice in manoeuvring in confined spaces, would you trust them offshore to recover a man overboard?

TECHNOLOGY – PROS AND CONS

COMMUNICATIONS THROUGH THE AGES

'Communication with shore used to be a hit-and-miss affair, but now it's all at the touch of a button are we actually over-connected?'

June 2019

I often wax lyrical to my two teenage children about how the ease of communication has changed the entire fabric of our lives, sometimes for the better, sometimes for the worse. You would have thought that my stories of how exciting it was anticipating and then receiving my letters and postcards from a variety of lovers via *poste restante* (those under 40, Google it) in all those exotic port cities would really get them going – but their eyes glaze over and stay glazed over as I go through the evolution from there to how a telex machine works. The first ones resembled a contraption right out of *Doctor Who*.

But it was that telex system whereby the owner of the Swan 65 *Independent Endeavour* found me stranded in the tropical hellhole of Manila in 1979 and offered me the skipper's job for the Parmelia Race. Then came the fax machines – a hand-drawn picture of a clew patch reinforcement was sent from Hood Sails in Lymington to our Portacabin in the Hamble during the *Drum* campaign in 1985 – we stared at this conjuring trick of A4 telemetry for some minutes in awe. But for the children today even email is consigned to their pre-history – it is all about thumbs down 'tap tapping' for them on an ever increasing number of platforms.

At sea we did have the pleasure of being totally out of touch often as the standard HF (high frequency) radio was frequently on the blink. Back during my first Whitbread Race in 1977 on *King's Legend* we took Morse code and drew weather maps from the dots and dashes – a labour of patience. By the time you finished this job the weather had changed. And the irony was that when the HF radio was working we were better informed about current events, routinely listening to the BBC World

Service, than at least I am today while at sea – in spite of getting the news at a press of a URL I now rarely bother.

Having filed several articles for *Yachting World* via email from the far south, I am reminded about the trials of doing my weekly *Daily Telegraph* column from the Soviet *Fazisi* in the 1989/90 Whitbread Race. You could say my contribution was a precursor to the blog. Inmarsat C was fully capable of sending a telex or a telex message to a fax machine back then, but the *Daily Telegraph* were having none of this as their copy takers were still employed; behind the pace even after Murdoch changed the face of the print industry with the controversial union-busting event at Wapping for his News International titles.

I was obliged to call a copy taker on a phone line patched through the HF radio while deep in the Southern Ocean, bombing along at speed, usually on the edge of control. This was a real game. First you had to connect to Portishead Radio bouncing a long wave signal off the ionosphere and when connected most likely you would have to queue for your turn to patch into the telephone system. This was not always wasted time. We would hear entertaining 'boiler burst' and 'car died' stories from wives ashore talking to their merchant seaman husbands. The wives would often demand their hubbies tell them, 'that you love me.' Sometimes, though, these conversations would be tragic when the wife announced she had left this poor bloke for his best friend, which made us all take a pull, feeling like voyeurs.

The time of day and night was critical as these signals came and went with the rotation of the planet. Once patched through to a sleepy copy taker in London, one who possibly had never been in a boat let alone at sea, I had to dictate an 800-word article word for word, often having to spell phonetically letter by letter what could have been for him obscure terms like storm spinnaker, Chinese gybe and mainsail leech.

In the middle of the article, two things could also happen. The frequency could go down forcing to you to start from scratch and re-connect. In the meantime, the copy taker could be in the loo, having a cuppa or he might have ended his shift and a new guy came in cold to the story. Or, after that over enthusiastic set of the storm spinnaker and subsequent

Chinese gybe laying waste to the leech of the mainsail, salvaging the carnage on deck put the column deadline firmly to the back burner.

Are we over connected now? This past January I was on a superyacht in Antarctica with connectivity better than I have at home in Cape Town. Sadly, I spent far too much time on my emails because of it.

THE WIND IS NOT FREE

'Sailing yachts might seem to offer a means of transport with a low carbon footprint, but don't delve too deeply'

December 2019

This column would not be complete without some focus on Greta Thunberg. A high latitude colleague of mine contacted me in the spring, knowing *Pelagic* was now in the northern hemisphere, and he asked if I was interested in taking Greta across to the United Nations Climate Summit in New York. Although this would have been good for one's CV, I never followed this up, more for practical reasons as we were then in Maine. In any event, I could not imagine my 30-year-old steel boat, with rust flowers in full bloom having just come up through the Atlantics, not to mention an engine with noticeable blow-by, could ever be the right vehicle for such a high-profile project. Not to mention the time it would take plodding along at 6 to 8 knots, albeit with a well-appointed plumbing system for Greta and her father to enjoy. The bucket system works of course, but it can be noted I like to hang it over the side if there are no facilities.

The IMOCA 60 *Malizia* was a sexy and indeed correct choice – a quick passage with zero carbon footprint. But as soon as I saw Greta on board, I rightly anticipated the reaction from the gainsayers that the carbon footprint to build that boat would far exceed a simple plane ticket. This was succinctly pointed out by the letter to the editor in the October issue of *Yachting World*. I think this reader would have been more pleased with *Pelagic* if his idea of a wooden boat with canvas sails was unavailable. Having said that you can also make a negative case for *Pelagic* with all that forged steel, all that marine plywood from all those trees, and that engine in need of a re-build that we would surely have to use to get across – how would it compare to the miles of carbon extruded to build *Malizia?* It is one of those questions to be avoided when you start looking into bottom lines of carbon footprint. The point is we have a voyage juxtaposed to the building of the vessel. Zero emissions on a voyage is a thing to strive for, but how did we get there in the first place is the awkward question.

Sailing superyacht vessels and even motor-driven superyachts are certainly on to achieving low emissions solutions, as we have seen featured in *Supersail World* many times. It is of course desirable to develop energy efficient systems while on passage, but once again if you start to add up the carbon equations to build what must be considered vanity projects of scale it might be best not to delve into this too deeply either.

Greta's voyage was a superbly well-orchestrated piece of publicity and the main thing is that she got over Stateside to carry on with her important message. Of note here is that we see how sailing and the 'wind is free concept' (being an oxymoron to those of us who know) continues to captivate the minds of the general public despite some unpleasant realities when costs of same are considered. The wind is not free. On the face of it, though, sailing rather than motoring makes so much more sense. It is quiet, generally a satisfying experience, partly sport but also partly an intellectual exercise and certainly cathartic, or should be.

However, if we look into the statistics of power versus sail, or by simple observation start to add up how many motorboats and sailboats you see in any marina, you realize that sailboats draw short straws every time. I tried to find some figures for this relationship but not all boats have to be registered in the UK, consequently it is thumb-suck guesswork, with no raw data to hand. I do remember in America a study by a sailing academic from a Wisconsin university calculated power versus sail at 10 to one. That was 20 years ago. And the trend was getting worse, at least if you were on the sailing side of the study. If you don't believe this is a sad reality, consider the number of trailerable motor boats, or if you have more expensive tastes, visit the Monaco Yacht Show where only a handful of sailing vessels are on display within a sea of motor yachts from toys, to tenders to ships.

The fascination of the motor (whether electric or fuel powered engine) seems all prevailing and is getting more so – we now have motor powered bicycles, scooters, skateboards, surfboards and all manner of toys to choose from – that we used to enjoy with the old-fashioned elbow grease. Carbon footprint? The hell you say!

COMMUNICATION OVERLOAD

'Shouldn't we all be getting off our phones when at sea?'

September 2022

The article in the June 2022 issue of *Yachting World* was timely as I need to upgrade the antiquated Iridium system I have on the original *Pelagic* (currently in Greenland). From feedback from the ARC, this was a superb technical piece and very informative indeed.

However, the somewhat disturbing lead photograph with the young sailor in the cockpit staring into his mobile phone provided me with an own goal for what can be construed as a sad, inevitable story of how we curmudgeons like to continually lament, 'Well, that's just the way it has all gone...' As sure as an incoming tide is unstoppable more sophisticated communications on board our yachts are inevitable. I am in no way advocating turning the clock back – however... read on.

I'm sure there must be at least one more of our readers who when having seen that picture said to themselves, 'But what about that magnificent sunset? Surely, a better screen (life size!) to stare into?' Possibly this young man had recently trekked to both poles and climbed the seven summits and he was on a sailing holiday to recover, so in this case I would let him off the hook. But looking at the picture I could not resist, with no disrespect, in thinking, 'Why don't you go play outside, son?'

Although deputy editor Toby Hodges does make the point early on that some of us still relish the idea of turning off the comms when we go sailing, he has left the philosophical argument of such a dilemma to yours truly. Well, someone needs to push back as counterbalance to trends that are clearly unstoppable, but can be mitigated and in this case by qualitative review of how we spend our time at sea. The analogy is the absolute necessity for a faction pushing back on woke issues that are obviously extreme, lest they become an ideology, soon evolving into a religion.

So, I will propose a separation of comms on yachts for utility and discourage comms on yachts for amusement. You would be a fool not to have the latest, when affordable, comms on board your yacht not least of all for basic safety considerations. In my view it should all end there. Let's face it, constant communication has become an addiction and this is obvious when coming from offshore and back on cell coverage along the coast, the phones come to life and sadly, instead of savouring those final days or maybe even moments right up to making the dock, your senses are turned off to wind, sea and current and that delightful motion they all bring to the vessel. Why distract yourself from those simple pleasures? Having said that we all default to our phones when there is signal. Why? Because we can.

I would hazard to guess, though, that when the WhatsApps, Instagrams and emails start cascading down on your device, there will be some welcome news from family and loved ones, but also some bad – bills in arrears, insurances expired, overdrafts left unattended, a flood in the kitchen, the dog on his last legs and more – all the usual frustrations we have learned to live with. In my view best to finish a voyage cleanly and get to your office or desk at home to clean the backlog, sitting down, calmly, soberly.

One bit of kit that was not mentioned in the article was the proliferation of the InReach system by Garmin. For expedition types on land and at sea this has become the system of choice, superseding a handheld Iridium, although using the same Iridium satellite array. It is a text only system, limited to 160 characters per send, and as the Garmin's publicity reads, 'You can stay in touch globally. You can send and receive messages, navigate your route, track and share your journey and, if necessary, trigger an SOS to a 24/7 staffed global emergency response coordination centre via the 100% global Iridium satellite network.'

Well, what more can one possibly need? I am certainly sold on this device as an unobtrusive solution for those basics. Although it is more than cumbersome to type in a message (like programming a GPS), you can link to your mobile phone via Bluetooth.

On the most recent projects on *Vinson of Antarctica* both high north and south, the scientists and film production staff all had one, claiming this is now required for work (lol). In other words, we could have 10 InReaches on board between the clients and crew. They are tiny devices, hung on carabiners in the cockpit or in the pilot house next to the windows. Although I sometimes found all six people in the cockpit or in the pilot house staring into phones when they should have been looking out for whales, it seems about the cheapest solution for doing the bare minimum of communication in this day and age when going remote.

No need to point out that I seem to have been 'hoist by my own petard' in this discussion. OK, I give up on push back for this discussion on comms. Maybe.

Postscript

Of course, all of the above is almost moot with the advent of Starlink. You can now stream BBC's Life in the Freezer *with David Attenborough while cruising in the Antarctica... or, you can stay at home, watching it there and save the pain and expense. Possibly the future to save somewhere like Antarctica from the ravages of mass tourism is indeed augmented reality.*

What will be lost against this apparent gain of being online at sea? To wit, on my last Arctic cruise with a now antiquated Iridium GO for basic comms, I (admittedly an email addict) would have foregone Hemingway, Conrad, Stevenson, Melville, Tilman, Chandler, Mowat and other lesser authors of the 20 books I read on that marvellous trip, more or less cut off from the realities ashore. And let's not forget Hergé. What a joy to have the time and space to re-read, yet again, the Tintin collection.

5 SAFETY AT SEA

Even I (who is well known for being not exactly manic about safety equipment – I mean one who does not continually feel obliged to buy and then ship on board every piece of new equipment that gets invented year on year) every now again take a pull when looking at the old Whitbread films and the photographs of how we sailed on the ocean racing circuit in the 70s and 80s. Barely a lifejacket or harness is in evidence. Liferafts and other pieces of equipment were even stored down below, for the most part inaccessible in a crisis. I cannot remember ever doing thorough safety briefings as we now do. I guess we were optimists just not focusing on what could happen, as it never did. I have yet to be on a boat, in charge or otherwise, that has lost a man overboard. In other words, no 'wake-up call.'

It must also be said that many of the classes of boats that are racing offshore today are arguably not fit for purpose. The deck layouts are in themselves 'unsafe', the safety factors of appendages and rigs are near '1' – these are dinghies on the ocean. Witness the results of the 2023 Fastnet Race where a quarter of the fleet dropped out due to gear and structural failures – or the crews just bottling out with a bit of wind against tide in the Channel.

The crews we sailed with all those decades ago were deep watermen, long on experience, and much was taken for granted, probably way too much. What has changed in the last few decades is the sheer proliferation of people going sailing, with little or no progression of experience from dinghies through boats of scale. Hence, more accidents happen through misadventure or inexperience, sometimes with loss of life, and every one of those incidents is put under the microscope of an inquisition. However, in being reasonable, we sometimes must accept an accident was just plain bad luck, and not make a meal of it.

There are two aspects to consider within this most sensitive subject of all my column foci (and one that has likely generated the most letters to the editor). On one hand, I feel there is today too much focus on 'safety' and less so on simple self-reliance that back in time we all seemed to have. We were never afraid of being on the ocean, but we respected it. On the other hand, the number of newcomers to sailing that are within teaching programmes, corporate charter, sailing rallies and yacht club activities, where duty of care is paramount and liability an underlying factor, means the free expression we enjoyed is now questionable.

Now, all bases must be covered, 'what if' scenarios imagined and risk assessments continually analysed, resulting in people going sailing with so much equipment on their person and so many gadgets to get you out of trouble that often what is engendered is a fear of a malevolent ocean, so much so that much of the joy and freedom of being at sea is lost. Certainly, paradoxically, complacency is on the rise due to too much safety equipment and instant communications on tap, which becomes a danger in itself.

The point is that this is as much a practical issue to contend with as it is a philosophical one. Let it remain so, philosophically at least for the individual, on his own boat, on his own voyage.

SEA TRIALS

'When it comes to sea trials for a new or refitted boat, it's a case of don't do what I do, do what I say'

November 2014

Anyone who owns a boat knows the subject. We've all done it, setting out to sea on an extended voyage, with little or no sea trials. I can consider myself an expert on this subject. To be honest, none of my four Whitbread entries had been extensively tested before the events. *King's Legend* in 1977 spent most of her time on the dock in Cowes in constant preparation in anticipation of the great unknown. *Alaska Eagle, ex Flyer I*, had been extensively modified in error and was late out of the shipyard in Holland. *Drum* did have a go for a month in Solent waters, but her summer's work up and big test offshore ended upside down in the 1985 Fastnet Race and put us back to sub square one five weeks before the start. On *Fazisi*, the Soviet entry in 1989, we just beat the bailiff to the start line.

Pelagic and *Pelagic Australis*, my two expedition boats, had similar chequered histories coming off the starting blocks. My ocean racing career culminated in the 'The Race' in 2001. It is one thing to start a delivery unprepared, or even Leg 1 of the Whitbread to Cape Town, but another to start what turned out to be a 64 day non-stop race around the world on a fresh off the blocks state-of-the-art Maxi catamaran. *Innovation Explorer* was her name.

How we survived these adventures and came through is a testament to the qualities of the crews who were always experienced sailors and/or technical experts able to deal with things on the go. I never felt unsafe in a sense, but rather the various predicaments that inevitably arose had to be simply embraced as we carried on.

But safety certainly can be an issue starting a long voyage untested, especially for debutante boat owners and their crews. New boat launches and post-refit situations are particularly vulnerable. The scenario goes something like this: The boat is launched, rig dropped in, systems run up and then day after day the sea trials are postponed due to the thousand and one other jobs, big and small, important and less so. It is the endless list syndrome – no matter how many things you tick off, at least the same or more are added as the scheduled departure time draws near. Add to this the usual delays from suppliers and technicians plus inclement weather, or no wind at all, and there is every reason not to leave the dock.

When I speak about sea trials, they should be just that – sailing or motoring in sheltered waters offer little difference to hoisting sails and running up systems at the dock. It is almost an irrelevance. Sea trials should imply going to sea, with enough time in hand to properly observe.

The high pressure hose test for deck leaks is a classic case in point. That is a static test of little value. It is much more conclusive to sail hard offshore with green water on the deck, and the boat working to the max, to reveal where the leaks will be. Plumbing is another aspect that should be always be fundamentally suspect. Given the motion of a boat offshore in heavy weather, will the engine cooling system work, ditto will the exhaust riser be sufficient in a big following sea? Will the port head suck seawater on port tack? Are the through-hull hose fittings really secure under load and motion? Chafe points on running rigging and sails, and ultimate mast tuning can only be resolved after a reasonable extended thrash in high winds and big seas.

In order to achieve this utopian situation two requirements are evident. Clear priorities – get offshore when the conditions are right. The guy delivering the cockpit cushions, already late, can come back another day. The second is will power. To muster the troops and willingly go out in gale conditions takes some.

I must try it one day.

Postscript

My story goes on. With Vinson of Antarctic, *launched in March of 2021, because of Covid I could not travel to the Netherlands to participate in the builder's trials at least, and then the Netherlands being what it is, hidden behind a dyke, the crew were anxious to get the boat out of there and over to the Hamble. And here history repeated itself once again, with little or no wind in the Solent and a thousand and* one details to sort out to finish the boat at the dock. I blame Covid for this one.

We left the Solent on our first real 'sea trial', thrashing our way up Channel and into the North Sea and on to Norway to stage ourselves for our first charter in Svalbard. Needless to say, the snag list was enormous, but once again we pulled it off.

THE GREAT LIFEJACKET DEBATE

'When to don a personal flotation device'

December 2014

Having had the impression that I should be keeping my head down about the topic of use or overuse of lifejackets, I welcomed reader's comments from the October 2014 issue of *Yachting World* in response to criticism of this magazine featuring pictures of people not wearing any. Well, never one to avoid sticking my neck out, I might as well get on with this one and get it over with.

I first realized there was something amiss when several years ago on a visit to the Hamble River during a dead calm weekend afternoon, I noticed that everyone on every craft (and they were not racing) were wearing lifejackets. I took note of this revelation and finally an old boy and local river rat rowed his dinghy on to the jetty. I struck up a conversation and then asked him if lifejackets were now legally mandatory. 'No,' he said as he hung his head down sadly, 'but that's the way it's gone.'

Let me make it very clear that if duty of care, for example in sailing schools, organized programmes or required by class rules stipulate that lifejackets are required as soon as you hit the water, I have no argument. It is rather on a purely personal level that is cause for concern when I get the impression that various authorities and pundits are advocating – no, almost demanding – that we all wear PFDs (personal flotation devices) or lifejackets on every floating object known to man. Well, how do we surf? How do we swim? Does this mean after swimming out to a raft on a lake or off a beach we have to don a PFD to 'be safe'? In short, how do we have a bit of fun on the water, unencumbered? Sailing in the raw, a very pleasurable experience – with a PFD on?

What I am driving at here is what I perceive as a move to instill a fear of the ocean among people, and a sense of reliance on one's own abilities is the collateral damage. In my not so humble opinion it is all about judgement when safety equipment is required – and we are fast on the verge of losing this ability to judge. Not only individuals are being brainwashed, but I also think some skippers can be at fault for making

143

the use of PFDs or lifejackets a given in various benign situations. If they can't judge the times when it is safe enough to be on deck without a PFD they are not doing their job in an educational sense. I mean, to see a crew motoring out into the Solent on a hot, dead calm day, all clad in PFDs and harnesses, seems strange and unnatural, let alone uncomfortable!

To put this way of thinking into a bold perspective I will use my own examples. Even in the Antarctic with 0 degree water, I don't require or encourage people to wear a lifejacket on deck in settled weather nor in the inflatable when going ashore. I don't expect them to suddenly fall over backwards, or throw themselves into the sea without notice – this just does not happen. If it gets tricky, though, lifejackets go on (harnesses more to the point than lifejackets on deck) and maybe survival suits for rough beach landings in the dinghy. It's a judgement call.

My kids sail Optimist dinghies in a sailing school and of course PFDs are required by the organization. Fine. We also bomb around on my Laser on our own time. If the wind is light neither myself nor the kids wear PFDs. As the wind comes up they put one on, but not me. When it really blows, I put mine on. I do this in principle to make very sure they do not get the idea that it is impossible to be on the water without flotation protection.

This is a common sense approach, but has serious implications if we get it wrong. Why? When the day comes when some bloke in the harbour urgently asks one of my kids to give him a hand with that boat that just broke free from its mooring ('Jump in, kid, I need help!') – and one of my kids says, 'Sorry, mister, I'm not allowed to be on the water without my lifejacket...' Well, there could be nothing sadder than that.

OK, dear readers, bring it on!

Postscript

In spite of push back by myself and others, this is a losing battle. It is almost a generational thing as we often see the old timers cruising around without personal flotation as they have always done. The younger crowd, especially those who have gone through 'training programmes', are lost to my cause it seems. Safety paranoia is well ingrained. Granted, the speeds being obtained by a variety of modern racing sailboats are such that wearing a PFD if not a lifejacket is more than justified. No question of that. But the test is when these same people get on an old clunker and still feel threatened and feel 'naked' without some sort of flotation device.

I see that the person who has inherited my column for Yachting World is a 100% advocate of never leaving the dock without flotation. For die-hards like myself this will be more difficult to argue against, especially when the 'one death could be prevented' justification comes up. By degrees we free spirits will start to appear like fools.

In 1998 the famous French sailor Eric Tabarly was swept off the foredeck of his boat off the coast of Wales and was lost at sea. He was not wearing a lifejacket nor harness. Like Tabarly, I am still happy to wing it, the end come what may.

JURY-RIG RUDDERS

'It is a measure of good seamanship that, should the rudder fail, you don't immediately think of the rescue services'

March 2016

What a pleasure to read in the December issue of *Yachting World* about the couple who sailed themselves halfway across an ocean after a complete rudder failure. No rescue was called out, this being my point. Granted, they had much support and advice via the cruising net, but as we all know the stories are legion of boats being towed in by overly stretched resources, for all sorts of reasons, many of which were unnecessary.

You can consider systems on board such as the rig with sails and of course the steering system as fundamental. The engine and propulsion system also, but debatable as secondary. Sailing back to a mooring or an anchorage, if not a jetty should be doable, for safety sake. If not, I suggest to practice this for when the engine fails as it surely will do, at some point in your sailing life. Getting towed in because of engine failure is unnecessary and just bad form.

If the rig comes down – and remember it takes the failure of only a single part of what are many pins and fittings – thinking of how you would jury-rig enough mast and sail out of the rubble left over is an exercise worth spending some thought on. Spare parts, materials, tools and a plan is what I mean.

Ditto rudders and steering systems. It is a bragging point that in my entire sailing career I have never lost a rig. But the bragging stops there when it comes to rudders (and for that matter a keel which when that happens you are surely screwed).

To save undue embarrassment I will recount only one incident. It was 1990 and we were on passage through the Southern Ocean from South Island, New Zealand, to Chile to begin our second Antarctic season. *Pelagic* was 800 miles from the Straits of Magellan when the hollow steel rudder shaft sheared off above the top section of the swing lifting rudder. This was not a sudden failure, as the blade had already started to flag in the heavy swell after the heel support gave way. We had attached a tag line to the rudder so when the shaft finally sheared as expected, we retrieved it with the spinnaker halyard with some drama, and lashed it to the deck, just on nightfall.

After sleeping fitfully on the dilemma we woke at first light, driven out of our bunks by the sickening roll and feeling at first quite helpless. Chile was a long way away. It would have taken a full naval and possibly an air operation to locate us and pull us in. This was never contemplated, and after all it was downwind to Chile. It took a full day and then continuous tweaking for Hamish Laird and I to build a sweep with our aluminium spinnaker pole with a piece of plywood attached to the end by threaded rod, all of which we had in stock. We went through three reductions in the plywood blade before we got it right. In fact it was not much wider than the diameter of the pole. It was quite a rig with two steering lines led from the end of the sweep through blocks on the quarters and then to winches, the port led across the cockpit to the starboard so one person could ease and trim. There were lashings here, lashings there, a line to hold the boat end of the sweep up and another to keep it from skying with our fenders as cushions. Although steering was strenuous, we averaged just under 100 miles per day and luckily arrived off Cabo Pillar at the entrance of the Magellan Straits in a rare spell of settled weather. Motoring on to Punta Arenas was straightforward.

We had avoided what could have been an even worse situation in calling out a rescue knowing that a tow through the Southern Ocean might mean abandonment. Clear thinking, calm and weighing it all up was what was required. The satisfaction felt when we cast that first dock line ashore was almost worth the pain.

STRETCHED RESCUE SERVICES

'Should something be done about the number of rescues in high-profile events? And if so, what?'

May 2016

Describing grand prix offshore sailors as 'idiots' (as a letter writer to *Yachting World* did) continually in need of rescue is a tad strong in the language. Nevertheless I can see this man's point and empathize with his frustration. The amount of rescues in ocean racing, mostly in solo and double-handed events, as the boats get ever more radical, is reaching endemic proportions. It's also not lost on this author how this seems to happen to many of the same people, time and time again. Yes, 'great publicity for the sponsor' is the usual litany from the press and pundits... and on the other side a very bemused and at times outraged audience. With a Vendée Globe fleet nearing 30 entries one can only speculate on the numbers that will be bailed out before they get to the equator, and certainly more beyond. Historical statistics back all this up quite clearly. But before we get too hot under the collar, it should be noted that most of these rescues are instigated and carried out by the project's shore team and paid for by the project's backers.

I was also amused to see on British television the story of a crew of two wannabe transatlantic sailors in a small cruiser having to be towed in by rescue services seven times in succession. The TV clip was telling as when the skipper was interviewed he seemed totally oblivious to the mayhem his crew has perpetrated.

Of course, with amateur cruisers and people afloat in general it is a conundrum, and to even mention charging for rescues is a bridge too far to contemplate, given maritime statutes in place and not least of all ethical considerations. Take note, though, in the mountaineering world, it is not so benevolent an environment. In the French Alps rescue services on standby charge for each call out and every climber and skier is advised to take out appropriate insurance – or else. At sea the rub is that although your insurance (if you have it) covers the cost of a vessel salvage, costs of a SAR (search and rescue) in order to prevent loss of life are impossible to recover by a government and harder to insure for.

Leaving rescues for cruisers aside as having no immediate solution, for high-profile racing campaigns there might be a system to ponder over, which might take some of the sting out of an SAR when the public bemoan over-stretched rescue services, risk of life for the rescuers and sometimes the enormous costs incurred to the tax payer.

Race organizers can impose a sizable refundable bond to be lodged by every entry sponsor and held in trust by the event. If the vessel is rescued whereby government services are called upon, this bond is forfeited by the entry – but not paid out to any government rescue service as they won't be able to accept it for the reasons given above. Rather, the bond is donated to a not-for-profit organization or charity which can be earmarked as the recipient for that event. It is a somewhat macabre way of raising funds, but this could temper the gainsayers who criticize these test pilots of maritime guided missiles. In other words if you screw up, and let's make no mistake when these mishaps happen it is due to human error either on the water, in the drawing office or on the builders floor – not an act of God or *force majeure,* and government rescue services are brought in to the equation, there should be a price to pay.

Whether this would make the skippers throttle back at times, or for that matter the designers to take a pull and increase safety factors probably is over optimistic thinking. And I hope they don't as the cutting edge in this game must be maintained and not watered down. But maybe it's time to somehow do away with the free lunch when all goes pear-shaped.

STAYING ON BOARD

'Ocean racing carries risks and great sailors have been lost overboard. It takes just a moment when your guard is down'

June 2016

The recent loss of Sarah Young from the yacht *Ichorcoal* during the Clipper Race is a tragedy. We should be under no illusions, though, that ocean racing does carry risks and it is the law of averages that loss of life will occasionally happen. This is not the first time and it won't be the last. No matter how much we dwell on safety issues we must all realize the ocean is not a golf course nor a tennis court. Unpredictable forces are continually at play. Remember the great Eric Tabarly? He was washed off the foredeck in the Irish Sea in 1998 and drowned. Given the man and his experience this was at the time simply considered bad luck.

The people who elect to do what can be described as hardcore offshore sailing must certainly know the risks and they take those risks willingly. That should hopefully be the end of this story. It was a credit to the crew of *Ichorcoal* that they decided to continue the race after a burial at sea. It was the only logical thing to have done and out of respect to a competitor, the race must go on.

An inquiry will no doubt follow. Why wasn't she clipped on, apparently against the usual protocols? I suspect it was simply a moment of letting her guard down. I am a big fan of life harnesses, make no mistake. My philosophy has always been a life harness is more fundamental than a lifejacket. Sticking on board is everything. Having said that, in my early sailing career I can barely remember wearing them. When I look back through my Whitbread photos it is amazing how many there are of the crew sitting on the weather rail or doing manoeuvres in heavy weather with no harnesses nor lifejackets. Rest assured, though, when it got to a certain point of severity no one had to be told it was time to put one on.

It is a good rule that at a certain wind speed or during the hours of darkness in all conditions harnesses are worn and clipped on at all times, but it is an overly optimistic expectation to achieve this 100% of the time. Anyone who has spun the handles of a coffee grinder or for that matter any top handle winch while wearing a harness knows what it's like to have the tether wound up in the handles, not to mention bruised knuckles from the harness buckles. Tether design is greatly improved to mitigate this, but there are times when they simply get in the way of a job to hand. Moving about the deck while always clipped on is another case in point. Yes, it should be possible if the jack lines are well run, but being brought up short by the tether while trying to reach for something is an annoyance. So we sometimes forego the attachment for speed and efficiency. Moving fore and aft or across the yacht with alacrity and in safety, all the while gauging the pitch and heave of the yacht while keeping an eye on the waves is a skill like any other.

I have come very close to being washed overboard twice in my sailing career. I didn't learn my lesson the first time, but the second time it stuck. On both occasions it was not at the height of the storm when our senses are finally tuned. The heavy weather had passed; the wind was right down, but the sea was still running. I had my back to the ocean sitting on the high side of the cockpit, mind in neutral, relaxed and taking in the view. Without warning a wave gently came over the quarter and floated me right out of the cockpit and over the leeward lifelines. I snatched a hold and leveraged myself back on board. Lesson? When you start thinking a harness is probably not necessary, you can be at your most vulnerable.

Postscript

The author Peter Nichols summed up this subject well when he wrote in his celebrated book about the Golden Globe Race, A Voyage for Madmen: *'Harnesses have unquestionably saved people from going overboard, but they have also failed, come undone, broken, chafed through, and sent people to their deaths. An overreliance on them breeds atrophy of the best of all devices to keep a sailor aboard: a fully developed horror of going overboard.'*

This is a debatable take on the issue, but the message is clear, and pertains to all safety equipment – don't rely on it! Avoidance of the need for it is the key and the complacency that is engendered by safety equipment is a Trojan Horse.

WHEN TO ABANDON

'I'm just going to come out and say it: too many yachtsmen are being rescued at sea from seaworthy hulls'

July 2017

It is the situation that most if not all sailors who roam the oceans dream about. Finding an abandoned yacht drifting around is booty, matey. Well at least to some extent before insurers get involved and take their slice. The scenario might go something like this: The vessel is sighted by chance, drifting, apparently not under command possibly down by her waterline. No contact is made by radio. You come in close to hailing distance and still nothing heard. Then the heroic decision is made to board which will involve some risks and certainly gymnastics. Heart rates go up. In a seaway it is a challenge and hopefully after sliding the companionway hatch open you will not find a mummified skipper and crew in their bunks. The bilges are awash but obviously the hull seems sound otherwise. You pump her out, throw up over the side several times then tidy up and take her in tow. At some point you notify the authorities and when in port stake your claim officially.

Although this is usually an apocryphal scenario it does happen and if news reports during the last few years are anything to go by the chance of getting lucky out there in the briny is increasing not decreasing.

The old adage that you get in the liferaft when the boat is sinking underneath you seems to have gone by the board. 'Stand by the boat' is another old favourite – when the boat was your lifeblood, your home, your all. Now it seems boats can be cast aside for very arguable reasons becoming almost an expendable item.

Mast failures, rudder failures, engine failures and just worn out crew have been the reasons that otherwise seaworthy hulls have been abandoned after the rescue is made. And with EPIRBS connected to Maritime Rescue Coordination Centres worldwide, satellite phones to hand and AIS recommended if not required the rescue is easier than ever to put in motion – maybe too easy.

Easy for me to say, right? I have never been rescued – if you ignore *Drum* capsizing when the keel spectacularly fell off in the Fastnet Race in 1985; then we had no choice other than a long cold swim ashore. So it might seem arrogant of me (not the first time) to criticize a decision to ask for a bail out. Whatever the failure might be it happens more often than not in heavy weather. A mast falling over the side or drifting around rudderless is disconcerting at the very least, more likely a panic will already have set in. Dealing with the aftermath to stay afloat, save the hull and keep the crew safe will be exhausting. It will take some will power and clear thinking to realize that all is not lost if the hull, no matter how uncomfortable she is riding is not going down any time soon. This is the time when a MAYDAY should have been a PAN.

Granted, complicating factors could be injuries on board or drifting close on to a lee shore rudderless and rigless with no power. Once the decision is made to call out the rescue services or take help from a re-routed passing ship, there is usually no turning back. The pressure from the rescuers to leave the vessel, having come all that way, will be enormous and 'no second chances' will be made clear. The onus on the skipper to take the safest course of action is paramount. So in the interests of ultimate safety of the crew the boat is abandoned and left to its fate – or worse with the hull rammed or shot through with military ordinance to remove a 'hazard to navigation.'

Of course, every abandonment has its particular story so it is difficult or impossible to suggest a different course of action that could have been taken in order to save the boat. This cannot be done from any armchair. It just happens and it is all accepted, with no guilt or embarrassment attached. When these stories hit the press it is simply reported and no one seems to wonder about the 'what ifs?'

Collect the insurance money and start again? Or best to contemplate another activity? There are a few things that we who go to sea should never forget – the weather will always change for the better and with adequate sea room there is always hope.

OVERSIGHT ON THE CLIPPER RACE

'Is there a lack of oversight on the Clipper Round the World Race yachts? Manning improvements could be in order'

February 2018

It came as a welcome development that the Clipper Race decided during the stopover in Fremantle to sign on a second professional sailor as the first mate. Clearly pressure was brought to bear. Three deaths in the last two events and several groundings, recently one with the total loss of the vessel is, no matter how you cut it, not a good score sheet.

What started as a rally many years ago in the wake of Chay Blyth's Global Challenge, The Clipper Race has taken on the sole mantle of the 'amateurs' around the world race. In light of these tragic events it is easy for pundits to put the boot in but the reality is that this race is otherwise a great success evidenced by the uptake of people willing to engage in what is surely a great maritime adventure. I would never gainsay them.

However, it was time (you could say all too late) to re-assess the structure of how it all works, in spite of what appears to be the thorough preparation the teams go through. Or do they? Well, the fact is in view of this being an amateur event, you cannot expect the paying crews to put much more time in before the event than the compulsory four weeks – or the event wouldn't work. After all this is a business.

No, I think the critique should not be on the preparation phase before the race but rather on what had been a lack of oversight on board during the race. Never having followed the Clipper that closely I was frankly surprised to learn there was only one true professional on board – the skipper. This was apparently mitigated by at least another one of the amateur crew taking the two week Coxswain's Course that focuses on safety at sea. This sounds terribly similar to the 'zero to hero' Yachtmaster programmes that have had their detractors. The idea was that this crew member with his two week Coxswain's Course behind him could 'take over' and possibly lead the crew in the event the skipper is incapacitated or worse, like having to be rescued if overboard. That sounds like a big ask.

Surely, I would have gone one better than the organizers recommending a skipper plus two other professional sailors who have some serious sea miles under their belts. This would provide for an experienced sailor as watch leader no matter what watch system you use. If cost to the organization is an issue, surely there are enough youngish people qualified with experience where they might even be engaged by the organizers for free, as this would look good on a careerist's CV. When I look at a sailing CV for my crews on the *Pelagics* my eyes always glaze over reading the lengthy list of certificates all candidates have nowadays – instead I go straight to the sea miles and the record of races and deliveries. Enough miles: 25,000 is very light; 50,000 you can talk to me; 100,000 is more like it. By that point you can assume they have seen a few things at sea and have dealt with them.

The point is, given the fact that many of the amateur crew are of a certain age and maybe not fit as they should be without the depth of experience that only many sea miles can give you, we have to assume they will often be prone to making mistakes, some life-threatening – things that come to mind are standing in vulnerable positions (leeward of booms, hands on blocks, standing in bights of sheets), not being able to anticipate wave motion, clipping on in the wrong places with respect to heel angles – just to name a few. These sorts of mistakes are rare with experienced sailors. The only way to get around this is to have a knowing pair of eyes at all times looking out for potential accidents. This was quite impossible with only one qualified person on board.

Undoubtedly the Clipper Race has become more sophisticated. It is sailed on, let's describe them as, 'sporty' boats compared to the fleet in the early editions. And it is surely more competitive. It is not enough just to 'get around.' This is an understandable evolution. It is never good to turn the clock back on an ocean race that does have its place, but these manning enhancements to keep pace with the expectations of the crews will not go amiss.

Postscript

I am told that the Clipper format is sticking to two professionals on board, assuming they always have a two watch system. Of course, for an around-the-world race (especially with the number people on a Clipper boat, which is many) a three-watch system is much more practical as you have an active watch, a standby watch and a watch at full rest. Whether a two-watch system is mandated and stuck to in all situations is not clear.

SEAMANSHIP BELOW DECK

'How can you have an interior that's comfortable in port but also safe offshore? Advocating for simple materials and some creativity'

July 2018

Accidents offshore, some with tragic consequences, will always occur if your playground is an ocean environment, which is a true wilderness. If you don't accept that, best to stay landside. No matter how much safety equipment you have and how you use it, often it's a case of being in the wrong place at the wrong time as something gives way. That's pure bad luck.

It might be just plain good luck, though, that I have had, in my long ocean sailing career, very few trauma injuries on board with people working the deck. And luckily no one has gone over the side. I'm certainly not complacent about any of that.

Funny thing, though, is that I can recall even up to recently several injuries that happened below deck. And this was in spite of being aware of the risks of getting knocked about below with some mitigation measures implemented.

When you are on deck, at least if you are not sleeping on watch, your senses are naturally heightened. Anticipation of motion in a big seaway should be a given. You hang on at the right moment. You try not to sit with your back to the sea. You position your life harness tether not to have slack in the wrong direction.

Below decks it is much easier to be caught off guard simply because you just don't know what is coming at you. To be thrown across the beam of a boat in a violent roll or coming off a companionway ladder as she pitches can be serious. Unlike on deck, I have not heard of anyone wearing a harness, helmet and body armour while below, at least not yet! The problem is that when we go down the companionway, especially in heavy weather, we have the false sense of security of entering a secure cocoon which is true enough – and that is when you relax and your guard is let down.

I'm pretty sure they don't exist but if there were statistics comparing injuries below to injuries on deck on sailing yachts in general it would tell a cautionary tale. Banged up heads, bruised and twisted limbs if not broken and plenty of cracked ribs come to mind. Although rarely life threatening they are all cause for concern, especially when far offshore and help is days away.

Every yacht is vulnerable to injuries below no matter how safe you design and equip the interior. The conundrum is that if the interior is ultimately safe at sea, you would not be able to move around it and live aboard at anchor or in port as the spaces would be too constrictive. Open floor space is always desirable to live in but this needs to be mitigated when offshore.

Most yachts big and small have some handholds, but never enough it seems. And there are examples of interiors with almost no handholds. By the way, for me a handhold is a 25mm tube that you can get your big fist right around and is strong enough to swing on with your full weight – might be ugly but utilitarian. A lack of proper handholds coupled with expansive designer interiors and furniture with sharp corners aplenty and you have the perfect storm below.

There are ways to make these void spaces safe and this can be accomplished right in the design phase if not retro fitted using removable safety features. Pipework at chest level from bulkhead to bulkhead can break up and divide the big spaces. Ropes can do the same. Chest level is important because at waist level a handhold/grab bar can become a trip point with people flying over the top. These temporary fixtures need to be quick to install and also have dedicated stowage so they are easy to use and are used often. Likewise for seating that becomes a launch pad with no way to wedge yourself in. No matter how many times you remind people to sit to leeward, they will still sit to windward, nodding off and off they go in full flight.

On *Pelagic Australis* we have gone one better, after years of experimentation. We now have a custom webbed cargo net arrangement tensioned by handy billies that breaks the main saloon in two. This extends from deckhead to cabin sole and you pass from port to starboard through a narrow gap between the net and the saloon table. Not pretty, but a sure way to catch flying bodies with a soft landing, plus cheap as chips to make and easy to install. With some simple materials and some creativity your below decks will be much more enjoyable at sea.

Postscript

Take note that on many of the foiling mono and multihulls, they now are wearing helmets and body armour down below!

SEASICKNESS MITIGATION MEASURES

'What should you do if you or any of your crew suffer from seasickness?'

February 2019

Throughout the Antarctic charter season I get asked the same question by many of our guests, 'What about seasickness?' We take many landlubbers down south who would, of course, be concerned but also seasoned sailors who know what it means to be crossing the dreaded Drake Passage. They are also curious if we have a magic bullet in hand. We do but it will mean missing out on a large part of the Drake itself – and I don't mean simply staying at home. However, this 'cure' might be preferable to trying to watch the great wandering albatross with your head in a bucket. Read on.

A combination of the cold, the anxiety of an unknown and the reputation of the Drake for enormous seas and howling storms could all add up for encouraging anyone who is prone to seasickness in going down, but any science behind those presumptions is specious at best.

Years ago in my reckless youth (or was it midlife?) I was severely reprimanded by a reader from an American magazine for making light of seasickness by relating our methods of prevention and care by giving our guests a bucket each and letting them get on with it – he demanded that I be taken off the magazine's masthead (I wasn't). I do take seasickness seriously. I know what it's like as I get seasick myself so there is an empathy – and yes, dying might be preferable.

Unless you are lucky enough to be bombproof at sea I have seen all the degrees from mildly queasy to abject subjugation followed by the onset of dehydration. When I set sail with a head sea where pitching motion is even mild, I will go down. Rolling and yawing are fine, but I don't do pitching. Over the counter Stugeron is my cure, taken the night before, the morning of departure and one or two for the first day – and then I can stop my pill popping. From that point force 9 on the nose can fill in and I will be fine. I am completely predictable and consider myself one of the lucky ones.

People come on board with all sorts of alternative cures both chemical and natural taken by mouth and also the paraphernalia of pressure point contraptions which may or may not be placebo. I encourage them all, if they have anything to do with mitigating the effects. Whether you take the Scopoderm patch or the variety of pills that work for you, it is vital to start taking them well before departure. When going out of the heads it is usually all too late. The 'patch' does seem to work for many who have medium to severe issues although it can affect your balance – not the greatest situation at sea. I had one woman on board whose pupil on the same side of the patch alarmingly dilated which caused minor panic until we came to the conclusion it was a normal side effect.

Seasickness can be strangely considered a rite of passage for the Drake and for many other infamous parts of the briny – The Bay of Biscay is one example closer to home. It is something you lived to tell about. But preparation is key to avoiding it in the first place or at least mitigating it if it does happen. A short skipper's lecture the night before departure about starting your medication of choice early (I recommend after dinner) is the starting point. Have a bucket near to hand for every bunk and one in the cockpit. If a patient/victim is outside of a safe cockpit area and intends to chunder over the side, they must be clipped on – in any weather. If they insist on staying outside keep them warm, but in cold climates this is impossible for any length of time. Sipping small amounts of clear water will keep them hydrated and forget about food – they don't need it. After an episode, encourage them to go below and get into their bunk. Being supine and staying in that position is sometimes the best cure. And check on them often.

We have had some serious cases. When retching comes every 15 minutes or so and the noise becomes intolerable for the rest of us, we inject intermuscularly with 25mg of Promethazine (Phenergan is a tradename), a sedative/antihistamine cocktail. It knocks them out for 12 to 15 hours and in more cases than not when they come to, they are 'cured' for the remainder of the passage. When *in extremis* they will not mind the needle, and if they protest you can threaten them with re-hydration, anally, with a rubber tube and funnel. But don't take my advice on any of this, best first to consult your doctor.

A PARA SEA ANCHOR TEST

'Heaving to is a necessary skill, but is a parachute-type sea anchor aimed at reducing drift worth the investment?'

May 2020

To be honest, when in heavy weather verging on extremis I was never a fan of sea anchors, nor drogues trailing off the stern – all too complicated. At least with the size of vessels I am dealing with I have always found it easy just to 'heave to' when strong headwinds and seas made forward progress unsafe or just plain too uncomfortable. Heaving to is a simple manoeuvre and when conditions get even worse there is nothing more that can be done.

In the days before GRIB files, while on the 54-foot, 28-tonne *Pelagic*, we hove to often when caught out in the Drake Passage. Every boat 'heaves to' differently (some not at all) depending on the hull, appendages and rig configurations. We simply dropped the main, backed the staysail, lashed the wheel to windward and that was about it. We gently rolled around, at a reasonable angle to the wind and sea but of course sailing backwards at 1 to 2 knots. If we had to wait 12 or even 20 hours for the system to pass, this was more than acceptable rather than bashing into it and going nowhere.

Having said all this, to heave to for any length of time in extreme weather you need ample sea room. The alternative to mitigate the risk of fetching up onshore is deploying a sea anchor. I was asked by a supplier of safety equipment to test a para sea anchor during our recent trip to South Georgia and the South Sandwich Islands including filming the deployment and recovery and commenting on the exercise.

In view of our science charter commitment I left this task to last, knowing that throwing tackle over the side can have unwelcome consequences, not to mention my inexperience with this equipment to be frank, ditto my crew. We had a good look at the sea anchor on the dock in Stanley before we started and made a plan.

Note that *Pelagic Australis* is 74 feet and weighs 60 tonnes.

From a 'hove to' configuration the bag it lives in is simply thrown off the windward bow attached to an anchor line. The other end of the parachute is the trip end and that is attached to a float/fender big enough to support the weight of parachute and anchor line in the deflated mode for recovery. Another floating line is attached to the main float and ending in a smaller float the scope of which is long enough to provide a wide target for recovering with a boat hook. You can begin to appreciate the complication. And for me running the trip line back on board is a non-starter. Letters to the editor always welcome.

We first did a trial in 15 knots of wind and flat sea off the coast of South Georgia. Deploying it in this condition was straightforward, and the para anchor on 50m of our 22mm floating polyprop shore line did hold the bow dead into the wind. So far so good. Though on recovery after snatching the floating line the weight of the tackle was such that we had to attach our gennaker halyard and hoist the main float to the masthead , the aim being to raise the contraption up and over the lifelines and land it on the foredeck – but we had too much line between the parachute and the float, so that line had to be shortened for the real trial.

The mission was to test this in more wind and a moderate seaway, which we left until just before arriving back in Stanley. This we did (the expletives have been edited out of the film) but note that it took three of us on the foredeck to deploy and pay out and for the recovery another body on the wheel steering up to the small float. There is no doubt the sea anchor cuts the drift to leeward substantially, I would venture to say by half. This is reason enough to have this rig stashed away somewhere in the forepeak.

The caveats, though, are many. The load on the main rode is enormous when paying out after the parachute catches. Even with our clean leads forward, run to a coffee grinder it was a dangerous manoeuvre to ease the rode under load and with full turns on the drum you could just hold it. There are chafe issues to consider, and a lot more. Does the average family production cruiser measure up to accommodate handling this tackle safely ? I doubt it.

In the final analysis, this manoeuvre must be practiced and even more important when used for real it must be deployed well before the storm hits and recovered well after it has passed. To pull this off at the height of the storm is a big ask for a full crew, even more so for a single or short-hander. And the temptation to cut it away instead of the difficult recovery is great – but it would be a very bad meal for a sperm whale.

THE RYA EVOLUTION

'Even after thousands upon thousands of sea miles, you can still get caught out by the basics'

September 2021

When first taking *Vinson of Antarctica* out of the Hamble River I had to think quickly on my feet which way those black triangles face on west and east cardinal marks... I hadn't been out in the Solent in not years, but decades.

I got a further shock on our maiden voyage up the channel, through the Dover Straits and into the North Sea. Traffic Separation Schemes, buoys lit and unlit, wind farms and oil rigs to dodge, with endless heads-ups and chatter on the VHF channels. The Admiralty paper chart of the southern North Sea was indecipherable due to the amount of information on that scale of 1:750,000.

For those sailors used to this where on watch attention span means everything, by comparison I must admit that it is a pleasure leaving Port Stanley in the Falklands. When you are abeam of Pembroke Light-house, there is a bank to dodge and that's it. Time to relax, feet up on the pilot house console with a Tintin adventure to hand and a cuppa.

The reader will be thinking, surely this guy must know about this stuff. I do sort of, but much has been lost to memory due to lack of use while in the Southern Ocean environs. Rest assured I got back in the frame quickly and became comfortable by the time we sailed by the East Goodwin lightship.

Yes, I do have a Yachtmaster Offshore ticket and the Ocean. Which brings me to a story I often tell people when the RYA training scheme comes into conversation and which I was reminded of when we crossed the Solent on *Vinson* on our way to Cowes during a photo shoot.

It must have been in the late 70s, possibly the early 80s when I took the one-day assessment for the Yachtmaster Offshore, well before it was a de facto requirement for a yacht skipper. This one-day assessment is still in force – a day out where an examiner assesses your competency. It is not necessary to do any prior coursework although much of the RYA menu of courses leads up to prepare you for it.

As you do, I borrowed a 40 footer in Port Hamble from my friend Archie and seconded another friend and sailor Geoff to be my crew. The examiner arrived on time at 0900 and while stepping into the cockpit badly twisted her ankle. Geoff, who was a sweety, called for the ice and massaged her ankle, all the while me thinking, quite inappropriately, this could all work in my favour.

We were brought up sharp, though, when motoring out the river not having cleared the entrance buoy, Archie poked his head up in the companionway and asked who would like a gin and tonic... which we made light of while signalling to Archie to stand down. Archie, with a face like a red traffic signal, had been serious.

The first and probably the most important task was the blind navigation exercise in fog, which began off the Hamble River entrance. From down below I had to dead reckon with the occasional cue ('I hear a bell off to starboard...') from the examiner on deck, and navigate across to Cowes Green, surprising myself with this success when allowed on deck. With that in the bag, and Geoff mentioning without prompting I had been around the world a few times already, we sailed for the Beaulieu River on a tidal calculation and picked up a piling, all part of the syllabus. While tied up, it was time to go through the Morse Code, signal flags (now both obsolete), buoys, lights and shapes, ColRegs, which I certainly had to swot up for prior. Getting the first few questions in each category right, we dispensed with the rest, as she said, 'seems like you know them!' And then we had a nice lunch – and that was it.

Was this rigorous enough then as it is now? Certainly, it is a case of the examiner having full confidence you know what you are on about. Nothing more needs to be done. But like any surveyor, if they find rot in the bilges or a corroded frame in one place they will dig deeper and no doubt find more. Same here in the RYA and rightly so; confuse the lights on a fishing vessel with the lights on a fishing vessel that's trawling and you might be headed for Davy Jones.

The RYA now has become the blue chip standard for training and small boat licensing represented in 58 countries by 2,400 training centres and 25,000 instructors. The strengths, in spite of the criticism (ad nauseam in dock talk) of the 'zero to hero' possibilities, are that in all stages of the progression up to Yachtmaster Offshore there are practical aspects on the water that you must do to prove you can handle small craft.

Compare this with the US Coast Guard system where, I believe, with the appropriate sea time in no matter what capacity (the galley dishwasher is the usual example) if you sit the written exams successfully you can get a license to navigate a 100-tonne vessel. American exceptionalism? Surely, along with red right returning.

Postscript

The RYA system goes from strength to strength and is now without question the global standard for training in small yachts.

Pelagic Expeditions in conjunction with the Vinson of Antarctica *expedition vessel, run the Ocean Yachtmaster Theory course in Chile, before the 21-day delivery to Cape Town, which is arguably the most comprehensive programme for celestial navigation.*

ABANDONMENT YET AGAIN

'Abandoning your yacht should be a last resort, but how desperate should you be before making that decision?'

March 2022

The two yachts that were abandoned in the 2021 edition of the Atlantic Rally for Cruisers (ARC) brought into question issues that need attention, but as is often the case, will not be easily resolved.

Let me first say that anyone making judgements on these two incidents is sticking his/her neck out to be chopped off as it can be nothing more than armchair speculation. You would have had to be there in person and then later willing to talk about it. Certainly, in the case of the yacht *Agecanonix* where they had a fatality, the psychological pressure just to 'get off' must have been enormous. Understandable and case closed.

The case of *Charlotte Jane III* is not so cut and dry, though, and there are not many actual facts forthcoming, no doubt for legal reasons. So, at the risk of being de-platformed or 'cancelled' by *Yachting World*, below are my opinions, by me and me only. Having said that, if you have read the pages *ad nauseam* on various sailing forums there is an echo chamber at play to some extent asking the obvious question of how can you abandon, no matter how uncomfortable the conditions, a perfectly sound hull, as evidenced by the successful salvage.

Having steered this column now for over seven years (gulp!), I have to be careful in repeating myself. But note that in the March 2016 column (see page 146) I dwelled on rudder failures of my own and how to carry on. In the July issue of 2017 (see page 152) I asked the question of why there are so many unneeded rescues after another similar loss of steering incident off the Canaries.

There is no point in delving too deeply into the *Charlotte Jane III* affair, but it is worth looking at some generic factors that are in the least interesting to contemplate. In an ocean race a rudder or rig (let's also include it in this discussion) failure does put you out of the running. Is there, or should there be then, some sense of responsibility in trying to get to the finish without assistance by jury-rigging these fundamental systems? They do it in the Vendée Globe often and the stories are the stuff of legend. Many cruisers have had to jury-rig rudders and masts, some out of pride adhering to a maxim of self-sufficiency, others out of necessity being alone in the middle of nowhere.

Let's remember, though, those sailors are the elite, or at least experienced enough to be resourceful. The inarguable fact is that the proliferation of people going sailing naturally lends itself to less experienced sailors tending towards the herding instinct of 'strength in numbers.' Consequently, the ocean sailing rally concept has evolved and the ARC has superbly led the way. If there is any doubt in how many rallies you can do in various parts of the world, see the January 2022 issue of *Yachting World*. It is also patently obvious that with more boats on the ocean there will be more failures of fundamental equipment like steering systems for a variety of reasons; poor construction and installation, hitting floating objects and lately the phenomenon of whale strikes among them.

In some ocean going events like the Golden Globe Race, to enter you have to prove *in practice* and demonstrate a jury rig and jury steering system. But this is a tiny fleet with a long lead time for the entries to accomplish this none-to-easy feat of seamanship. In the ARC it is written in the *Safety Equipment Regulations* under sub heading 'The following equipment shall also be fitted/carried', that you have to have, 'A proven method of emergency steering with the rudder disabled.'

The 2021 ARC had an upper limit of 225 boats and only 144 entered due no doubt to Covid. When it is otherwise fully subscribed, we can appreciate that for the organizers to fully check and have demonstrated the solutions to these somewhat statistically unlikely scenarios of failure is clearly out of the question. I will venture to say many entries will have let this one slip under the wire with a hypothetical jury rig and not well thought out, if at all. If you didn't take the time pre-rally to actually build something to test you would be operating on speculation if you had to invent the system *in extremis* – adequate materials and the right tools come to mind, and these modern boats don't like extra weight and usually have not much room for 'stuff.'

And as one forum contributor pointed out, to rig a rudderless steering solution on these modern boats with tiny keels is not as easy as with the more traditional full keel yachts of yore, where directional stability was built in. I might even be arguing completely out of turn, postulating that modern 'blue water cruisers' as is the popular marketing catch line, are so vulnerably designed and built that I, as an old deep waterman would think twice before setting sail in one. Have we really arrived to that point? I don't think so, but it's food for thought.

Another thing that has generated a talking point is the idea of getting everyone into a liferaft in high winds and a four-metre swell as being a safer option than sticking with your rudderless, but floating shelter. The old adage 'never step down into a liferaft, only up as your boat sinks underneath you' is a good one to remember, when making that call to step down. Easy for me to say from my armchair, though.

6 EXPEDITION SAILING AND CRUISING

This has been my forte for more than 35 years, overlapping with my ocean racing career that took place from 1987 to 2001. It was quite clear that continuing to race at top level and start a business at the far side of the world in the southern high latitudes was not compatible. And if truth be known, I was obvious to me in order to compete at that level against Olympians and America's Cup sailors now going offshore, I was simply not good enough.

The 54-foot original *Pelagic* had set the scene in the 90s and by 2000 it was evident that to stay at the leading edge of expedition sailing I would need to build a bigger platform. *Pelagic Australis* was launched in Durban in 2003 and returned to our base in Tierra del Fuego as the only custom, purpose-built vessel of the genre.

We were a 'vessel of fortune' taking tourists (in many forms including climbers, divers, skiers, photographers) to Antarctica, Patagonia, South Georgia and also testing the waters of Greenland and Svalbard. This was the bread and butter of the business. If your track record speaks for itself, other opportunities soon arise with professional film teams and science projects needing transportation and logistic support to these remote areas. Ships for this application are too expensive and it has been recognized of late that the national science programme vessels juggling schedules of several if not many multidisciplinary science projects do have their drawbacks. Small dedicated teams on small vessels are now the vogue.

This dynamic is unique in chartering, at least the way we do it. Whether film, science or adventure, the crews of the vessel, by definition few in number, need help from the charterer to manage the boat at times. And the crew often need to help the charterer do their work, often onshore. It becomes one team working together, unlike the classic 'them and us.' On our new Pelagic 77 *Vinson of Antarctica*, soon to be joined by a sister ship, we have been on back-to-back film and science projects since her launch in 2021.

CRUISING GUIDES AND PARADISE LOST

'Does the plan for a cruising guide to Antarctica represent another "paradise lost", another remote area tidied and packaged?'

July 2015

There is a plan afoot for a cruising guide to Antarctica. I know this as I was asked to contribute to it.

At risk of alienating a large part of the cruising sailors around the world, and not a few publishers, I would like to throw this curve ball out there.

Although we all use cruising guides once they appear – it would be silly and irresponsible not to – I cannot help being amazed at their proliferation for all points on the globe, however remote. They have their place of course; in well-travelled areas to facilitate cruisers that have no time to do the research on the ground – fair enough. What's done is done. What will happen, though, and we are not far off it now, when there is nowhere else to go to discover on our own (even if it is an illusion as it is rare now to be the first – anywhere)?

In the 1980s I 'discovered' the far south where no cruising guide existed. It was exactly what I was looking for – if 'exploration' was an exaggeration, then a 'cruising frontier' was a fairly accurate description. The joy, and often the struggle and sometimes downright pain in finding our way through the fjords of Chile and the archipelago of the Antarctic Peninsula was experimental to put it mildly. Uncertainty was a given. We ran aground often, wound up in untenable anchorages and survived various dramas and in doing so also made 'discoveries' that we revelled in. To record our wanderings we sketched 'mud maps' and kept them (still do) in a book we called our 'Rutter.'

Of course we were not the only ones roaming around. Many pleasant evenings were spent rafted up with other likeminded voyagers where we freely traded the sketches and local knowledge – in the beginning with tracing paper and pencil, glass of whisky in hand. A guide book of sorts, but not one you buy off the shelf, rather one purchased with time. This tradition of information exchange continues on web forums and, although far less personal, is at least a point by point approach rather than compendium. It should be selective. After hastily introducing himself on the dock in Ushuaia, one visiting boat owner immediately asked if he could photocopy my entire Rutter. Not liking the 'cut of his jib', the request was politely denied.

Then, in the early 90s a Chilean ex-admiral had a go at a cruising guide for Chile which was of no consequence. In 1991 Jerome and Sally Poncet published *Southern Ocean Cruising*, which was mainly about aspects of environmental awareness on the Antarctic Peninsula. Sally states in the introduction, 'I recognize that for some, the handbook may come as a disappointment: there are no sailing instructions here, no anchorage descriptions, no handy hints on where to shop or change your dollars. I leave that kind of book to someone else, to a future time. But the day that book is written will signal an end of the Antarctic as a true wilderness area, the end of voyages of exploration and discovery...'

Back in Chile, during 1998, the Royal Cruising Club published a cruising guide that was a simple overview and non-comprehensive. And shortly after, the magisterial *Patagonia – Tierra del Fuego* was published by an Italian couple after 10 years of cruising and documenting. This truly signalled the end of an era. Hilaire Belloc got it right when he said, 'When the unknown becomes known, it loses that mysterious power of attraction that the unknown always possesses.'

The motives for writing cruising guides can be several. Marking territory? Financial gain? Opening up new cruising grounds for all those who will follow – resulting in another 'paradise lost'? Well, it will be pointed out that I am partially guilty in all of the above. The difference is I wrote about what we did, but not necessarily where to go. That I left up to those who made the effort to discover it all for themselves.

Postscript

The proliferation of cruising guides for especially remote areas continues at pace and not only the published hard copy editions but now most have online forums where information can be added ad hoc. They are undoubtedly resources of immense importance for cruisers, more so for those on tight schedules in our world of quick fixes, and also for those who have a certain fear of the unknown and don't necessarily like poking around without a daily game plan. Kind of like following the dots.

I have now changed my attitude almost 10 years on from when this was written as one of my 'axe grinding' columns, and I have come to the conclusion that what for me were those 'voyages of discovery' are truly over for everyone and I am not fussed about making contributions of what I know when asked. Fancy that!

CATAMARANS

'A catamaran is faster, safer and more comfortable than anything with a single hull – but you have to pay attention'

February 2016

If you don't believe your own eyes, there is no doubt if the statistics are to be believed that catamarans are taking the sailing world by storm, both racing and cruising offshore, and not least of all inshore in stadium events. Having raced and made passages on high performance Maxi cats I can certainly attest to the allure of the genre. They are faster, safer and more comfortable than anything with a single hull. Faster is easily understood, but it is justifiable to question the safety aspect. Of course, an offshore cat or trimaran can go upside down with a moment's lack of concentration. Up until that point, consider that compared to a monohull you are much higher off the water with waves by and large passing under the net and beams. Sail handling is a dream, compared to grappling with sails tangled up in the lifelines on the foredeck of a monohull heeled at 20 degrees. Drop the foresail halyard and the sail falls on to the net. Reefing the main is also easy by comparison, as you stroll around on a flat platform tweaking this and that.

Look at the Volvo Ocean Race images and then compare them to the pictures from any offshore multis where the crew are riding above the water rather than in it. And if the whole shebang does go upside down the crew can still live in the hulls, and in fact plans for communication, power generation, cooking, water making and all else are taken into account in the inverted configuration. Monohull keel failures, which seem to occur with alarming frequency, often leave holes in the boat – she still floats, but it can be a more desperate situation surviving until rescue. In ocean racing terms at least, when you add up speed, safety and comfort it seems multihulls are a more intelligent approach for ocean racing.

I have less experience on cruising catamarans. One holiday in the Seychelles, though, was enough to convince me that this is the only way to go for at least the tropics. We had two families of four on a 43-foot cat. Each to his own hull, with two heads in each! The other family were non-sailors, which made absolutely no difference to managing the holiday nor to their enjoyment as it was, as some readers have pointed out, like living on a floating caravan. We were there to enjoy the islands, to do so by sail, but the sailing was secondary. By contrast, just to test this conclusion, our family is cruising the Falkland Islands and Tierra del Fuego with another family, eight all up, this December/January. *Pelagic* is an old style, narrow 54 footer. If you don't see my next column (see page 146) you can assume we have all killed each other.

Is it the sailing or the destination that is of prime interest? If the latter, the catamaran formula wins hands down. Granted, most charter cats sail like dogs, are in the main chartered by less experienced sailors and are ultimately very safe inter-island. It would take a tropical storm force 9 if not a hurricane to overturn them.

Hence the rise of the performance cruising catamaran; ultra-light, all souped up with a powerful rig and minimum scantlings, but still sporting a living room with a picture window and en suite bedrooms. These are different animals requiring skilled hands to keep them on the right side of heaven. I see the dilemma. If you are a sailor with a racing background, this is the perfect toy to 'cruise' which might be a contradiction in terms – cruising at 25 knots is not relaxing no matter what anyone tells you. Letting the ocean slide by at 8 to 10 is more like it. In the hands of less than skilled people who are not paying attention every second to wind, waves and trim, these 'performance' cruising catamarans can be on the right side of hell in a jiffy. A 'performance' indeed.

Postscript

To carry this story of cruising catamarans even further, mainly in the bareboat charter genre, take note that these charter companies are fast eliminating an interesting piece of equipment – the mast and sails! I can attest to this with some knowledge as Cape Town, being the base for many of the world's constructors, are hatching 'power cats' at alarming rate. The conclusion is and I have seen it myself, that most people who charter these boats are not really interested in the sailing as stated above – they just want to get from one anchorage to the next to have fun. The sails have become an unneeded distraction and to roll out a jib is one thing, to hoist the main just too much trouble. The evolution is driven by demand, or let's say lack of it in your own desire to 'go sailing.' A shame for energy consumption, certainly. A shame for the proliferation of noise and lack of sailing aesthetics, yet again.

SMALL IS BEAUTIFUL

'It can make sense to keep going for larger and larger yachts, but you lose something in the process'

April 2016

Some years ago I piloted a 170-foot superyacht down the coast of Chile. It was the owner's twelfth sailboat, each one progressively larger than his original 40 footer. I assume the size of the vessels increased as a function of the owner's business success and aspirations. This is an understandable progression. For the marine industry these repeat clients are fundamental to the lifeblood of many of the world's premiere production and custom yacht builders. Four or five yachts, always larger and more extravagant, are not uncommon through the life of a keen yacht owner.

Sometimes perplexing from the point of view of a dockside observer, the reasons for going larger are several; faster passagemaking is a given; more privacy perhaps; more separation between the professional crew and the owner's party; more luxury for sure; more space for household conveniences and gadgets and dare I say it – more status. Ramping up is obvious, but going back down? It takes some will power!

This past Christmas holiday on board the 54-foot *Pelagic* mentioned in my February column (see page 178) where I speculated on our chances of survival in a confined space for a month was in fact a great success; both families of four all accounted for. We cruised north about the Falkland Islands then on through the eastern entrance of the Straits of Magellan to Punta Arenas and then down through the channels of Tierra del Fuego to Puerto Williams near Cape Horn. It was a cool to cold voyage, which means a lot of time below living on top of each other. I never did but I should have kept track of the amount of times one needs to say 'excuse me' when navigating below or trying to extract yourself out of the companionway hatch. This is part of the human price we pay (with the smells) for benefits that are only clear when we do scale down to smaller sized vessels.

Granted, on the larger *Pelagic Australis* the capabilities are obvious – mainly speed and space on board, both on deck and below. Although we are still very creative with pushing the boundaries of exploratory cruising, there is no doubt that when I fall back on board *Pelagic*, I feel a sense of liberation. Not only do we have fewer systems on board, the systems are by nature more simple, and the cruises usually are more trouble-free technically. If things do go wrong the size of the objects that fail are more manageable.

The real advantage of 'small', though, is just the size of the floating object. We can do things with *Pelagic* that we wouldn't dare with *Pelagic Australis*. *Pelagic* is 'man-handleable', while the big boat at 74 feet and 55 tonnes displacement is not. She is also about the maximum size you would want to entertain hanging from shore lines in confined spaces where it is likely to blow. With *Pelagic* we can literally run her up on beaches for safety, with the confidence that we can refloat her. With the bigger boat, we can't play this game. Looking back over the *Pelagic* history through my photo archives, it is quite clear we found ourselves, by design or circumstance in many more interesting and satisfying situations, which translate into memories. I speak here about the motives and the essence of exploratory cruising.

When I see ever bigger and bigger yachts venturing into far corners of the world I do question the logic. Anchored in some cases way offshore, and limited in their inshore navigation, they not only remove themselves to a great extent from the environment they chose to cruise in, but they also potentially remove themselves from some human contact. When it is not possible to play it close and cavalier laying to a broken down jetty in some far flung outpost which sports no marinas, you are really missing something in the spectators that you will attract.

Postscript

Never more true. I write these words from Ilulissat, Greenland. We are inside the crowded harbour with a motley collection of fishing boats, big and small and all sorts of interesting locals to observe and who observe us. We get polite nods and smiles. Meanwhile there are four superyachts anchored outside – too big to get in, too precious to lay alongside the awkward and smelly wall of the fish factory. They don't know what they are missing.

SOUTHERN OCEAN LOGISTICS

'Preparing for summer in the far south involves a supply run to Cape Town from the Falklands and a boatload of bureaucracy'

November 2016

Pelagic Australis, my flagship of the two boat fleet, which includes the original *Pelagic* (my 'Pelagians' call me The Commodore), was back on station in the Falkland Islands at the end of August after our annual refit in Cape Town. While the bigger of the two boats made this annual 3,500-mile voyage from Chile with charter crew on board, *Pelagic* sat decommissioned in Stanley for the southern winter. The high latitude charter season has now begun in the far south. When this goes to press I will be on South Georgia with both boats engaged. Although I have never been one to follow a routine, this is a routine nonetheless and one that we have been keeping since *Pelagic Australis* was launched in 2003.

Preplanning such a season is fundamental. Yacht services can be described as primitive in the Falklands, not due to lack of expertise on the ground – the Falkland Islanders are a resourceful bunch, but rather because of the continuing economic and logistic strangle hold Argentina keeps over this British outpost since they fought the war of possession in 1982. A bilateral agreement allows only one over flight of Argentine airspace per week from Chile. The alternative is a twice weekly service from Brise Norton in Oxfordshire with the RAF 'air bridge', subject to availability from the UK Ministry of Defence. Hence, no yacht type spare parts kept in stock in Stanley.

This also goes for Puerto Williams in Chile, a charming venue at the 'uttermost part of the earth', but where it is impossible to buy a spark plug. Ushuaia is agriculturally better supplied, but whatever services there are in that city of 70,000 people is offset by oceans of bureaucratic inconsistencies for customs, port clearances and other arcane regulations. There is not even a fuel jetty for small craft in

Ushuaia – we roll 200-litre barrels down the dock, one by one and siphon the diesel into the tanks.

Consequently, refitting *Pelagic* is done by remote control to a great extent. This means an end-of-season audit, then loading *Pelagic Australis* with things like her liferaft for the annual inspection, outboards, inflatables, any motors and alternators for servicing and of course the sails for loft inspection and repairs. Without our 'walk in' forepeak on *Pelagic Australis* that is a virtual cargo hold, this would be otherwise impossible with a full contingent of charter crew. On the return 'dead heading' journey the big boat is full to the brim with spares, supplies and provisions – and often spares and supplies for my colleagues on other boats in the area.

I am left on the dock in Cape Town. My other moniker is 'The Cheque Book Captain' – I do the rounds and pay the bills. The pre-season checklist is also a substantial office job. Cruising permits with the South Georgia government must be finalized. Same for Antarctica with the Foreign Office who processes our Antarctic Treaty permit applications. All our charter guests are subject to biosecurity requirements for the prevention of introduction of alien species to these fragile polar environments so several reminders are sent out to make sure everyone is on side with their equipment and clothing.

The International Association of Antarctic Tour Operators (IAATO) also has pre-season checks including logging our applications and permits with our flag states. Verifying things like our company information, vessel call data, shoreside emergency contacts, crisis management plans and our schedules for the entire season are necessary for a smooth operating season for the organization, and for us.

Like all things today, it has become more complicated with more due diligence required, at least if you play by the rules. Sometimes it is hard to stomach especially having been south in the golden period where decades ago we asked no one, just cast off and went.

However, having jumped through all these hoops, whether it be for your first time, or in my case 27 seasons later, there is always that reward on making landfall – snowy mountains and icebergs.

Postscript

Eight years on and things have changed – incrementally in terms of what technical support we can get in these locations and monumentally in terms of the avalanche of paperwork and documentation we have to comply with. No doubt this is due to the proliferation of cruise ships into the Southern Ocean theatre. The pressure on the environment is becoming very real.

ALONE ON AN ISLAND

'Destinations that were once off the beaten path are now either controlled by permits or crowded with other boats'

December 2016

It is rare to be left to your own devices on a wild island. From the tropics to high latitudes more often than not when you think you are alone and have achieved a sense of isolation allowing your imagination to conjure up allusions of first contact as in the voyages of Captain Cook, someone usually comes steaming around the headland and drops anchor next door. Or possibly the prefecture or a park warden will materialize out of thin air asking for your cruising permit.

Indicative of the interest in worldwide cruising (in large part thanks to Jimmy Cornell) beyond the pedestrian waterways of the Mediterranean and Caribbean, over time many of the uninhabited islands in far flung locations have seen a steady traffic, well-publicized, even more so now with social media and cruising forums. Tropical island destinations were first on the hit list, a trend that began in the middle of the last century. The average cruiser was more than capable of dealing with the challenges of coral atolls, fringing reefs, the heat, jungle environments and the critters that infest them that might make the experience in part miserable. The shoal waters would provide, by fishing or diving for your dinner, no permit needed, which satisfied the primeval desire of otherwise urbanites to 'live off the land' in solitude. For any cruisers less adventurous flotillas now regularly ply these waters which in one sense seems to deflate the purpose of getting away from it all.

High latitude destinations certainly offered more challenges. Considerations for the cold, risk of ice, short seasons and generally heavier weather meant these austere outposts only in relatively recent times have found focus. Many sub-Antarctic islands as well as Arctic equivalents were, as a rule, ravaged by sealers and whalers for hundreds of years and then forgotten about by territorial governments. This created a vacuum opening up a golden period for bold small boat navigators willing to make the necessary preparations and take the necessary risks to visit them.

Lately, though, sovereignty has had to be reinforced either for potential mineral exploitation or to altruistically protect a unique ecosystem for scientific study. An organized tourist destination is also a motive. At present there are no sub-Antarctic islands you can visit without a permit and many where no permits will be issued at all. A few are even off limits for the scientists. This due diligence also extends to the entire Antarctic continent as per the terms of the Antarctic Treaty. Everywhere in the Arctic, which is all sovereign territory, is also slowly following suit with permitting regimes. In many cases daily position reporting is a requirement. The 'golden period' of showing up on a voyage of personal discovery unencumbered by bureaucracy seems to be truly over.

In September 2016 our early season South Georgia mountaineering expedition on *Pelagic Australis* was as usual well planned out and transparent with the South Georgia government having gone through a rigorous permitting process. The difference, though, in going down in early September meant that we would be the only yacht on the island and well before the tour ship season opened in mid to late October. Although the administrative base at King Edward Point alongside the abandoned whaling station of Grytviken, now a museum, is manned by a British magistrate and a harbour master plus a retinue of British Antarctic Survey scientists, this staff is restricted to their station and the immediate environs of Cumberland Bay.

The point was that while roaming around on the beaches and in the mountains we were utterly alone – not counting the penguins, seals and other flying birds numbering in hundreds of thousands. Although we are aware of and adhere to all the guidelines regarding the wildlife and biosecurity protocols there was a certain sense of freedom knowing there would be no one sharing our anchorages and no one to 'bump into.' A liberating experience indeed.

OFF-SEASON SOUTHERN OCEAN EXPEDITIONING

'Summer weather on South Georgia became so problematic that we decided to head south in winter instead, with some success'

January 2017

Although we are in the business of providing uncertainty as one of the mainstays of the *Pelagic* experience, at times, after so many struggles with weather putting the kibosh on otherwise well laid plans, you do sometimes feel your head 'banging against a wall' – especially if it is the mountainous wall of South Georgia.

A sub-Antarctic island which lies between 54 and 55 degrees south and cuts through the Polar Front – an ecological boundary between the cold South Atlantic water and the really cold Antarctic water – it is probably the most problematic region we travel to especially if the goals are mountaineering. Seven hundred and fifty miles from Port Stanley in the Falkland Islands to first shelter at the north-western tip of the island, it is not that far a sail especially going east downwind. Getting back west is another matter of course, but the sailing is always accepted as a rough and tumble affair.

When we started voyaging to South Georgia back in the late 1980s the obvious time of year was late spring or high summer which is November through February. The theory that holds true in high latitude regions, which is certainly the case for Antarctica and the high Arctic, is that the summer period will be the most settled with high pressure having moved in. The ferocious weather we always encountered in summer was apparently the norm so we soldiered on through several years of supporting climbing expeditions along with various colleagues doing the same. The fact is although South Georgia is a high latitude destination it is not really high enough.

With better weather analysis and some trial and error we realized that the winter to early spring period was preferable. Tracks of the depressions that pass through the Drake Passage follow a path south of the island in the southern summer so the speed of the system is additive to the wind speed around the low. During early winter through early spring storm tracks move north, just enough to pass over or north of the island with some frequency. This results in either a dead spot under an elongated area of low pressure or better still a less intense easterly airflow as the low moves up and through.

During those early years in summer our failures in the mountains had outnumbered the successes and times of not even getting started off the beach were many. In winter and early spring not only is the weather somewhat kinder, but colder temperatures make for easier sled pulling with skis.

In September/October 2016 we again embarked on an ambitious mountaineering programme which in fact was a repeat of our August 2014 expedition when in spite of a deep winter itinerary even a landing at the south end of the island was untenable because of gale force south-west winds produced from a stationary high pressure out to the west. This year that high pressure eventually cooperated. We managed to sail and motor in light winds directly to the south-west corner of the island and land at a seldom visited shelter called Trollhul. The next day we were off and up on the glaciated terrain – just in time to get caught out in a five-day storm that kept us pinned down in our tents in relative comfort. Then a dream scenario unfolded. The high to the west moved over the island and stayed there for the next two weeks. During the next 12 days we traversed 65 kilometres of glacier to St Andrews Bay on the north coast. We climbed two virgin summits on the way – Mt Starbuck and Mt Baume. We were in a comfort zone that is rarely experienced on the island where technical climbing was feasible with little chance of getting caught in *extremis*. A nice place for those of us with short memories. To top things off we sailed back to Stanley in three and a half days flat – the all-time record. Dangerous complacency had set in on all fronts!

THE FREEDOM OF BOAT OWNERSHIP

'It doesn't matter how much or how little you use your yacht, it's a symbol of freedom – an escape pod from reality'

March 2017

How many times have you heard, or said yourself, something like, 'Look at all those yachts in the marina, and you seldom see them go out.' It is true. And it is a worldwide phenomenon. From the marinas of Europe, the Americas, Australasia and everywhere in between yachts of all sizes are probably the most visible of expensive recreational assets that can be considered grossly under-utilized. Vintage cars might be another example, but they are normally out of sight locked up in garages. Horses might qualify and although they do need to be fed and exercised daily at the minimum, a parallel also holds true for yachts. Anyone who leaves their yacht unattended for lengthy periods knows the possible outcome – a dead ignition system on the engine and winches that won't turn. Like horses, boats with myriad moving parts need to have their 'muscles' flexed on a regular basis.

Standing fully clothed under a cold shower tearing up 100 dollar bills is often how boat ownership is described. A floating black hole is another. Poor sod, bloody owner, Captain Bligh and the 'cheque book captain' are just some of the possible sobriquets that a boat owner usually suffers at the hands of his crew whether in appreciative jest or otherwise.

No matter how it is cut, if we consider a cost-benefit analysis, the benefit being time on the water after casting off from moorings, yachting can be a mugs game and any accounting system used in justification, no matter how you creatively cut it, a potential embarrassment. I for one cannot envisage owning a yacht unless it is working its way. Granted, racing yachts are a particular genre as the season's racing schedule sets the scene and the boat does get used by this imperative.

Most cruising boats, though, are not bound by an organized itinerary, so many represent what I call an 'unmovable feast', spending most of

EXPEDITION SAILING AND CRUISING

their time in marinas. However, where you are expected to show up (and having paid an entry fee) the ocean rally concept represents the alternative. The Atlantic Rally for Cruisers (ARC) and other maritime 'get togethers' have become hugely popular, but they represent a drop in the bucket of the ocean. To really get your cruising bang for your buck, 'live aboards' make sense of it all. The yacht is the permanent home or possibly a planned itinerary qualifies which might be an around the world cruise with the family. Then there is the proliferation of charter flotillas worldwide *a la* The Moorings and Sunsail which points to an obvious alternative to boat ownership, although the fine print in the business model does mean you ultimately inherit the yacht at some point, with all its usual problems.

Nonetheless the sheer numbers of yachts, apparently idle tied up to the dock on 'standby', points to something more profound at work. In 1979 myself and a young crew on the *Independent Endeavour* won the Parmelia Race that started from Plymouth and ended in Fremantle with a stop in Cape Town. This was a one-off event that was celebrating the 150th anniversary of the founding of the Swan River Colony in Western Australia. Soon after the finish I delivered the Swan 65 up to the Mediterranean for a charter season. The elderly owner, a mining tycoon and newspaper owner from Perth sailed with me as far as the Seychelles. One starry night as he and I were alone in the cockpit he admitted the only reason he bought the boat in the first place was to have an escape mechanism for his family when the Chinese invaded Australia. A novel idea and he was dead serious.

The point to that story is that boat ownership, however under-utilized the boat becomes, if not simply a status symbol – and there are plenty of those examples – provides that escape vehicle on standby is always ready to go. Not for a Chinese invasion nor to run from some cataclysmic event, but rather just to break free, even if only for a day or a weekend from our everyday work-a-day world. Even if it is seldom used it is always there in waiting for you, anxiously tugging at the mooring lines which can easily be cast off with a few flicks of the wrist. Freedom.

A VOYAGE OF PARTICIPATION

'Not every charter guest wants to learn the ropes but becoming a useful member of the crew is a fulfilling goal for anyone'

April 2017

It's usually an interesting conversation talking to charter guests about their experiences. Yacht charter – there are so many ways to go about it from the operator's perspective. More often than not you do hear plenty of positives; the beautiful boat, an impeccably turned out and capable crew and the location being superb. Then the bombshell is dropped when they admit it was great but how useless they felt, never having been asked to lift a finger.

Bareboat chartering I can fully understand. The charterer is in control of the operation of the vessel, come what may. It is DIY sailing. Even if the laying of the anchor is not executed every time with textbook precision, much the same as that slightly skewed bit of woodwork or that corner cut in a plumbing operation you did in our own home, there is a great sense of satisfaction in not having called in the experts, nor having to pay for them.

Granted, skippered chartering really exists for those who are either incapable of safely running the show, or are simply those sailors and non-sailors alike looking for a full service holiday, where by some magic the meals appear and afterwards the dishes disappear leaving the charter guests alone to socialize obliviously or maybe to wonder what they are actually doing there in the first place. This is the classic Mediterranean and Caribbean model that we who sail are all familiar with – either as the waiters for, or the consumers of, the fine meals and wines on offer.

Discounting superyacht chartering which always falls into that full service category by virtue of scale I am a firm believer that in the medium size range of skippered chartered yachts, most of the guests would rather be crew or considered thereof at least in some degree. Everyone, even the most rank beginner or a non-sailor if asked can do something useful on deck under supervision and they will with few exceptions rise to the occasion and enjoy it. Grabbing the tail of a jib sheet and just pulling or winding that winch handle, and working up a sweat in the process, will in my view give more satisfaction to a charter guest than that sunset rum cocktail which will be even more appreciated having in some fashion or another contributed to the day's sailing. Following on, if they hadn't got stuck into the deck work, it is mightily hard to ask them to help wash or dry the dishes.

This is certainly the Pelagic way. Everyone who signs on is crew and immediately is melded with the professional team. We take many sailors of minimal experience and many people who have none at all. These folks are there to witness Antarctica, South Georgia or Patagonia by boat. This means standing watches, working the deck, launching the Zodiac, cooking and washing up to name a few of the daily chores required from a working crew. We don't entertain, we engage with people who want to live aboard, learn the ropes, try some navigation and help maintain the vessel during an adventure sail. I would venture to say that most everyone who charters a yacht would like to say the same, but that is usually not on offer. Most often charter guests are left to languish staring out to sea...

Instead, the norm with exceptions is a professional crew who have a mindset of handling what they assume are useless guests which cannot be trusted to touch any sail control systems nor are encouraged to help out with the obvious where no harm can be done. It is true that on the two *Pelagics* we have no electric winches where unsuspecting people can wind themselves into pretzels by pushing the wrong button. Nevertheless it is incumbent on a professional charter crew to encourage people in some fashion or other to partake rather than simply chivvying them out of the way for every manoeuvre. Of course, a professional charter crew is ultimately responsible for the safety of the guests so this is always a judgment call. It is clear, though, the more experienced the professional crew with the confidence and skill of oversight the more they are likely to get the charter guests onside and contributing, making for a happy ship.

Postscript

We have built the entire Pelagic business model on this concept of a 'voyage of participation.' And, some of the ambitious things we do absolutely require the help of our guests (usually brawn, not brains). It is all about uncertainty as the attraction. We never guarantee we can go anywhere and do anything but we will try. In the end, when all is said and done these people can honestly say they have been on a sailing expedition, and not a charter cruise.

SAIL SOUTH, AND FAST

'Since 2011 the number of vessels visiting Antarctica has risen steadily and in 2016–17 exceeded the all-time high. If you are going to go, don't leave it long!'

June 2017

After the month of February on the Antarctic Peninsula I migrated north to thaw out in Miami for three days. Well, not completely as I spent the three days in an air conditioned hotel meeting room participating in an IAATO Executive Committee meeting. One of the topics we discussed that is now firmly in the sites of the organization's strategic plan is how to manage what is an explosion in expedition ship tourism. Read Chinese coming into the fray as tourists (already the second biggest demographic) and new ship companies.

This is of interest to anyone who has dreamed of taking their yacht to the Antarctic or for that matter anywhere in high latitudes north or south. High latitudes cruising is considered to be an exotic destination – what some call 'wilderness' and the perception has been of untraveled cruising grounds, managed to some extent but not overrun like a national park *a la* Yellowstone. That was what Lars Lindblad and the *Explorer* was offering as an Antarctic experience for cruise ship tourists with his first trip to the Antarctic in 1966. That was the same year Bill Tilman on *Mischief* dipped down to Deception Island as the first yacht, followed by Dr David Lewis on *Ice Bird* in 1973.

Like so many changes and upheavals we have seen in the world in recent memory the story begins with Perestroika. Overnight the Russian Academy of Science fleet of ice-capable vessels, and there were hundreds, with some exceptions were mothballed when their budget was cut by the new government. Clever tourist entrepreneurs from Europe, the States and Australia saw an opportunity and did deals to charter these vessels, with an accommodation conversion, along with the deck crew and hotel staff – for peanuts. A look at the statistics tells the story. In the 1991/1992 season there were roughly 4,000 shipborne tourists to the Antarctic. By 2006/2007 it was closing in on 38,000 and at the time this was considered a saturation level. The economic crash that followed in 2008 softened the numbers back down to 25,000 for a few years and then an International Maritime Organization (IMO) ban on heavy fuel oil burned or carried in the Antarctic also put some ships out of the game which was also welcomed by the Antarctic Treaty community who were beginning to take serious notice of the upward trends.

Since 2011 the numbers have risen steadily and in the 2016/2017 season we exceeded the all-time high with over 40,000 visitors, mostly shipborne. But this is not all. Although the old Russian ships have by and large been outdated, new companies are joining the party and the established tour ship companies are building more modern expedition ships. The numbers of expedition ships is predicted to rise by 50% by 2019. The conundrum for the Antarctic is that it is non sovereign territory so there is no obvious way to limit the number of operators. IAATO is therefore looking at self-regulating by various means; possibly by the companies agreeing to one landing per day where they now offer two in their itineraries. The Antarctic Treaty on the other hand might restrict what is on offer by designating more landing sites 'Specially Protected Area' (SPAs) which would squeeze landing opportunities and might create a self-limiting effect where some companies would bow out. In the high north it is a different dynamic. The Arctic rim countries claiming sovereignty can be more proactive with limitations imposed at short notice as tourist pressure increases.

And gone are the days of being alone or at least one of a handful of yachts in any of these high latitude destinations, let alone sharing them with the ships. The reality, though, is that the total number of yachts anywhere in high latitudes at a given time is still very small. In the Antarctic it is measured in the tens not hundreds. Luckily for us, high latitudes are not every sailor's cup of tea for obvious reasons.

Having said all this, a well-equipped and properly manned yacht, preferably steel or aluminium construction, whether a Mom and Pop cruiser or a super/mega version, can still duck and dive away from the ship traffic using some creative exploratory navigation and, to some extent, mitigate the crowding effect. Recent arrivals of fibreglass hulls, catamarans and those worried about their paint job I'm afraid will be stuck in the rush hour traffic lane. Whoever you are, if contemplating a high north or high south voyage, don't leave it too long. *Carpe diem!*

Postscript

Only six years after I wrote this column, the crowding is now a serious subject. Within IAATO's and the Antarctic Treaty's remit what they refer to euphemistically as 'tourism growth' is actually a tourist explosion and is already unsustainable by most people's opinions. Yes, yacht visits have increased over the decades, but their numbers of visitors measure in the hundreds per season – the shipborne visitors were well over 100,000 in 2022/23 and set to double in a few years' time.

Frankly I am now having a hard time with my hand on my heart to promise our tourist clients a cruise that was to a remote, pristine environment on a flexible schedule. The Antarctic at least, is no longer a wilderness area; it is a managed wilderness park.

VOYAGING TO THE SAME OLD PLACES

'The best part about being a boat owner is that every morning you get to choose whether you see something new and unknown or the old familiar'

October 2017

At the age of 65 I have realized I am in a rut of sorts. I am again returning to South Georgia this October for another month's expedition to this splendid wilderness. I have lost count but it must be well over twenty expeditions to the island, almost always involving deep field activities. As is usual we have charter guests but also a three-man climate change team from the University of Maine, and I will be helping them drill ice cores on the Szielasko Ice Cap. This is a rewarding project combining recreation on one hand and a bit of serious science on the other – a great way to get our charter guests involved. There is some heavy lifting to and from the glacier which they don't know about yet. For them it is a chance to participate in something very relevant to the island's rapidly retreating glacier systems. The science team has been with us twice before – so all this is familiar ground for them and us.

I was reminded of what has been this enjoyable routine that has lasted for decades during a recent correspondence with my friend Jerome Poncet in the Falkland Islands. If I am indeed in a routine in the far south with *Pelagic*, he has made it his life's work and pleasure with his *Damien II* and *Golden Fleece*. He and his family have logged well over forty years in the area and in large part are responsible for many of the classic 'ice with everything' BBC filming epics we see on TV. With unparalleled knowledge of where the wildlife is hiding, the Poncets are famous for getting the film teams there and back safely with some very creative navigation in between.

Jerome is now on what he describes as his 'semi-retirement' and is joining his second son Leif who is cruising his own boat in Alaska this northern summer. That will be his first foray into that 'far side of the world.' This made me think – I have never been to Alaska or any of the Pacific Northwest other than an illicit cruise with an old girlfriend in Puget Sound many years ago. I guess it has been a full immersion with southern South America and points further south in that there was always scope for new places to explore and discover. I had no real desire to look elsewhere. On the other hand, it has evolved into a business. There is that question of sustenance that must be considered.

While mulling this over there is evidence that there are two very different styles of cruising and 'exploring' (if I might belabour that much misconstrued word again). On one hand, you have the globe girdling crowd that island hop endlessly whether it be for a year's cruise or a ten-year cycle. They never spend much time in any one place, content to always experience the new and then move on. Seeing the coastal world is the object and arguably there is no better way to do this than on your own boat with complete freedom. It is a kaleidoscope of experiences.

Then there are the mugs like me and many others content to return again and again to those same venues, which in the case of the south is in fact a very condensed region. In effect we are living the region rather than visiting. Familiarity is the main attraction; meeting old friends in remote farms and villages (and sometimes delivering essentials). Coming into anchorages with the knowledge of the shoals and other navigational hazards in your head, rather than reminding yourself from the chart we take for granted. Then there is waking up to the morning's bird song without having to get the bird book out for identification.

However, the interesting thing I have observed is that the globe girdling crowd can be much more inspirational in their writing about their voyages than the 'stay at home' grounded bunch of which I include myself. We were inspirational once, but their continually fresh experience lends itself to better and more colourful descriptions in print it would seem. Those of us who have been time and time again to the same waters having similar adventures are no less enthusiastic, but might be more philosophically at ease. If asked, I would not have it in me to write another article about Cape Horn.

Tom Price, the British mountaineer who was a member of the South Georgia surveys in the 50s, spent many months roaming around the interior. He sums it up: 'The more one becomes familiar with such grandeur, the less one has to say about it, the less in fact one thinks about it. But it is there nevertheless, and has its effect upon the soul.'

Postscript

I must write the Pelagic memoir one day. Publishers have asked me for it. Friends keep reminding me. Maybe when the knees finally give out and I can no longer carry my load, or pull my sled, I will have the time. Maybe just after that next expedition…

THE NORTHWEST PASSAGE

'The Northwest Passage is still a treacherous way to travel between the Atlantic and the Pacific. A fallback plan is essential'

November 2017

I checked the Canadian Ice Service's website just before the deadline for this copy – one last time, lest this column proves to be totally irrelevant by the time it goes to print.

I was partially relieved. Why? Because it appears, now in early September, close on the onset of winter that the Northwest Passage might be a no go, at least for flimsy yachts, due to heavy concentrations of first year sea ice in the Franklin and Victoria Straits – the normal route through this labyrinthine archipelago. There are alternative ways through, but they, at the time of writing, are also problematic. Of course, with a big change in wind, some vessels might squeak through and I will be a laughing stock – but as always in this column I will take that risk.

I attempted the Northwest Passage on *Pelagic Australis* in 2005 – and failed due to ice in this very area. Although we were too early in the season, the decision to retreat back down Baffin Bay was justified as it never cleared. A few small yachts did make it through – one on the deck of a Canadian icebreaker and another following behind in their wake resulting in serious hull damage. Following an icebreaker is not be undertaken lightly, unless in *extremis*. Thereafter if your yacht floats at all you will be sailing a squashed tin can.

Since 2005 the Northwest Passage has gained the reputation of being not only always possible, but almost a given for robust small craft and even precious superyachts with hulls that are not ice-strengthened. The optimum period for planning a successful transit of the critical 'choke points' is the last week in August into the beginning of September, which is really near to the onset of winter and not long before the freeze up.

Irrespective of how this season pans out, it is worth noting that although the seasonal sea ice is fast disappearing all over the Arctic as a trend, there is still plenty of multi-year ice persisting through the summers, getting harder and more dense with time, which shifts about on the vagaries of wind and current. So if last winter's sea ice doesn't melt off, this accumulation of 'heavy ice' might still stop you. This inherent risk of possible failure for small (or precious) craft must be gladly accepted if an attempt on the Northwest Passage is to be made.

The big mistake when planning this voyage is to lock yourself into another cruising itinerary immediately on the back of it assuming you will get through. You might find yourself at the end of the season in the wrong ocean having retreated back down into the North Atlantic when you were supposed to be approaching Hawaii. It is noteworthy that the coast of Baffin Island opens up late in the summer so this is a good backup plan if you have to retreat back out to the east. In fact it is a much more interesting cruising ground than the western sector of the passage itself, if box ticking is not your primary motive.

Meanwhile, on the Alaska side the British polar adventurer Pen Hadow is attempting to sail to the North Pole with two 50-foot yachts to publicize the disappearing environment of Arctic summer sea ice. I was asked to attempt this on *Pelagic* about eight years ago. It was a far-fetched project then and it still is today. However, successful or not this bold project will draw further attention to climate change. Russian icebreakers have been breaking their way to the north pole for decades, but to arrive at the top of the world in a lead of open water on a small craft will be an event worth noting – even more so if they manage to extract themselves. Getting up there is one thing, getting back another. If their leads close out and the yachts become beset in the pack, the team will certainly be evacuated somehow, but then the environmentalists will put the boot in for what has become trash – the two yachts – adrift in a pristine environment.

From their blog it seems already apparent that the pole might not be attainable and they are falling back on a short course menu of science projects while on the edge of the pack ice. By the time you read this column they will have either attained the pole or have been stuck in the ice trying, which will, in both cases create a media frenzy. The irony is if they are sensible, stick to the science on the edge of the pack and retreat before getting caught out you might not hear about them at all.

Postscript

The idea of taking a small yacht all the way to the pole is still being mooted, but the reality of a successful voyage there and back is still a pipe dream. These stunts, because that is what they are, do little or nothing for enhancing climate change awareness when we are now inundated with this issue daily.

SAILING VESSEL SCIENCE SUPPORT

'The retreat of glaciers on South Georgia points to climate change and a recent voyage there helped gather more compelling scientific evidence'

January 2018

There is no better way to appreciate climate change as a reality than returning year on year to South Georgia, that most celebrated of sub-Antarctic islands in the Southern Ocean. For whatever reasons – and there are possibly many – in an environment like this with temperatures for the large part of the year hovering around 0 degrees C, whether the temperature is just below, or just above, makes all the difference. Clearly, in the last three decades that I have been coming here the trend has been upward and this is backed up statistically as the island had been occupied by Norwegian and English whaling companies since the turn of the last century into the late 50s and since then by a British Antarctic Survey field station. These carefully-kept records tell the tale of an increase in temperature over the medium to long term, no doubt about it. That is scientific fact and you would have to be partially blind coming here over the years and not notice the dramatic changes in the landscape which are so evident.

For example, the Neumayer Glacier that I camped on and walked across to attempt to climb the highest peak of the Three Brothers in 2002 is now open ocean. The glacial front has retreated six kilometres from its position on the 2004 edition of the South Georgia map, compared to where it is now on the map's September 2017 edition. This is an extreme example, but the retreating glacial trend is typical of nearly all the glaciers on the island especially on the warmer north side. Interestingly, though, on the southern side that takes the brunt of the weather first there is more snowfall so the recession is less severe and actually advancing in a few places. But this must be considered anomaly rather than contra-argument in the climate change debate.

In consequence those of us using South Georgia as a playground looking for snowy conditions with colder temperatures to ski and climb have been tending to come here earlier during late winter/early spring to run our expeditions, in spite of risking dark nights offshore which can be nerve-wracking if ice is reported en route. Not long ago we would have been guaranteed a metre of snow on the shorelines in September into October. This has not been the case, though, during the last two seasons. In September 2017 the shoreline and foothills were in a high summer condition. Of course, this is probably a short-term climatic hiccup, but it makes you think, and worry.

Because the sub-Antarctic islands are on the edge of the Antarctic ecosystem, climate change scientists are keen to learn all they can from these fast disappearing glacial systems. Ice cores can tell the story. In October 2017 we hosted for the third time since 2012 a team from the Climate Change Institute, University of Maine – one of the leaders in the field of interpreting historical climate information from ice cores in order to better predict what the future may hold. I was seconded in as 'grunt' to assist the three researchers working on the Szielasko Ice Cap on the Barff Peninsula who were attempting to drill ice cores 30m down to the bed rock and also chainsaw ice pits at various elevations to take block samples. This vestigial glacier (our team says in 20 years it will all be gone) might help to not only determine the age of the ice laid down, but also by chemical analysis tell the story of historical weather patterns (and other catastrophic events like volcanic eruptions that can mask weather patterns) which could help predict the future. Unfortunately we were, for a variety of reasons, only partially successful in getting the samples, but what we did get we hoped would provide the justification for another reconnaissance voyage in 2019.

Finally getting to the point of this column, it must be said that it is possible for a small yacht like ours to provide logistic support for what are significant scientific pilot projects, especially in a remote location like South Georgia, where there is not even an airstrip. Also, there is now a growing trend among philanthropic super and mega motor yacht owners to donate time on board their vessels for science projects, helicopters included. I can't think of a better way to use your vessel.

THE FALKLANDS IN ITS AUTHENTICITY

'Taking a yacht to the Falkland Islands, where marine facilities are primitive, is truly a frontier experience'

June 2018

Upon returning from the Antarctic Peninsula at the end of March 2018 my skipper on *Pelagic Australis* reported with no exclamation mark that there were seven cruising boats in Port Stanley, our base of operations. He didn't have to elaborate as I got what he meant. There is hardly enough safe dockage in Port Stanley for three or four yachts. There is no marina as such.

As a remote and exotic safe haven location Port Stanley probably ranks down there with the most primitive with regards a marina environment. It is a tough place to hang in to. The narrow harbour is a four mile reach aligned dead east–west. With an average wind speed over the islands of a bracing 17 knots and continuous frontal weather passing through – coming mostly from the westerly quadrant – it can be an untenable situation if you are at anchor in front of the town, or caught out on the wrong side of the very few rough and ready jetties that can be utilized by small craft. You have to be ready to rock and roll. And if you have precious topsides, I suggest to stay well clear.

The choices to tie in to are somewhat unique. Working from the eastern extremity going west you have FIPAS which stands for Falkland Interim Port and Storage System – a floating amalgam of six enormous barges lashed together, left over from the 1982 conflict with Argentina. Apparently, this structure is long past any chance of a clean bill of health survey and has never been dry docked. It is kept afloat by patching up and pumping out. This is the main terminal for ships to bunker, offload and re-supply. Warehousing is available and the port captain's office is a container perched on barge No 1. Yachts can use the eastern butt end of a RoRo pontoon to gain some shelter but the drawbacks are soon obvious due to continuous maintenance. Showers of rust and shot blast grit that in a westerly peppers rig, sails and the deck can be pretty grim.

The favoured alternative is at the FIC East Jetty on the foreshore of the town. The Falkland Islands Company recently re-structured the eastern end which is much appreciated. Another is the new public jetty, which we sometimes use in calm conditions, but this is intended and prioritized for the tenders offloading tourists from the many cruise ships that now visit the town and we are warned that the pontoons and structure supporting them are not to be trusted in supporting any tonnage.

Actually, things have gone backwards from the early days as the government jetty, which was further along the foreshore to the west, was a great spot either on the end or tucked behind an 'L' that gave the best protection for small craft under about 60 feet albeit with lifting keels. That was sadly condemned in the early 2000s and broken up, and no replacement is forthcoming.

The government has bigger fish to fry, namely the fishing fleet itself, both local and foreign going, that is licensed in the Falklands Maritime Zone and is the biggest earner for government. Also, the nascent oil and gas industry. Their enthusiasm and infrastructure building waxes and wanes with the price of crude while the locals are always anticipating the 'boom' a la Shetlands. Currently the oilmen are taking a rain check. And tour ships bring in a £15 per passenger landing tax plus their spending on tours, cream teas and knick-knacks – and they come in the many thousands annually.

The yacht traffic is therefore small beer. Frequently plans are mooted for a redevelopment of the foreshore with a proper yacht marina being fundamental. Us regulars are frequently asked to comment on the plans and put our two cents worth in the design. Alas, we frequently are disappointed when nothing seems to materialize. And so it goes.

But is it so bad? I have never been a fan of marina environments. They can take over as a life of their own and in a way cut you off from the port and its people, if all services and conveniences are laid on. We continually complain about the lack of facilities in Port Stanley and there is no doubt that if the marina does materialize it will be most welcome. But it will also be closure to the endless struggles that we accept as part and parcel of what can be considered a frontier experience. Having thought about this, long may it be so.

Postscript

Strangely, facilities for yachts have gone backwards still since I wrote this column. There are now no dockage situations that are completely reliable, because of other improvements that have left yachts right out of the agenda. Plans are still discussed and mooted and discussions I have been involved in with government always revert back to 'payback' via a marina for the infrastructure. But there is also a reputational issue at stake here, as places like Puerto Williams and Ushuaia, although not having marinas per se, do have some facilities for visiting yachts. Stanley still has zero.

THE POLAR CODE RAISES ITS HEAD

'The introduction of new Polar codes for vessels visiting high latitudes could have profound implications for yachtsmen'

November 2018

It is a fact that what us old-timers fondly call the 'Golden Era' of sailing to high latitudes had ended some time ago. I won't belabour that point for newcomers lest I discourage them. To venture to these regions will always have rich rewards for sailors.

The bureaucracy in order to get there is another matter that must be noted by the uninitiated. With the exponential increase in cruise ship traffic in recent decades to the Antarctic and Arctic regions, rigorous environmental and safety considerations have had to be imposed by authorities which are understandable. Permitting has been, for some years now, required by every vessel and aircraft that enters into the non-sovereign Antarctic Treaty area which is defined by all areas below 60 degrees south. In the Arctic, the national governments of Denmark, Norway, Canada, the United States and Russia, and the local governments of Svalbard and Greenland are inventing new due diligence requirements year on year, making things more complicated for ship operators. As these rules and regulations have been applied to all floating objects, yachts which are in small numbers and for the most part small in size have also been impacted, certainly in the Antarctic, less so up north in parts – for now.

It is no longer possible for a yacht to claim that they were unaware of the need for permits, or in effect, to do some serious preparation to complete a safe and environmentally friendly voyage to these particularly sensitive areas of our planet. But things can go overboard in this respect, and the latest example to raise its head above the sheer is the Polar Code.

In brief explanation, the Polar Code is an IMO invention in response to this increase in ship traffic in polar regions and was a direct result of the loss of the expedition cruise ship M/V *Explorer* that sank in the Antarctic in 2008 after hitting heavy glacial ice, luckily without loss of life. After many years of deliberations, consultations and lobbying for and against certain aspects by flag states, the Polar Code, a 57 page document, took effect in January 2017 for SOLAS vessels. This Polar Code is an add-on to SOLAS (International Convention for the Safety of Life at Sea) requirements and in the main is all about safety – scantlings on ships, safety and lifesaving equipment, manning and where in ice covered waters you can go with certain ice classed vessels at certain times of the year. The environmental side is a mere six pages which is an add-on to existing MARPOL (International Convention for the Prevention of Pollution from Ships) regulations defining pollution issues near or in ice covered areas.

That was Phase I – for SOLAS vessels – which is all about carrying passengers. Phase II has just started and the intention is to apply a Polar Code to non-SOLAS vessels, meaning specifically fishing vessels (which by record are very prone to accidents in polar regions) and recreational vessels – and that is us. The dilemma here, which is only beginning to be recognized by the IMO is that whereas SOLAS vessels had a set of regulations to start from as they were all of a certain size greater than 500 gross tonnes, non-SOLAS vessels range from fishing boats to mega yachts, to superyachts to yachts like *Pelagic Australis* that was built to the MCA MGN280 standard for commercial craft of less than 24 metres with 12 passengers or less – to *Pelagic*, homebuilt 30 years ago, and proudly in the Mom and Pop cruiser variety without a stitch of certification. And knock on wood, having sailed *Pelagic* in polar waters for 30 years without incident will count for nothing if and when Phase II kicks in following in the same vein as Phase I.

It is obvious Phase II yachts, let alone lumping them in with fishing vessels, are a dog's dinner of types and sizes which will be impossible to regulate under one set of rules. There is a rumour of guidelines rather than regulations by statute, but don't count on it.

The messages here are twofold: if you are contemplating a new build in the next one to three years and can't wait for what Polar Code Phase II might actually legally require, then build to the highest specification you can, which for small yachts is currently MCA MGN280 which has become a global standard to a great extent. If you are thinking of spending time in high latitudes with an existing vessel I would not wait too long to make a plan. Go high north, go low south. *Carpe diem!*

Postscript

Pursuant to this panic, a small advisory group (me included) of polar yachtsmen was formed to try and forestall what was on the horizon. The Polar Yacht Guide (PYG) is the result and gives a set of recommendations to yachtsmen who wish to sail in high latitudes. It is very general rather than being over-prescriptive, precisely because of the wide range of vessels in this small vessel category. Under 300 gross tonnes seems to be the magic number where the Polar Code has agreed that setting binding regulations is not practical – for now.

THE RAW FORCES OF NATURE

'Failure to reach a planned goal is a strong likelihood in adventure sailing, so we might as well embrace the fact we may not get there'

December 2018

It doesn't take a sailing-to-climb expedition like the one I just finished in October to realize how the raw forces of nature can lay waste to well-made plans. The same can happen on a planned weekend crossing of the English Channel where dinner in St Malo has to be cancelled due to a raging southwesterly in the western approaches.

Granted, voyaging to South Georgia through the Southern Ocean does raise the bar of vulnerability, no doubt about it. And once you are there, what can be accomplished in the mountains is a gamble in the truest sense of the word. If totted up, our mountaineering failures over three decades far outweigh the successes. But we are not masochists, as the successes, when they came, were sweet and well-appreciated.

The uncertainty of this game of chance is part of the attraction, but sometimes that uncertainty becomes the theme rather than a prelude. The 2018 season's objective was to repeat our stunning success of 2016 with the same 65-kilometre ski traverse from the southern tip of the wild south-west coast of the island starting in Trollhul Bay and ending at St Andrews Bay on the north-east coast central section, and home to the largest king penguin rookery in the world. In 2016 we cherry-picked two fine targets of major virgin summits in a rare spell of high pressure. We were out for 16 days including 6 days storm bound in glacier camps. Looking back this was the icing on the many layered cake of previous battles lost with the island.

The optimism that expedition engendered (and we always have the struggles and failures filed somewhere in the back of the memory bank) led us to believe we could do the same again, as there are many more summits to de-flower in what must be one of the world's most remote and committing exploratory mountaineering environments. There is no one to call for a search and rescue on South Georgia. In any event this time the island's weather punished us handsomely and we are now humbled, once again.

We had five weeks in hand from Port Stanley and return and we got off to a good start arriving on the island after a four-day passage. No chance to land at Trollhul Bay, though, due to strong winds onshore. So we waited on the north coast for five days making day ski trips before retreating to the base at King Edward Point where the small contingent of eight overwintering British Antarctic Survey staff and two government harbour masters who control the fishing fleet in the maritime zone offered to give us the west-facing jetty for what would be a major easterly storm on the rise – making the north coast un-navigable. That storm lasted a full four days and to top it off King Edward Cove, facing south-east, was big enough to accommodate all the brash ice in Cumberland Bay discharging off the Nordenskjold glacier. We couldn't move if we wanted to trapped by the ice under pressure from the wind.

When the storm force winds abated down to variable and the pressure on the ice lessened we escaped incarceration and made a beeline for the south-west coast, south about, as Trollhul, usually prone to heavy swell would be as flat as it gets in the lee of that easterly storm. Five of us were put ashore with ten days of supplies, camping and climbing gear, all carried in sleds. The traverse took twelve, which says something in itself and we accomplished nothing in mountaineering terms other than a journey in very arduous conditions of heavy snowfall, high winds and little or no visibility. It was hard work pulling the sleds in the deep snow and few rewarding views were had in among otherwise white-out conditions day after day.

And how lucky we are to be able to play this game of Russian roulette on land and sea, where success is never guaranteed, where patience wins out when one takes the long view of the overall experience of attempt and failure being not time wasted but cherished. There is a surfeit of canned and packaged adventure travel today where assured gratification is by contract. Not so when the quest has failure always looming large.

So next time that dinner in St Malo has to be cancelled, hunker down in the marina on this side of the channel and enjoy just being there with the wind blowing in the rigging and tinned beans on toast on the table.

THE REAL CAPE HORN ROUNDING

'Rounding Cape Horn is an experience to cherish, but what really qualifies for the achievement?'

April 2019

I distinctly recall telling a magazine editor that if asked to write another article about Cape Horn, I would shoot myself. That was a long time ago. The time has passed.

In January 2019 after piloting a superyacht in the Antarctic we re-crossed the Drake Passage and came in slightly from the west, 'rounded the Horn', and then managed to land on Cape Horn Island. One of the guests, vaguely aware of my sailing history both racing and cruising in the south asked me how many times I have 'rounded'. Years ago I would have arrogantly told him only five, for to actually round Cape Horn in the classic sense you need to start from somewhere like New Zealand. The implication is there are some miles to do before and after and just rounding the Horn on a day trip as I have done many times with our charter guests during the Beagle Channel/Cape Horn cruises doesn't really cut it. To answer the gentleman I just said 'many', not having any idea exactly. No point in giving him a lecture and spoiling his moment.

Indeed, to be a member of the International Association of Cape Horners (I have never joined for one reason or another) you have to be on a non-stop sailing passage of at least 3,000 nautical miles and double 50 degrees south from the Atlantic to the Pacific or vice versa. I guess they had to draw the line somewhere as that would have been lots of ears to pierce if every cruise ship contingent including those coming back from the Peninsula qualified.

On my first rounding during the Whitbread Race in 1977, the visual experience was locked in a mystery. We rounded at night, the feeble light on the island barely visible, and when dawn broke we vaguely had a view of the mountainous terrain falling behind in our wake as we began to climb north towards Staten Island. We remained largely ignorant of what we had seen. Indeed, in those days you would have had to be an academic to find out any of the recondite history of Tierra del Fuego let alone its then present place in the politics of southern South American. Other than the well-worn Cape Horn sagas known to all sailors there were precious few popular books on offer about the region in general.

It was only when I started my second life in the late 80s as a pioneer of the Southern Ocean charter game that we came to grips with the region. Our two-week routine cruises included a short trip around the Horn launched from the spectacular anchorage of Caleta Maxwell just to the west on Isla Hermite. If it wasn't blowing a gale, the Southern Ocean swell was always rolling through. After only a few hours we rounded up into Caleta Leon on the lee side of Cape Horn Island and dropped a hook off the kelp line.

In the early days getting ashore and up the rickety staircase on the sheer cliff to the station was quite an original experience. Manned by a Chilean naval rating with his family, and maybe a three-legged dog, we were always sincerely welcome and invited in for tea or coffee. Our visit was even more appreciated when we brought a cabbage or two and some potatoes. This family was on station for a year straight and supplied infrequently so any contributions to augment their supplies which were always a bit short, went down well.

Over time more yachts started to visit and the interior of the station was decorated with yacht club burgees from around the globe. Inevitably this most famous point of land was put on the cruise ship itineraries and the numbers of visitors increased to what now must be many thousands per season. A gift shop with Cape Horn paraphernalia even evolved.

In January, we landed with 10 people, climbed those same steep stairs – still rickety – and made a very brief visit to the lighthouse and chapel. The naval officer, smartly dressed for the occasion, was courteous, but no coffee or tea was on offer, the gift shop was gone and it turned out to be a slightly stilted encounter. Possibly he was about to be overwhelmed with another ship arrival.

We took the time to stroll out on the boardwalk to the statue – the albatross cut out of outsize steel plates (which could do with a lick of paint) that overlooks the vast expanse of the Southern Ocean. One thing that will never change.

Postscript

In March of 2023 I was inducted on the second round to the newly formed Cape Hall of Fame in Les Sable d'Olonne, along with Dame Ellen MacArthur, the Kiwi empresario Grant Dalton, two French sailing supremos, Franck Cammas and Michel Desjoyeaux, and single-hander Jean Socrates. I was the only one who turned up for the ceremony. Does that say something?

PELAGIC GOES NORTH

'When his yacht *Pelagic* was launched, Skip vowed he'd never return her to the Northern Hemisphere. Now he explains why he's doing just that'

July 2019

When *Pelagic* was launched in Southampton in the autumn of 1987 and sailed immediately south I claimed, in a very 'Bernard Moitessier moment', that she would never return to the crowded waters of northern Europe, or for that matter the northern hemisphere. To demonstrate I was serious about that statement while on our first expedition to the Antarctic, while caught in a prolonged storm well tied in to the shore, I cut up our UK and European delivery charts and stitched them together to make a log book, using some spare pieces of Treadmaster deck material and leftover joinery to make an attractive cover. Mind you this log book had nothing to do with position, course, speed and weather but was immediately the record of what fun we were having. The backsides of those charts were filled with nonsense prose, satire, cartoons, facile watercolours and some impressive ballads. The ballads were invariably authored by the public schoolboys in our crew. I have this log book still. Hard to tell if my teenage children were amused, bemused or simply confused when they found it and had a read.

You saw it coming. Never say never. At time of this column's publication *Pelagic* will hopefully be somewhere off Newfoundland after having arrived on the mid coast of Maine to prep for an Arctic season. She sailed it in one, non-stop from the Falklands, arriving on the smell of an oily rag. The decision to move her north for the foreseeable future was ironically due in part to the fact that the Antarctic is getting so crowded with tour ships that we can no longer function with that vessel in what was our pioneering spirit. As my colleagues say – those who are still standing – 'We were lucky to have had the *epoch d'or*.' I use the French as most of those pioneers were French, plus me. Instead, *Pelagic* will now seek out pockets of solitude in Greenland and Arctic Canada leaving the more commercial *Pelagic Australis* to continue with the southern charter business that continues with yet more and more demand. It is painful to say, but in the highly organized and oversubscribed tourist business in the Antarctic *Pelagic* is now marginally unfit for purpose according to some bureaucracies. I never did get around to putting in that watertight bulkhead. Better to exit the region gracefully.

While *Pelagic* sailed north during those six weeks of open passage delivery I have been the absentee owner onshore, comfortable in my armchair with my laptop waiting for the weekly position report from Kirsten the skipper. Not being on board during these long hauls, with a schedule hanging over your head and a commitment halfway around the world makes for an anxious time. Email reports of fuel delivery problems to the engine, a broken furling drum, an unsolved oil leak, sat-phone low on minutes and other minor snafus – if not complaints, were at least useful pieces of information to file and is of course all part of this game and must be appreciated. Luckily, I never had a satphone call from the boat. When I see that telltale +8816 number on my mobile, I always find a chair to sit down on before answering to hear about a major incident that has occurred or one that is unfolding.

Worse than the worry, though, was the envy I was experiencing. Reports of 'great sailing' and 'wind aft the beam for the last 10 days' plus things like 'got becalmed finally, lots of swimming and today we caught a dorado' had a more profound effect on me than the list of repairs and spares needed that would cost me money and possibly compromise the schedule at the other end. Those good news stories made me think, 'Hey, that is what I used to do!' Long passages were my passion. Dragging behind the boat on a bit of old rope as shark bait, sailing butt naked, having a libation at sunset, eating simply and being on watch alone under all those stars while anticipating another new landfall and a run ashore in a strange port was my *raison d'etre*. Well, having missed that warm tropical experience with some regret, I can now look forward to pushing some northern ice. Why not?

THE LIMITS OF CITIZEN SCIENCE ON YACHTS

'Can you make a serious contribution to science while sailing?'

March 2020

Sailing, whether it be peripatetic cruising simply as lifestyle or carving up the seas in competitive around the world ocean racing, can harbour if not a tinge of guilt, then maybe at least engender a thought towards saving the watery part of our planet that we sailors so enjoy.

Making a scientific contribution in one form or another while at the same time living our passion is now a trend, but the idea is nothing new. In fact, explorers through the ages have often relied on a scientific mission to help launch through patronage projects over and above basic geographical discovery. Captain Cook's voyages immediately come to mind. Fitzroy and Darwin on the *Beagle* was another, both producing enormous amounts of new specimens and data, some of which still needs to be studied, stashed away in the vaults of the Natural History Museum in London. Sometimes, though, a scientific quest can be costly – let's not forget Scott died coming back from the South Pole hauling rock specimens for science – while the Norwegian Nansen made no compromises in his bid to be first to the Pole, and live to tell about it.

Today this dynamic persists. There is a surfeit of no compromise 'adventure expeditions' – verging on a circus. And there are many others that Bill Tilman described as having a 'thin veil of science' to justify themselves. Famously Tilman hated having to help carry a plane table theodolite to map parts of the Himalayas when all he wanted was to go mountaineering. I wholeheartedly agree. There is nothing wrong with having a go at a challenge for the satisfaction and fun of it. It needs no scientific justification.

My experience dabbling with science projects within the prime motive of simply having an adventure has rarely been satisfactory. 'Doing some science' always sounds good, and it might help you get funding from commercial sponsors or even via some naïve university budgets, but it usually winds up to be a dog's dinner of agendas and the scientific output is minimal. Ask any fieldworker who has tried this, especially on small sailboats, and they will happily vent their frustration *in vino veritas.*

A few super and mega yachts, on the other hand, have embraced this trend in a big way, often with significant results. The Five Deeps Expedition is a case in point. A wealthy American and his mega motor yacht took a submersible to the five deepest trenches in the world's oceans. This was the real deal in terms of an adventure challenge where not only new geographical ground was explored, but also new species, unique habitats and behaviours of benthic marine organisms were documented. Other superyachts have been donated at little or no cost for less ambitious projects. The message here is these vessels have the capacity and logistic capability to produce outcomes. Sort of a sea-going version of Elon Musk in outer space.

Where does this leave little guys like ourselves? There have been some noteworthy examples that do work. Dee Caffari's *Turning the Tide on Plastic* was a winner. Sampling microplastics en route on the Volvo Ocean Race did produce worthwhile results, and shocking results at that. In the far south some of my colleagues in the charter business are making repetitive trips with the same scientific institutions taking samples of marine life and making observations on a dedicated basis. The so-called Expedition cruise ships of 100 to 400 passengers have also bought into this idea in giving their guests something worthwhile to do. The Polar Collective (www.polarcollective.org) is an adjunct committee aligned with the International Association of Antarctic Tour Operators that has five citizen science projects ongoing including: cloud observation, seabird surveys, phytoplankton concentration measurements, phytoplankton sampling and sea ice concentrations. These five do require expedition staff to train up in order to lead the passengers, but anyone on a yacht can be trained up to do the same.

The problem with most of these initiatives is how to give the feedback to those citizen scientists, the payback if you will. This is tricky with esoteric sampling, observations and measurements that often need years of analysis to produce a conclusion.

One stands out, though. Happywhale.com. How many of us have seen a humpback whale sound, and how many of us have gotten that tail fluke photo? Yes, plenty of us. It is easy to do. Happywhale, conceived and developed by Ted Cheeseman, a colleague from Antarctic tourism, is probably the most gratifying for the citizen scientist. You can upload your photo into a recognition database, even name your whale if it is a first sighting (how about Willy, or something more original?) and then track it from future sightings. A humpback feeding in the Antarctic was later sighted off Nicaragua. This should be a buy-in for any yachtsman. Check it out.

Postscript

Certainly, it is trending for scientific projects to use small, dedicated vessels for their programmes, rather than sharing expedition time on big ships like the new Sir David Attenborough. *We have been involved in several such projects on* Pelagic Australis *and now on* Vinson of Antarctica. *The researchers often say these dedicated trips are much more cost-effective when the cost is compared to the results they can produce. Often on the big ships these projects are marginalized, sharing time with many other science groups, and there are winners and losers when weather and the inflexible schedule of a big ship is taken into account.*

The caveat is that any yacht wanting to play this game must have all their ducks in a row with their certificates of vessel inspection and manning plus comprehensive, verifiable insurance policies. When dealing with universities and governments it is all about due diligence and risk assessments.

SOUTH SANDWICH ISLANDS, DEEP IN THE SOUTHERN OCEAN

'Returning from an impressively ambitious scientific sailing expedition in Antarctic waters'

April 2020

To prove a point made in my last column (see page 219), we did accept a science-based charter to the South Sandwich Islands in January 2020 which was, if truth be known, a huge gamble. This semi-active volcanic arc of seven main islands and their outliers begin in the north with the impressive volcanic cone of Zavodovski, 300 miles south-east from the southern tip of South Georgia. The chain lies right in the teeth of travelling depressions that form in the Drake Passage below the toe of South America and is notorious for gale force winds, ice risk and generally miserable conditions. It is no tourist destination for sure.

The southernmost island aptly named South Thule is 200 miles south of Zavodovski and sits just above 60 degrees south, on the edge of the winter sea ice band around the Antarctic continent. It is not quite in the Antarctic Treaty territory so the UK owns this stretch of hostile real estate which together with South Georgia is officially called the UK Overseas Territory of South Georgia and the South Sandwich Islands.

Partly discovered and charted by Captain James Cook in 1775 and partly by the Russian explorer Captain Thaddeus von Bellingshausen in 1819 the islands have hosted only a handful of visitors since. Attempts at sealing and shore-based whaling in the nineteenth and into the twentieth century were unsuccessful due mainly to a lack of natural harbours and not least of all the ferocious weather conditions. In recent years a few science expeditions have landed by ship with helicopter support or via expedition yachts to make baseline surveys of the wildlife – Zavodovski boasts the largest vertebrate wildlife aggregation of any species anywhere in the world with over 1.3 million pairs of chinstrap penguins. Volcanism is also an obvious focus, with the island chain lying on a shallow submarine ledge with a deep water trench immediately to the east. Zavodovski and Saunders, an island in the middle of the chain, erupted violently in 2016. This eruption was picked up by satellite imagery, but until we arrived in January, no one had been back to see the effects on those penguin colonies. Were they even there?

The two volcanologists from University College London (Team Volcano) collected rock samples and measured CO_2 and SO_2 gases with drones flying into the plume that was always streaming downwind from the top of the crater. Getting to the rim was out of the question, though, as high winds and cloud persisted for the three days we were on site. A two-man team from the University of Maine Climate Change Institute (Team Ice) took ice cores on the glacier and water and snow samples. Meanwhile 'Team Penguin' from Oxford censused the entire island of chinstraps and Adelie penguins with drones in addition to collecting penguin faecal and blood samples for DNA analysis, and satellite tagged twenty chinstraps to record their foraging range. Dr Tom Hart, who had made three previous trips to the islands and was the science coordinator for this trip was the pioneer of a system developed over the last decade of placing hunting camera traps in penguin colonies to monitor activity year round. One of the two cameras on Saunders survived the eruption in 2016 and the time code nailed the date down to between 4th and 9th April as the hourly images went black!

In an eight day window we repeated these surveys on Thule Island in the South Thule group, Bellingshausen Island where we swam ashore in dry suits and got towed back out through the surf, and on Candlemas Island further north where we had to abort one landing, but managed it the next day, again swimming in and being towed out in breaking surf. Our last objective was to survey Zavodovski, the most difficult landing, but the sea was so chaotic around this tiny island of only 3 kilometres in diameter it was impossible to safely launch the Bombard C5 inflatable off the deck. Instead, Team Penguin were able to survey the entire chinstrap colony on all sides of the island with drone flights – a remarkable achievement, not least in making hand recoveries in a big swell and a 25 knot wind.

Thereafter we set sail and hightailed it upwind to the southern tip of South Georgia in a favourable weather window, and then spent a

SKIP NOVAK ON SAILING

relaxing 10 days along the coast making more surveys, collecting ice and biological samples, and changing camera trap batteries and memory chips.

The scientists reckon we achieved 90% of our objectives on what was a most cost effective formula in using a small sailing yacht in one of the most difficult areas of study in the world. That translates to an A+ report card for *Pelagic Australis* in the Southern Ocean School of Hard Knocks.

Postscript

In January of 2023 we returned to Zavodovski on Vinson of Antarctica with another team of 'penguinologists', a volcanologist, and a five-person film team shooting for the Disney Channel. We camped for nine days near the coast, covered 80% of the island on foot and summitted the volcano. And in November/December of 2023 we returned again with a British Antarctic Survey team to continue their research. The South Sandwich Islands are firmly on the scientist's map, and the facility of using a small dedicated vessel has been proven three times over, in one of the most hostile of Southern Ocean environments.

POLAR CODE PHASE II FOR ARCTIC WATERS

'Could technical rules being set by non-sailors signal the end of free roaming in high latitudes?'

August 2020

In the November 2018 column (see page 209) I wrote about the looming Polar Code Phase II for non-SOLAS vessels which is intended to regulate fishing vessels, small cargo vessels less than 500GT and recreational craft in polar waters. It was a heads-up, nay warning, that if you were thinking of building a new yacht with the idea of venturing into high latitudes, best to build to the highest spec available which is the UK's MGN280 Code for Small Commercial Vessels that governs boats of 24m and 12 passengers or less, which has evolved pretty much as an international standard.

If you can achieve this or as close as you can, you might well be covered when Phase II kicks in sometime in the near future. I also recommended back in 2018 that this was a *carpe diem* moment for existing vessels to go high north and low south before new rules take effect, which we had hoped would be recommendations and guidelines only, at least for our sizes of humble yachts, as it looked unfeasible to lump all the disparate kinds of recreational craft in size, type and specification together, from superyachts to Mom and Pop cruisers, let alone fishing vessels.

Over the intervening year and a half, reading through various IMO notifications generated from a stable of 20 delegations indicated they were starting to address this dilemma through a lengthy multistage process. They seemed to be veering for a sensible approach of using a lower limit of 300GT for recreational vessels to be considered for 'technical analysis' as a cut-off point. Consequently, with my two boats and those of my colleagues down south being well below, I rather ignored the whole process for a time – until now.

Although the International Association for Antarctic Tour Operators is a correspondent group within the IMO representing the yachts that charter in the Antarctic, World Sailing has recently entered the fray. This was prompted by mainly northern voyaging yachtsman who were very concerned about where the IMO was heading with the Phase II Polar Code. Rumours were of mandatory regulations for 'all ships' regardless of size being strongly advocated among some member states, in spite of the 300GT lower limit advocated by others. Another point of complexity is the idea of differentiating Arctic and Antarctic waters, which also has roughly an equal number for and against.

It must be noted that the Antarctic Treaty, along with IAATO have developed a set of recommended guidelines for yachts wishing to sail to the Antarctic and this is a template for what could be applicable to small craft in the Phase II Polar Code regime. AECO, the Association of Arctic Expedition Cruise Operators, also has something similar but less detailed with regards technical issues, and more about conduct ashore and environment.

The worry is that either of those might not weather what the IMO has in store, and this was recently brought home to me by the World Sailing correspondent group led by well-known yachtsman and former Royal Ocean Racing Club director Alan Green. And here the distinction of north and south needs to be made.

In the Antarctic we have had very few SAR call-outs involving yachts (unlike fishing boats). The yachtsmen who venture across that great leveller the Drake Passage are generally well prepared and IAATO has a well-known outreach programme to help those looking for information on piloting and equipping. Basically, all of us in IAATO are there to lend a hand. Additionally, we get less traffic as the Antarctic is so far away from population centres and traditional cruising grounds.

Northern destinations like Alaska, the Canadian Arctic, Greenland, Svalbard and Russia are at America's and Europe's doorstep. Consequently, there is more traffic, and what I wasn't aware of is the frequency of SAR call-outs due to yachts ill-prepared and/or yachtsmen out of their depths. The afterguard of well-seasoned sailors, under the auspices of World Sailing, is extremely concerned that if the Polar

Code doesn't implement severe restrictions on the privilege to sail far north, those sovereign nations will do. Any set of enforceable rules with technical demands that are out of proportion and unachievable for small craft could signal the end of free roaming in high latitude sailing as we know it.

Therefore, World Sailing's experts have drafted a set of recommendations for lightly prescriptive guidelines for small craft that they hope will be taken on board by not only the Polar Code, but by the Arctic community of nations at large, and in turn used as an educational tool, as we do with the Antarctic guidelines in the south.

It must be noted that although experienced yachtsmen are contributing the expertise to what is a long-winded inter-governmental process, and one that raises more questions than it answers, these decisions of how it will play out will ultimately be made by the IMO delegates who have little or no experience of sailing in high latitudes, let alone sailing at all.

Postscript

As I pointed out in the Postscript to my earlier column (see page 211), the Polar Yacht Guide that World Sailing instigated seems to have assuaged the situation, for now. But we, as high latitude yachtsmen, must keep out ears to the ground and not let our guard down.

MARION ISLAND IN THE TIME OF COVID

'Looking forward to visiting the isolated Marion Island, after sneaking glimpses of the remote spot while racing past it'

February 2021

While my high latitude colleagues were languishing in various ports in South America, either blocked by port authorities or dead in the water for all practical purposes due to Covid lockdowns, or simply lack of demand, I found myself flat out in Cape Town. Why? A simple case of being in the right place at the right time, with the right contacts. Out of the 52 companies in the International Association of Antarctic Tour Operators which includes expedition ships, superyachts, air operators and vessels like *Pelagic Australis*, I was the only one in operation, at least for the first half of the season.

Pelagic Australis arrived from Marion Island mid-November 2020 after a fortuitous 70-day charter supporting a science team. Marion is a South African outlier, 1,200 nautical miles south-east from Cape Agulhas. At 46 degrees south it is well above the polar front, but is still considered a sub-Antarctic island, with all the wildlife you would expect in albatrosses, penguins, seals and many other species of burrowing birds. The South Africans maintain a meteorological station and support a marine biology contingent of 10 people. It is a very isolated piece of real estate, and much more remote and off the beaten track then even South Georgia. No tourists are allowed and the permits to land are hard to come by.

I have sailed by Marion, actually one of two islands known as the Prince Edward Islands – the other being Prince Edward Island, a few times during the Whitbread Races. It is more or less on the route to New Zealand, which also takes in the Possession Islands, Kerguelen Island and Heard Island. If truth be known, and I don't mind admitting this decades later, I often cooked up navigational justifications to alter course slightly just in order to get a closer look at these wild places. I don't think it would have changed the race results much. You will never get one of the Volvo or Ocean Race skippers trying this on now!

On the trip to Marion Island, skipper Chris Kobusch was joined by Dion Poncet and Juliette Hennequin, friends from the Falklands who lent a much needed hand. Dion is a master at tricky surf landings and also driving inflatables around marine mammals, from many years doing the same for the BBC films we have all enjoyed. The mission was to deliver seven scientists down to the base. They were supposed to go in March on the SA *Agulhas II*, the South African icebreaker, but got caught out like the rest of us with the Covid lockdown.

This project frankly saved my business, but to pull this off was three months in the planning during a severe lockdown in South Africa, and involved problems with visas, work permits, quarantine and Covid testing and then clearing the port. It was touch and go right to the send-off as so many things bureaucratic could have scuppered us.

Pelagic Australis departed Cape Town on 16th September with 14 people coming on board straight out of quarantine, plus two and half tonnes of cargo. A six-day sleigh ride in the 'roaring 40s' brought them to the lee side of the island. The reports back to base were the anchorages were rocky and poor, constant swell was running and 60 knot katabatic winds poured off the extinct volcano almost every night. No country for old men... They arrived back in Cape Town on 17th November, ahead of the return schedule.

It is not easy for me to relate this adventure second hand, having missed the voyage myself and I remain envious. The good news is I will be going down in April to recover the film team who have been left on the island. This is finally realizing the dream to see Marion, after those glimpses through the mist back in the Whitbread days.

The Cape Town story lives on. In January I will be doing the first of two back-to-back trips down to Gough Island, in the Tristan da Cunha group. 1,500 miles south-west of Cape Town. We are supporting a mice eradication project sponsored by the Royal Society for the Protection of Birds (RSPB). Again, quarantines and Covid testing are required by both teams, specifically in order to protect the current staff on Gough who man the meteorological station. None of this is easy and adds layer upon layer of complications – so we soldier on.

Meanwhile, we have been tracking the Vendée Globe and given the level of technical problems thus far I might be reporting from the pit stop here – which is their last chance to bail before the Southern Ocean.

Postscript

After that extraction of the film team on Marion, which was an interesting challenge to say the least, upon arrival back in Cape Town the final negotiations were taking place to sell Pelagic Australis *to Greenpeace. This was a discussion ongoing from October 2020 and was a long-winded affair. After 19 years of operation the keys were handed over in May and she sailed north to the Netherlands to be re-christened the* Witness. *With many things considered it was a win-win for Pelagic Expeditions and a good home for the boat with Greenpeace. See my column on page 280.*

ANOTHER COVID STORY – TO GOUGH ISLAND

'Getting involved in the helicopter bombardment of a remote island... all in the name of a war against mice'

May 2021

If you are in the yacht charter business, there is not much you won't do to earn a crust. A time to pull your finger out and adapt before the falling tide of marina fees, crew salaries, insurances and various expenses to keep things afloat pull you down to meet Davy Jones.

I love these wonderful projects that are so out of the ordinary I immediately buy into them without much logical thought, sorting out the details downstream. The RSPB (Royal Society for the Protection of Birds) got wind that *Pelagic Australis* was stuck in Cape Town, which was fortuitous for both parties. In March 2020 the RSPB had to abort their project to eradicate mice on Gough Island, a tiny volcanic outlier in the Tristan da Cunha group in the South Atlantic when Covid locked things down. The vanguard had sailed to the island only to be marooned by the news. They had to eventually re-deploy the yacht to sail the stranded team on to Ascension Island as they could not return to Cape Town. The mice, having arrived 150 years ago with the sealers, have gone aggressively carnivorous devastating the seabird population, so they would feast for another year, hopefully their last. You can YouTube these critters attacking and eating the flesh off the live chicks... Not a pretty sight.

We are doing the repeat voyages to establish a team of 15 on the island, with two tonnes of bird seed and other equipment, who will, over the next two months, sequester two species of fragile endemic land birds and care for them during the bombardment of 'bait' (read poison) from helicopters. In May the SA *Agulhas II*, the South African icebreaker, will deliver the three choppers and the Kiwi pilots who have the necessary expertise. Needless to say, this is logistically an ambitious project in every way, shape and form.

Although Gough is British territory, there has long been a South African meteorological station on the island, and in the time of Covid all visitors by definition are suspect. My crew of four plus eight RSPB staff had to quarantine for 14 days before departure from Cape Town. Note, this was not one of those 'self-isolation' jobs where you go home and cheat your way through out of necessity. No, this was a full 14 days in a box in a hotel room with kitchen and nothing coming in and nothing going out except your trash in the corridor and of course what goes down the drains in sink and toilet. No hotel food, no Uber Eats.

Unlike arriving at Heathrow with a bag and being taken to a Covid hotel, our crew, all Cape Town locals, had time to prepare. I brought in some dumbbells to keep fit (more symbolic than used), plus an enormous box of old slide transparencies and a clapped out light box. The idea was making selections for scanning later. Some of this material was over 40 years old, going back to *King's Legend* on my first Whitbread Around the World Race and, of course, the building of *Pelagic* in Southampton in 1986/87 right through those early expedition years until I went digital in 2005. Through this 'magic lantern' I reunited with old girlfriends, paid respects to many shipmates who have departed and generally was amused on re-visiting what we used to get up to.

On 1st February the 12 of us were bussed down from the hotel in negative pressure, jumped on board (the boat having been theoretically sanitized well before) and after stowage of personal kit and household and safety briefings we were off that afternoon, maskless, in a howling southeaster, wind aft of the beam with a five-metre swell. For the landlubbers this was a bumpy start, heads down in buckets.

After that blow died down, we motor sailed on and off for four days going due west on about 35 degrees south before a nice northwester filled allowing a close reach down to the island. It was a pleasant trip in mild conditions and when the autopilot failed halfway it was actually a bonus, as people enjoyed taking half hour stints on the wheel in the generally sunny and warm weather.

On arrival we were lucky with a calm 'open roads' anchorage just off the kelp line, and within the hour, the RSPB contingent was offloaded (rats, not mice, leaving a sinking ship came to mind) with their day bags on to a rocky shore line under the met station. That afternoon we offloaded their kit bags by crane from the inflatable, a 30m drop along the cliff face. The next day all the other cargo was uplifted in gravel bags just before increasing swell made the last trips precarious. We moved around the corner for two days to a better shelter to recover and prepare for the return, and not least of all to admire this most rugged of volcanic islands and cruise the shore by Zodiac.

Upon leaving the island we circumnavigated and then went wing and wing, main down to 4th reef trimmed amidships and kept that rig for the next 36 hours. With only four of us on board, and my 18-year-old daughter Lara on her first crew contract, I was reminded how pleasant sailing in these mid latitudes could be, from my early years of yacht deliveries – shorts and T-shirt stuff, fishing line over the side, making sushi and swimming mid ocean.

To all my high latitude colleagues and diehard aficionados of the cold I would say, try it, you might like it.

Postscript

Sadly, the mice eradication programme failed. Mice were discovered not long after the bombardment ended. If there is one breeding pair left, or one pregnant female, it is a failure. Having followed closely the successful South Georgia rat eradication project, and having done one ground truthing expedition with Pelagic Australis, *my conclusion is that the nature of the terrain being extremely steep in most places and heavily vegetated meant that much of the bait did not reach the ground. The RSPB plans to try again one day, but that is a big ask. There is also a project afoot to tackle the rodents on Marion Island – easier terrain similar to South Georgia, but much worse weather on average if you can believe it.*

SPITSBERGEN SEA TRIAL ON VINSON

'Sailing a brand new custom boat off the edge of the charts requires a return to first principles'

October 2021

I am writing from 80 degrees north – in truth 79 degrees 45.' The Pelagic 77 *Vinson of Antarctica* bit off a lot to chew on with her first real offshore sea trial sailing from the UK direct to Tromso. We had to enter Norwegian waters in order to deal with a quarantine and then carry on to Longyearbyen in Svalbard. A gamble for sure given a new custom boat straight of the box.

This was our first charter that was seven months in the negotiation – supporting a German government team of geologists in their long-term study of the geophysical structures of that archipelago and taking samples for age analysis – what will be 1.5 tonnes of rocks in the forepeak after 30 days in the field. We are in VOA's polar environment and no show stoppers from our side, so far, testament to our design and project management team and KM Yachts in Holland. The 130 items on the 'snag list', some warranty but most modifications, when she returns to KM in September are par for the course in a new build and not in any way excessive in our case.

The big question was whether we could enter Norway at all, and this was not clear until we presented ourselves in Tromso. Likewise, the German team scheduled to meet us in Longyearbyen were also clueless if they would be allowed into Oslo by air. Unlike the UK, which had dates for things opening up, Norway did so with no prior plan to work to, only if and when the data gave a green light. We were all working on spec right up to the day, all acceptable for a professional project of small scale, but this uncertainty blew the Arctic tourism cruise ship sector right out of the water for the season.

So our 10 days spent in the port Longyearbyen prepping and waiting for the geologists was like going back in time to 1983 when I first visited on the 61-foot sloop *War Baby*, when there was a tiny population in this mining town and no tourism whatsoever. Now, we could enjoy the proliferation of cafés, restaurants, museums and gift shops with the few locals who have hung in during the Covid washout.

The last time I was up in this region was 2004 with *Pelagic Australis* and although cruise ships were certainly a feature they were not excessive in number. Pre-Covid in 2019 there were over 55,000 tourist visitors, many shipborne, and we were told in normal times we would hardly ever be left alone in any of the fjords.

Fooling around at 80 degrees of latitude is interesting. In 2004 we hit 80 degrees, in the fog, and miraculously all our instrumentation went down – a total black out; no speed, no wind, no GPS, but more to the point no radar and sounder. It was as if one of those clever young programmers of these increasingly complex and integrated systems thought no one will be going that far north or south, so why bother extending the algorithm beyond that convenient arbitrary figure... After many reboots, a few anxious Iridium calls to the company, who were perplexed and remained so, and some hours with a few nail biting moments as we untangled the leadline, it just as miraculously came to life. We were on paper charts in those days but without the fundamentals of radar and a sounder we were playing a tricky game, sort of like Willem Barentsz in 1596.

Fast forward to the present and although the electronic chart plotter worked meticulously until about 79 degrees 45' the folio does end about there. So, it was no surprise when we were once again on and off in the fog in relatively shallow waters and back to 1983 techniques of taking transits, back bearings and using the fundamentals of radar for distance off. All this requires a level of concentration not found when using a chart plotter, at least in well-surveyed areas where you can bring a boat in to a quay 'blind.'

Luckily, I was not fazed by this transition into the past, nor was Kenneth, my understudy and an RYA instructor. One wonders, however (and I am reminded of celestial navigation in the same context), although you have to learn these first principles on paper at some point in a training progression, how often will you actually use them if the chart plotter works, which it seems to most of the time?

It might seem cavalier to turn your plotter off and spend time navigating in the Solent and English Channel and getting these techniques down pat, but make sure you don't go aground (especially on my advice!) as you will then be accused of not using the tools available to you. Or, you can do the real thing and sail up to 80 degrees north and literally fall off the end of the electronic chart. It can be a liberating – or sobering – experience.

THE ALTERNATIVE SHACKLETON TRAVERSE

'A return visit to South Georgia never fails to excite, especially exploring the "alternative" Shackleton route'

December 2022

I'm not a counter. I'm not the sort of guy to add up things like ocean miles sailed (I get asked that continually and don't have a clue what the answer is other than 'a lot') or how many around the world races I've done. At least the latter is easy to remember, it's the fingers on one hand.

Another one is how many times I have been to Antarctica and places like South Georgia. For these I have also lost count. It is not the volume of trips that is important during a life's passion but rather the quality of each of those trips. And South Georgia tops the list in that category. It's getting on to 35 years of involvement at the cutting edge of high latitude sailing in the deep south. Every project is different, special, carries risk, is physical, can be stressful at times, and if you add up all of this it implies a certain level of satisfaction. Although going to South Georgia might be considered a routine for me, I never take it for granted and I am as enthusiastic about it now as I was on our first trip there during the southern winter of 1988 on the original *Pelagic*.

In fact, recently I came back from a month's expedition to the island at the very front of this season. Based from the *Vinson of Antarctica*, the focus was a ski traverse starting in King Haakon Bay that took six days in the field skiing 50 kilometres across snow and ice of five glacier systems (the Murray, Briggs, Esmark, Kohl Plateau, and the Konig) and crossing four cols. After five camps, our party of nine arrived into Stromness Bay late in the afternoon of the 26th September.

For Shackleton aficionados some of those names will ring a bell if you have read Shackleton's *South* or *Shackleton's Boat Journey* by Worsley, not to mention the plethora of Shackleton 'on the bandwagon' take-offs of one thing or another, which seem to be endless. But rather than doing

237

the classic Shackleton Traverse (also counted by me on the fingers of my other hand) this was the 'alternative Shackleton route' – one that in 1916 his party of three could have done from where they landed with the *James Caird* in King Haakon Bay and arrived at the same point of refuge at the whaling station at Stromness. The advantages of our route were the avoidance of the famous 'come what may' slide into the unknown off the Razorback Ridge above the Compass Glacier and also the steep descent down from the Breakwind Gap into Fortuna Bay off the Fortuna Glacier. When I say 'downside' I mean a technical part of that route which is in fact the main attraction for us who have followed. Dealing with those obstacles is not to be missed! But the objective difficulty for us on our alternative route was having to cross three glacial cols instead of two to reach Fortuna Bay. Of course, this is all useless speculation; the important thing from my co-leader Stephen Venables and my perspective was to cross some new ground on the island. Uncertainty is what it is all about!

The sub-Antarctic Islands of the Southern Ocean are where the wildlife proliferates, glaciated or not, and these fragile environments are now protected by convention to an extent of either not being available to land at all, or so highly regulated that if you are allowed onshore you see things from a prepared boardwalk and the story of what you are seeing is articulated by a dedicated, obligatory guide. And here is where South Georgia is an exception. Because of the long history of human contact with the island from the sealing, then the whaling on an industrial scale, the government of this UK overseas territory does manage it strictly, but does not forego the tradition of expeditions into the interior, although with a rigorous vetting process to achieve the permit to do so.

This coupled with the fact of no airstrip on the island and the distance of 800 miles from Port Stanley, both there and back across a stormy Southern Ocean is a self-limiting mechanism. It is a boat trip, and usually a rough one. Also, the cost of mounting a campaign certainly comes into this. So, in effect we see a mere handful per annum of these self-supported expeditions that venture beyond the cruise ship landing sites. It is the lowest of the low impact activities you can do on South Georgia, camped well above the shoreline in sort of a biological vacuum, but one of stunning and dramatic alpine scenery, always with one eye on the outlook for what can be very volatile weather.

One of our group summed things up quite nicely on the *Vinson* blog: 'You don't find outings like this at your exclusive high class travel agents. Thrilling, unique, physical and highly recommended but not for the faint-hearted.'

I look at it like this, 'South Georgia is a demanding mistress. When she beckons, you just gotta go and perform.'

7 STORIES FROM BACK IN THE DAY

There is no doubt this 'category' in among all the technical and opinion pieces was the most fun to write. In fact, this could be a book on its own, but many of the stories left untold are unpublishable in today's snowflake culture. There is also a limit in rehashing your life where, if the narrative goes overboard, the narrative becomes your life. I know a few of my old sailing buddies that fall into this category, as amusing as their repartee is *ad infinitum*. My ex-wife often remarked I would remind anyone who would listen that everything that happened in the 70s was the best, and it is true in part. When another of life's enhancements – further questionable technological advances, the plethora of useless conveniences and further ease of communication – raises its head, I can't help but fall into a reverie of 'back in the day.'

In counterbalance I try to look forward as much possible, anticipating the next project before we have finished the one we are on, always adding to my quiver of stories. And yes, memoirs sell books if you have a certain notoriety. So, when the knees give out completely I might get around to writing the *magnum opus* of the *Pelagic* years. Wait for it.

THE DRUM CREW REUNION

'Remember when the Maxi *Drum* capsized during the Fastnet Race? The crew do and a 30-year reunion brought it all back'

January 2016

In August 1985 the Maxi yacht *Drum* capsized in the Fastnet Race with 24 crew aboard. The keel had fallen off near Dodman Point in Cornwall, which was dramatic enough, but the fuel that fed the ensuing firestorm was the fact that crewman Simon Le Bon from Duran Duran had been trapped below. After our timely rescue, happily with no loss of life, both he and the managers of the rock group, Mike and Paul Berrow, were put in the unenviable position of backing an optimistic and very expensive salvage and refit in only five weeks to make the start of the 1985 Whitbread Round the World Race. Reputations were at stake and the press was salivating. We had to pick ourselves up, shake off any doubts and react.

The miracle of completely rebuilding the yacht in time was due to blind perseverance by our three backers and the crew. We held firm and got on with the job. Required: salvage, righting, pumping out and towing back to the Hamble. Then, new keel, new sails, new mast, new electronics, complete rewiring of the electrics, paint job in and out and servicing all else that survived. Making the start and carrying on around the world for a respectable third place in the Maxi class is the stuff of Whitbread legend. It is not an exaggeration to look back on it as a defining experience for all of us.

In 2005 we chartered *Drum* from subsequent owner Sir Arnold Clark for the Fastnet Race. What better way to celebrate the twenty year reunion finishing what we had set out to do in rounding Fastnet Rock and sailing into Plymouth. Unfortunately, I found myself in the Canadian Arctic attempting the Northwest Passage on *Pelagic Australis*. I had a plan to fly in and straight back if we made it halfway to a safe haven, but it was a bad ice year so I would miss the Fastnet reunion. Rounding the rock was not to be, however, as it was a windless race and *Drum* retired.

Ten years on and time to gather the troops once again. This time in Monaco during the Monaco Yacht Show, as not a few of our crew graduated into the superyacht game, and by consensus this venue made sense. Twenty of the capsize crew and the Whitbread crew flew in from all points on the globe and gathered for a two day affair of lunches, dinners and repartee at Neil Cheston's villa above Monaco. Many of the guys I see on a regular basis. Several I have not seen for decades. Sadly, Simon was on a roll, on tour in America and couldn't attend.

Though never having been to one, I can imagine what a classic school reunion is like – everyone sizing each other up and how well they did in life or didn't do, with envy and *schadenfreude* dished out as an aperitif in equal measure. Not so with the *Drum* crew. There is something singular about having shared what was a life-threatening experience the day we found ourselves upside down in the English Channel. The refit against all the odds strengthened that bond and stood us in good stead for the protracted challenge of the Whitbread Race itself, which was no mere outing. It was not the accomplishment that mattered most, but rather the total experience.

When we all reconnected in September it was straight back to 1985, save for the bald and grey heads and sun-lined faces. Most of us have continued a life at sea, more or less. Immediately slipping into the same silly conversations that got us around the world got us through the reunion. After watching Rick Tomlinson's slideshow (twice) accompanied by vintage 1980s Duran Duran, we came to the conclusion that, as in our youth, we still might be somewhat immortal with a job left undone. Finishing the Fastnet, finally, on *Drum* in 2017?

Postscript

Phil Wade and the Berrow brothers made a serious effort to get the boat once again, but the deal collapsed. Shortly after, Drum broke off her mooring on the Clyde and washed ashore, breaking her rudder. The latest story is that she is headed for the breaker's yard.

ST BARTHS BUCKET

'Feeling a little like a fish out of water, Skip tries out the St Barths Bucket superyacht regatta'

July 2016

Superyacht regattas are not my chosen cup of tea. The last time I did one was 2001 on *Timoneer* during the America's Cup Jubilee in Cowes, with my former *Pelagic* partner and Whitbread shipmate Phil Wade. So it was with some reluctance when I was parachuted into St Barths for the Bucket Regatta in March 2016. If truth be known I was there doing two polar inspections on yachts going high north and south. In the warm sunshine and a trade wind breeze it was frankly hard to concentrate on that job at hand. Likewise, the crews on board both boats were understandably preoccupied with preparing their yachts from cruising mode to racing mode. Very difficult to get our minds around growlers and bergy bits.

There were 39 entries for the Bucket, which apparently is the most popular superyacht regatta on both sides of the Atlantic. This was a record year. These regattas are always a 'who's who' of professional racing. Flown in from all points on the globe in between their main racing campaigns the young guys provide the muscle, still required on the foredeck wrestling acres of light canvas; the older, wiser hands push the buttons that operate sophisticated hydraulic control systems while the sailing celebrities drive, do tactics and navigate. On *Surama*, a 40-metre Huisman ketch built in 1997 and on her first outing as a racer, we had none other than the Volvo Ocean Race winner Ian Walker on the wheel.

During pre-race coffee ($6 for a cappuccino) and post-race drinks I ran into old shipmates I hadn't seen in years, in some cases decades. Surprised to see me in a pair of shorts and flip flops, I came in for some light-hearted flak, many kindly commenting on how I hadn't changed, some coming to the same conclusion that it must be something to do with life in the cold – sort of like pulling a salmon fresh out of the freezer, unlike the long process of curing a sardine or a kipper with

30 years of tropical sun. And that's right. For all those who were there that are reading this, I don't dye my hair – yet.

Superyacht racing is not for the inexperienced or for that matter the faint-hearted, even if an old hand. The loads on the sheets are measured in tens of tonnes, and things do break, having resulted in a few horrendous accidents that are sometimes mentioned, but not belaboured. They are now lessons to keep in the back of one's mind, always.

As sort of a superyacht beginner, I was given a starter role as trimmer of the mizzen staysail. This might have been in jest assuming Jon Morris, the crew boss, had read my column in *Yachting World* – as the mizzen staysail winch was the only winch aboard operated by a winch handle, something I am at least familiar with. Other responsibilities were keeping Ian's hat from blowing off his head – potentially serious under the tropical sun given he sports a cue ball. I couldn't help but sprinting forward uninvited, though – a 30-metre sprint – to gather the spinnaker on take downs and also overhaul the spinnaker sheet on the gybes before sprinting back to set the mizzen staysail. I have to admit that every time I did this it made me feel my age a bit.

The superyacht racing rules are adjuncts that have been invented to make things safe for the crews piloting these vessels, some up to 600 tonnes displacement. There is a 40-metre distance rule that is monitored by range finders for crossing and mark roundings. What we guessed was 40 metres (our boat length) turned out to be 80m, so my conclusion was that 40 metres is real, real close. A hydraulic failure on the mainsheet winch for a bear away duck on a port–starboard situation was a frightening thought. Quite rightly, a mature approach is certainly needed – no cowboys need apply. Superyachts? No, they are ships with sails.

THE SHACKLETON CENTENARY

'Modern day adventurers pale into insignificance when you consider the exploits of Shackleton 100 years ago'

August 2016

On 20th May 2016 I had the privilege of attending the Shackleton Memorial Service at Westminster Abbey. One hundred years ago on that date Ernest Shackleton, Frank Worsley and Tom Crean stumbled into the Stromness whaling station having made their desperate trek across the unsurveyed spine of the sub-Antarctic island of South Georgia.

The Shackleton story is well known but it is always worth repeating if only in brief. In the summer of 1914 they set sail from the UK just after the outbreak of World War I – Churchill telling them to 'Proceed' when they offered their services to the war effort. Their ship, the *Endurance*, was beset in the pack ice of the Weddell Sea in the southern summer of 1915 after a failed attempt to land a party for an overland traverse of the entire continent to the Ross Sea, planned for the following spring. The *Endurance* slowly succumbed to the pressure of the pack during that winter and eventually broke up, the ship's company now 'safely' camped on the pack ice by the 27th October. For the next five months they drifted with the vagaries of the pack in amongst attempts to man-haul their three boats and equipment north to reach open water. In the end they settled into a waiting game and by 9th April 2016 all 28 men were able to take to the boats, barely surviving the sail and row to Elephant Island during the onset of winter.

Shackleton's famous open boat voyage to South Georgia on the 22-foot *James Caird* and the subsequent rescue of the men left behind on Elephant Island with no loss of life is one of the greatest sea survival stories of all time, arguably all due to the leadership of Shackleton. His methods are now enshrined in syllabi in many business schools, in spite of his pre-expedition business ventures all ending in failures.

I had a chuckle, though, when the Bishop of London giving the address at the service compared Shackleton and his men as true explorers to the 'likes of the shallow modern day explorers we see today in the media.'

I am sure many Antarctic aficionados in the audience, either laughed to themselves as I did or choked depending on how serious one takes oneself.

A repeat of the 800-mile Shackleton boat journey was once considered the Holy Grail for a host of modern day adventurists. Trevor Potts and a UK crew managed to finally pull it off in 1994, making it to the island and managing to land safely (an even greater feat) – in the days before a support vessel was required. It has been tried three times since including one aborted attempt in dramatic circumstances. I know, as *Pelagic* was the support vessel for the South Aris project in 1997. When about halfway to the island at the height of a gale the Irish team capsized three times in succession, resulting in a flooded cabin and a banged up crew. With more heavy weather on the way, they wisely abandoned their splendid replica of the *James Caird* – named the *Tom Crean* – and *Pelagic* hightailed it to the safety of the island. They later completed the mountain traverse.

The German adventure supremo Arved Fuchs sailed all the way to near the island on his replica in 2000 and linked up the mountain section. This replica/re-enactment concept was taken to extremes by the 2013 project under the leadership of Tim Jarvis along with well-known sailors Paul Larsen, Nick Bubb and others. They did the boat journey and the mountain crossing, but the difference was they were dressed in traditional clothing and using equipment of the era. Although always impressive feats of research and organization, these recreations at any level are fundamentally flawed. Support vessels, GPS in case, and now connected to the internet, are givens – and they did not eat the seals and penguins. The Bishop of London had made a good point.

Postscript

The boat journey has been tried and mooted by several projects even more outlandish in recent years, one attempting to row across the Drake to Elephant Island and then to South Georgia solo. It ended in a fiasco needless to say. We have made a fundamental decision not to support any of these projects, lest we contribute to this very suspect circus-like genre of so-called professional 'adventurers.'

SKIPPERS AND OWNERS

'Does a paid skipper ever out-rank his or her yacht's owner?'

August 2017

Having been both a skipper of other people's yachts in my former life and for almost three decades a 'poor bloody owner' most of the time employing skippers, I can well comment on the interesting and often stressful dilemma that occurs often between the two when they are on board at the same time.

The size of a yacht always invites controversy and in this case it occurs in the range of between 60 and maybe 100 feet on the outside. On anything smaller a professional skipper would frankly be in the way. Nearing 80 feet, and certainly above the magic 100 that arbitrarily defines a 'superyacht', the game changes where a professional skipper is a requirement for his/her sailing expertise to keep things safe, and management skills are needed to keep the whole show on the road. And that might include making sure the cocktails are shaken not stirred.

It is also a given that in that midsize range a skipper will be more times than not a swashbuckler who is in it for the sailing and the travel. He/she would want to take on full responsibility and make their mark, most likely in hopes of climbing the ladder for running bigger vessels in future. And that means not counting time in too many marinas.

When the owner comes on board for a sail or a longer cruise, possibly also having come up through the ranks of owning smaller boats and knowing a thing or two, you might have the perfect storm brewing. It requires a certain maturity on both sides of the equation to weather that possible blow. But where should the line of responsibility be drawn in that shared experience of sailing together?

I can remember many occasions from my youth of being heartily disappointed, and at times disgusted and angry, at witnessing incompetence from owners on yachts while in their employ – so much so that one American gentleman nicknamed me the 'rebel without a cause.' Those were the days when I was living out of a seabag, fancy-free, and come what may, needing little in the way of sustenance other than a pint or six and certainly no regard for a pension. Only when a few financial prerogatives raised their ugly head did I realize that I had to toe the line and behave myself and swallow humble pie, even if that meant letting the owner crash into the jetty, leaving me to make the repairs. There was the next job to think of, and when you got it, a reputation to maintain.

I readily admit that it is nigh on impossible at times not to interfere with the running of my boats while I am on board – as a supernumerary during our various charters in southern waters. I have hired the best crew to run these boats for me and therein lies the dilemma – how to let go. Granted, my interest in being on board in the first place is really more about getting 'there' and engaging with the land, whether it be leading people in the mountains or simply walking with them among the penguins. I am an 'expedition leader' in the parlance.

If you, as an owner, are only sailing focused then it becomes more difficult and problematic in developing a mutual cooperation with your skipper. Where on one hand it is your boat and you should 'take the helm' so to speak, on the other hand when things get tricky step back and let the skipper and crew get on with it. That is what you hired them to do. By the same token, a skipper worth his salt will step back and let the owner take command without making an announcement, and even let him make a few mistakes. The more experienced the skipper, the more this will appear seamless and natural.

On the *Pelagics* my complaint seems to be that the mainsheet is always over trimmed. I claim to feel this in my guts and testicles while in my bunk. When I rise in my skivvies unasked for and rush into the cockpit to dump off a few metres of mainsheet, the crew, knowing my idiosyncrasies, are always highly amused. After having made many mistakes overly interfering as an owner I now have a foolproof formula, especially during those all critical docking manoeuvres in heavy winds: go below and make a cup of tea and do some emails. When you hear the engine shut down it is safe to come on deck. Your skipper and crew will appreciate this.

SOCIAL MEDIA NIGHTMARE

'Instant communications mean plans are constantly being changed and modified. Skip hankers after the long-term commitments of past decades'

October 2018

Recently, my old shipmate mate Phil Wade and I were reminiscing about his stamp collection. Phil is the most unlikely collector but his many books of stamps that depict all things that float are an impressive record of a lifetime of travel. I call Phil a 'collector of stamps, a collector of dreams.'

For not the first time we hashed over the evolution of communication over our lifetime. Sending postcards to friends, and more poignantly receiving them at 'poste restante' (for those under the age of 30, Google it) was such a joy.

Since social media and the way people now communicate, often while 'bowling alone', is ever more in the news – the good, the bad and the ugly aspects – I have to retell a favourite story (for probably the hundredth time) to demonstrate what was possible when making a long-term arrangement. This was a 1970s story, and I will gladly bore anyone who will listen about how everything that happened back then was pretty damn good.

In the spring of 1979 I delivered an IOR Maxi from Honolulu to Manila, and on arrival became stranded when the owner disappeared and the boat was eventually impounded. Living the adventure – going to cock fighting matches, an inexpensive distraction, kept me amused – but running out of cash I started putting out feelers by telex at the main post office downtown. I needed a bail out.

This was pre-fax machine. The first fax I saw was from Hood sailmakers in Lymington sent to our Portacabin office in the Hamble during the Whitbread Race work up on *Drum* in 1985. We gathered around and stared at this magic piece of paper detailing a hand-drawn clew patch for the mainsail. Telexes and telegrams were the mode of comms up until them. If in the field they required some legwork: marching around to post offices and standing in queues. Then returning daily to wait for an answer that might never come. One positive thing about this was it gave you a lot of time to contemplate your future – or lack of one.

In May after two months in Manila a welcome a telegram arrived from the UK. 'Need you as skipper. Parmelia Race to Fremantle. Start in August. Peter Wright.' I agreed by return. I was saved.

If you ignored the heat and humidity, the armies of mosquitos at night and the filth in the harbour, things weren't all bad in Manila. There was an incredible collection of yachties in what seemed to be permanent residence. Solo sailors, families and ne'er-do-wells and chancers aplenty. Many had bought cheap production boats in Asia and a year later, on the way to somewhere, got no further. They were always 'waiting for a part' in order to ship out and carry on.

While working out the details of my departure, a lone Frenchman and I struck up a chord in Franglais and we got on the subject of alpine mountains – as you do in the heat of the pre-monsoon with sweat running down your backside. He was on his way to Fremantle delivering a Choey Lee, one of those Hong Kong specials down by their waterlines with teak trim. Planning ahead now, and seeing as I would be in Australia by December for the Sydney Hobart, I sent a telex to mate Graham 'Frizzle' Freeman, the skipper, to get a berth on the new Frers Maxi *Bumble Bee* 4. I was all set for the next nine months – back in the day that was pretty good going.

The monsoon broke just as Patrick shoved off for points south and I was about to board a flight. It was like flushing a toilet – the toilet being the open sewers of Manila, the septic tank the harbour.

Patrick and I had agreed to meet at the Cruising Yacht Club of Australia in Sydney on Christmas Day on the eve of the Hobart Race. I was there on the day and so was he. For six months since Manila there had been no communication to the contrary. Indeed, no communication at all. When I finished the race we jetted over to New Zealand and spent the entire summer mountaineering.

How different it is today when all our plans (read: lack of) seem to be continually modified and adjusted – right up to the moment when you trip over the kerb while your friend almost walks off the dock, both on smartphones, within line of sight of each other. Ahhh, the 70s...

THE RUSSIAN FEDOR KONYUKHOV

'Skip is on standby to welcome or assist his friend Fedor Konyukhov, one of the world's most incredible, almost superhuman, adventurers'

March 2019

There is no denying that many things Russian are not the flavour of the month, any month in the last few years. In spite of somewhat bad press all around, there is a good news Russian story that is noteworthy and hard to ignore, at least for those of us who float.

On 5th December 2018 Fedor Konyukhov, a 67-year-young adventurer started an epic row from Dunedin in New Zealand through the Southern Ocean intending to complete a circumnavigation in three summer stages through 2020. Stage 1 to Cape Horn is expected to take 120 days. This is the 'holy grail' for rowers. Several people have tried in recent years and none have got very far. Attempts have been made from Tasmania, New Zealand and the Falklands. Some went around in circles and others almost froze to death. They all had to be rescued in one fashion or another.

This kind of adventure, which can rightly be considered a stunt, is not my cup of tea, but I am watching this one as I think Fedor might have a chance, at least of getting himself near to Cape Horn. The last time I met him was in 2012 when he was displaying his then rowing machine at the Southampton Boat Show. I didn't take much notice, but in 2014 he rowed her 9,400 nautical miles from Chile to Australia, non-stop and unsupported in 159 days. Of course, that was in warm water, but he has more than enough experience in the cold.

His life is an overwhelming history of adventure expeditions that is more than impressive, and I challenge anyone out there to best his record of adventure not only in volume but variety. He is a Knox-Johnston/Chris Bonington/Richard Branson et al all rolled into one. You name it; mountaineering (Seven Summits), polar journeys, around the world yacht racing, ballooning around the world, dog sledding journeys and racing and desert crossings are some of his fortes. Having said all of this, there are disbelievers out there. You can go online to read the scientific analysis disputing the trans-Pacific row is in the realm of possibility for a human. So, in addition to all of Fedor's accomplishments he is also an enigma wrapped in a mystery.

But there is still more to him. Eclectic is an accurate description of Fedor. He is a prolific artist, an author of 20 books, and builds Russian Orthodox chapels in his spare time – a deeply religious man, in 2010 he was ordained as a Russian Orthodox priest. His medals and accolades for adventure, his art and writing on the 'Russian front' go on and on. On an admittedly tamer voyage in 2011 his Russian group chartered *Pelagic* and *Pelagic Australis* for a Beagle Channel and around Cape Horn cruise. Fedor arrived on board bearing a Russian Orthodox cross, which they erected on Cape Horn Island.

I visited Fedor's chapel in downtown Moscow a few years ago to collaborate with his son and manager Oscar, who often provides Russian clients to Pelagic Expeditions. I recommend to anyone while on a visit to Moscow to arrange a visit to see Fedor's art and memorabilia that adorns the chapel along with many of his icons to seafarers. There is no doubt Fedor has God on his side, and no doubt quite a few Russian oligarchs, who back these campaigns either privately or through their businesses. If they are doing this altruistically good on them, but I suspect it also has a lot to do with projecting what is surely a Russian success story. It is strange, though, that Fedor is not better known outside of Russia beyond the various adventure genres he is so much part of.

Fedor's very high tech rowing boat *AKROS*, designed by Brit Phil Morrison, really looks the business and clearly a lot of thought has gone into this project, especially for life support systems. And the boat is well sea-trialled. Of course, most of these rowing expeditions must be down current and downwind as fundamental, so it is debatable how much time is actually spent propelling yourself by the oars, and how much is accountable to drift. Nevertheless, a Southern Ocean row is all about surviving it.

The point of this story is that I was recently given a heads-up on this project to provide support at Cape Horn for Fedor's arrival. Needless to say, the Chilean Navy has rescued more than their fair share of round-the-world yachts, both racing and cruising, and it would be nice if he does need help to do so privately, so both *Pelagics* will be standing by. I have to. One of Fedor's icons to seafarers is on our bulkhead on *Pelagic Australis.*

STORIES FROM BACK IN THE DAY

AWAHNEE – A MUST-SEE FILM

'A wonderful film about the voyages of Americans Bob and Nancy Griffith has Skip recalling wistfully a time of total freedom at sea'

May 2019

Every now and then you come across a gem of a story. Recently a friend swiped me over an MP4 file called 'Following Seas'. It sat on my desktop for some time. When I did run it I was spell bound for the hour and 25 minutes. The story is about a couple who I had vaguely heard of, Bob and Nancy Griffith, and their 20 years of world voyaging (cruising might not be an appropriate description) throughout the 60s and 70s on their two *Awahnees*. For some the film will be a revelation of what sailing around the world 'back in the day' was like, but for me, it was more of a reminder. Back in those days I was still a teenage fresh water pirate on Lake Michigan, and how it was all done by the Griffiths was very familiar.

Bob and Nancy met in Hawaii in 1959 when Bob sailed in (and brought the 53-foot *Awahnee* to the dock under sail in a crowded marina – something I can relate to). Bob had bailed on his landside life as a vet in California after having lost a young child. Nancy had a five-year-old son, Reid. They joined forces and the rest is history, documented in parts on 16mm film. This included a shipwreck on Vahanga Island, an atoll, not far from the soon to be radioactive Mururoa Atoll. The story of salvaging the gear, parts of the structure, and lifting the engine off its bed which was several metres under water stands out in stark contrast to so many of the stories we see today where yachts are abandoned at sea, still floating, for little or no reason at all.

They were eventually rescued after two months living a Robinson Crusoe existence on the beach having eventually met and enlisted the only other two people on the island – two French convicts – to help in the salvage. When finally taken off they were arrested as spies, immediately released. They made their way with the remains of their boat (down to the nuts and bolts) as cargo and landed in New Zealand. They then promptly set to work building a ferro cement boat along the same lines of their Uffa Fox original. They called her *Awahnee,* not *Awahnee II.* Nancy explained there was no point. *Awahnee I* did not exist.

Nancy Griffiths narrated this film a few years before she died in 2013. It is in the style of the beginning and ending of *Titanic* – an attractive and elderly, but very lucid woman recounting a life led by their own terms. She takes us through those decades of adventures which included a circumnavigation of Antarctica and a landing there in the early 70s.

Tragically her son Reid, at the age of 14, was killed in the Marquesas, having fallen off a cliff while hunting goats. Bob and Nancy had two children of their own (who also narrate parts of the film) and when Bob suddenly died of a heart attack in 1979, while they were living ashore for a time, she buried him at sea, which was still doable, if you were resourceful and had not much respect for authorities. She then went on to run a sailing school and later captain her own sailing cargo ship for a time. Much of the 16mm film now digitized was water damaged and ropey, but this adds to, not detracts from the overall quality of the production.

Neither of the *Awahnees* were precious yachts (it appears the interior was never really finished on the ferro version) and from what we see in the film, there were maintenance issues which would be criticized in the modern context of our standards. How they sailed would also be *grist to the mill* for today's marine thought police as decidedly cavalier. There is no evidence of a lifejacket nor life harness ever being worn. Granted, Nancy nonchalantly recounts the story of how she was thrown overboard when trying to furl the mainsail running downwind while wing and wing – it took them a half hour to return upwind, but she was never in doubt that they would find her.

I sat in a sad silence for a time after the credits rolled. I contemplated how we, by the virtue of our numbers, have out of convention tied ourselves up in bureaucratic knots and furthermore have entangled ourselves in so much safety equipment, gadgetry, tracking devices and contingency plans that there must come a time when there will be no point to taking that voyage, either for physical or philosophical motives. It can all be done by virtual reality!

THE ISLAND OF TRISTAN DA CUNHA

'The distant and remote island of Tristan da Cunha is a place where the sun still sets over the British Empire, but it is slowly changing'

August 2019

In the southern winter of 1988 *Pelagic* escaped the icy grip of South Georgia and made course for Cape Town. We had finished our first Antarctic expedition season and we were heading for the docks to finish building the boat. But that is another story.

The island of Tristan da Cunha lies right along that empty passage so it was a given that we would attempt a visit. Lying at 37 degrees south, this volcanic outlier of only 38 square miles sits right on the southern edge of the Atlantic high, 1,300 nautical miles west-south-west from Cape Town. Along with Pitcairn in the Pacific it is one of those very isolated islands on the edge of a horizon where the sun still rises and sets over what is left of the British Empire.

Luckily for us it was a relatively calm, sunny day when we dropped anchor in 20 metres on a steep slope of loose volcanic scree. While we were getting organized to go ashore at Edinburgh a small launch came alongside with a swarthy looking chap who without warning flung a four-foot slimy sea creature into our cockpit and said, 'We don't eat octopus, no sir!' and kept right on going. We had met Mike Repetto, descendant of a shipwrecked sailor.

Landing is never assured here as it is open roads, a swell is always running, and if an onshore wind sets in you have to pull up and go. The only shelter is a small boat harbour with a metre of water which is awash and unusable for most of the time. Their small lobster boats are craned on to cradles which are then pulled up a ramp to the cliff edge. Luckily, we had the rare good fortune to spend three days and two nights hanging on the hook, always with a crew on board at the ready to sound the alarm.

We were the only yacht that had stopped there that year, except a small German cruiser that had never left after being washed ashore and eventually salvaged by the islanders. Re-supply from the UK was twice a year, other supplies came in ad hoc with fishing boats from Cape Town. Communication with the outside was amateur radio. We were indeed a welcome distraction and received a congenial welcome from the curious islanders.

Today's roughly 285 souls still originate from only seven family names. When Napoleon was incarcerated on St Helena in 1816, Britain took possession as a safeguard against his escape. A garrison was installed but later recalled having been a fool's mission with respect to Napoleon. However, two of the soldiers were so enamoured with Tristan they promptly took wives back in the UK and returned. Shipwrecked sailors and other chancers followed, adding to the mix, and their descendants live on today.

The attraction of such an isolated lifestyle is not to be underestimated. In 1961 the island's volcanic crown blew its top and the entire population was evacuated and eventually billeted in RAF barracks on Calshot Spit, Southampton Water – not the most salubrious location in southern England. The British Government had reckoned they had been let off the hook by an act of God, a plug having been put into the drain on the exchequer from the Tristan subsidies. They were proved wrong of course, when after only two years the island was deemed safe to return and by god, all but 14 did.

In 1988, we had met the civil servants – a doctor, the teacher and the preacher – but not the magistrate. He never appeared to say hello, and it was explained he did not like nor encourage any visitors and intended to keep the island a 'human museum.'

Happily, this became an impossible proposition after satellite communication systems were installed and the internet age followed. I have never returned to Tristan but *Pelagic Australis* was able to briefly land during her end of season delivery cruise back to Cape Town for refit in May 2019. During the last decade a few cruise ships also have landed and there is more yacht traffic for sure. The islanders are still welcoming, but some rules have been imposed. No visitors allowed ashore after 1800 for example. Although short visits from yachts and ships are tolerated, long stays where people are dropped by fishing boats and picked up six weeks later are more popular with the islanders – a case of 'take some time to get to know us'. Apparently social media has raised an ugly head even here, with short-stay yacht and ship visitors depicting this exceptional collection of people an oddity in a none too favourable light.

IN COURT FOR DRUM'S
KEEL FAILURE

'This year's Fastnet Race triggers memories of the 1985 event – and subsequent court case – when Simon Le Bon's *Drum* lost her keel'

October 2019

The other day I was walking along The Strand and on into Fleet Street in London for no other reason than to find the expensive clinic that was dishing out that new and expensive vaccination for shingles – recommended by my GP given my age and stress levels (from owning two boats continually trying to sink themselves).

The landscape seemed vaguely familiar, but when passing the Royal Courts of Justice on my left I twigged. The last time I was in this neck of the woods was back in 1988 when I was required to appear on behalf of the owners of *Drum* (Simon Le Bon and co) in their lawsuit against the fabricator of that famous aluminium keel that fell off in the 1985 Fastnet Race.

There was a pub across the street we all retired to after the event – or was it before, in order to fortify ourselves? I can't quite remember. The pub was not to be found, which was strange – given the captive audience of endless winners and losers emerging from across the road.

In 1988 when I walked into the courtroom and sat down awaiting my interrogation by the defence counsel, I was shocked to see that every barrister, every barrister's assistant and the judge himself had a copy of *One Watch at a Time*, my *magnus opus* on *Drum's* Whitbread Race campaign. I can only assume these were all remaindered copies. Every book was festooned with Post-it notes, which made me start to sweat.

In his opening statements our barrister fumbled while 'untying the mooring lines' and it was clear he knew not bow from stern. I thought if he continues like this we will be holed and sunk at the dock. You soon realise why these people are highly paid because within minutes he seemed to have an epiphany, trimmed his sails sharply and charged off at speed down the race course.

Then the defence had a go. First up on the witness stand was our project manager. This was lucky for me. Almost immediately his head fell over on his left shoulder after the first barrage of questioning by the barrister attacking his integrity. The battering continued and he sank lower in stature with every question until he almost disappeared behind the lectern.

Like him I had no formal qualifications in the marine industry other than a skipper's ticket, so I saw it coming. When the barrister asked for mine I raised myself up on my toes slightly, stuck my chest out and said quite calmly '25 years of offshore experience.' This seemed to do the trick. The rest was attempting to recall the chronology as the pages of *One Watch At A Time* were thumbed through to corroborate my explanations.

As often happens, the ending was anti-climactic as the case was settled before lunchtime by the solicitors doing a deal in the corridor and all was adjourned. As I was filing out I received a request from Judge French to sign his copy of my book – an accolade indeed. At that point I'm sure our team *did re*tire to that pub.

You could say this was a watershed event in yacht construction. That keel failure was a calamity that was a bridge too far. Remember the problems with rudders, structures and all kinds of equipment during 1979 Fastnet Race? The information given to boat builders and fabricators of parts by the avant-garde of yacht designers of the day was sketchy at the best of times. The keel drawings for *Drum* merely said 'all welds will be structural', but there was no welding schedule attached. The fabricator claimed he had no idea what, or for what, he was actually building and that was his defence. He had no case, but our designer was criticized for a lack of technical information on his drawings.

In any event the *Drum* story was definitely a wake-up call from that point forward. Sound engineering came to the fore but the irony remains that as offshore racing yachts become more radical, in spite of better engineering and more reliable composite materials, the safety factors are lowered in order stay competitive. So, keels keep on falling off and things keep breaking, but that is the nature of the game. But I will never forget that big bang and the immediate roll over. Best not to be repeated too often.

Postscript

The 2023 Fastnet Race is a case in point when history repeats itself. Out of the 400 entries, 20 threw in the towel before the start, facing a stiff southwesterly in the Channel. Eighty others dropped out along the way in what was described as horrendous sea conditions. Many failures of rigs, structures and fittings occurred, and when you see the dinghies that are now entered in races like the Fastnet, you understand why. Luckily, no lives were lost in 2023, remembering what happened in 1979.

THIRTY YEARS LATER, STILL AT THE KING AND QUEEN

'Oddball projects and round-the-world heroics... Skip relishes the 30-year anniversary of a great Whitbread Race'

November 2019

When I started this column in October 2014 I began with a nostalgic tour down the Hamble River, which seemed like a good place to start – so much yachting history, so many stories fuelled by so many pints downed in all those pubs.

Well, we are back there again. On 31st August 2019 the King and Queen, the yachtsmen's favourite, was host to an ad hoc reunion of Whitbread crews from the 1989/90 event. Instigated by Howard Gibbons, the project manager of Tracy Edwards' *Maiden of Great Britain* campaign, the idea began with a simple mail shot to a few of the likely suspects in the area, and snowballed from there.

In the 1989 race the first all-female *Maiden* project, along with *Fazisi*, billed as the first ever Soviet entry, were the two media hooks – oddball projects to be sure, but both established themselves as iconic stories in around the world race history. The images for me are unforgettable. Tracy's girls in bikinis giving the bottom a wet sand – Soviets running around amusing and likewise impressing the locals as we struggled to finish the build of *Fazisi* at Hamble Yacht Services after flying the hull in from Soviet Georgia in an Antonov 124. Our mission was to get to the start line against all the odds, not to mention without a lien on the boat. As you would expect the Soviets were busy chasing the *Maiden* girls around the hard, along with all the other crews, with some success.

And, if it wasn't for Lawrie Smith's *Rothmans* ditching their keel for a better design, *Fazisi* would have not been able to enter. As one Kiwi crew said on the dock as we bolted the tiny fin on to the hull, 'if this thing rates we are in trouble.' Well, we didn't and luckily acquired *Rothman's* old keel which was twice the size and bolted that on.

Of course, the serious players like Peter Blake's team on *Steinlager*, Grant Dalton's *Fisher and Paykel* and Pierre Fehlman's *Merit* were in a different league – remember those were still the days of the International Offshore Rule where a Maxi could resemble a banana or a Sherman tank and still somehow rate the same. Those three and the other seven Maxis were the big beasts of the event. Many of the crews were paid to go sailing, and most were still not.

These were the nascent days of true professionalism in sailing, bridging the gap between the cornucopia of boats manned by sometimes questionable crews into the box rule where the boats looked the same to the general audience, but were not – and eventually evolved into the one-designs in recent editions with Volvo as the main sponsor. But no matter how you cut it, the 1989 edition was still more carnival than professional sport. And the Hamble village was where it all happened during that very special summer.

The Hamble reunion was basically a night in the pub. Nostalgic speeches were not given, nor other entertainments laid on other than Rick Tomlinson's rolling photo and video gallery on a modest screen in a corner. I am sure we were all delighted to see ourselves appear and gulped at how we looked 30 years ago.

Although the crowd was British in the main, people flew in from Sweden, Seattle, yours truly from Cape Town (with other business tacked on) and many points on the continent. A big ask for a pub night but it goes to show how strong these major yachting events – which took a year of your life – can linger in our memories. If you were around in the day, you will remember the names of the boats that were represented: *Maiden of Great Britain, Fazisi, Satquote British Defender, The Card, Rothmans, NCB Ireland, Creighton's Naturally, Liverpool Enterprise, Fisher and Paykel, Steinlager* and *Rucanor Tristar*.

I suppose the major difference from then to now was how somewhat civilized we had become. The 'heavy lifting' at the bar was left to a few of the sons of Whitbread sailors who were along. I wouldn't say we are now boring by any means – there was plenty of humour and innuendo, straight from the weather rail. But the days of six pints as standard on a typical pub night were a thing of the distant past. I nursed two for the four-hour gig. True professionalism indeed.

DODGY BEGINNINGS IN THE YACHT CHARTER GAME

'Skip recalls the formative experiences that led to his pioneering sailing in the Antarctic'

June 2020

I'm often asked by people more familiar with my ocean racing career how I got started in the high latitude charter business. Chartering for profit if not just for sustenance was never the reason I 'went south' and subsequently became recognized (I'm constantly reminded) as an entrepreneur of the genre.

The beginning had to do with what a quorum from the crew of *Drum* on the 1985/86 Whitbread Race thought was the next move. On the cusp, but certainly before a path was evident in making a decent living out of racing offshore, a few of us who were 'getting on' thought it time to do some sailing on our own agenda, before knuckling down, if ever.

Three of us put money into the DIY building of the 54-foot steel *Pelagic*, and each of us had a year on board doing our thing. Mine was Antarctic focused and after the second season that I was awarded an extra year for the sweat equity put in during the building (a year of high anxiety when the budget went pear-shaped). Before those four years were up we had to decide what to do. I had only scratched the surface of the southern regions and there was so much more pioneering in the offing.

We three partners drafted a buy-out agreement based on what I recognized as an opportunity. My father always told me in his wisdom, 'Son, whatever you do don't quit the Chicago Yacht Club', which of course I did soon after landing in the UK in 1976. But I was wise in my own way to keep the channels open with all the members who I had sailed with as a nipper. My first charter was with five gentlemen yacht owners for a two week junket to Cape Horn and the Beagle Channel. That was a success that lead to more of the same.

Contrast my second charter that same inaugural season of 1991 with my Kiwi mates that had saved the day with the *Fazisi* campaign in the 1989 Whitbread. Via an FM radio station they bought the rights to the Soviet story and funds raised were enough cash to get us around the second half of the world. It was stressful, but from these situations you get mates for life.

This was before the days I had legal a charter agreement. I will never forget Kiwi Paul Smit telling me, 'Not to worry, we'll sort it all out later,' during the first night while we were cavorting on the dance floor of the Tropicana Club in Ushuaia as I kept reminding him he had the entire $10,000 charter fee in cash in his back pocket. Everything about that trip was cavalier in the extreme. We capsized the Zodiac twice, one from a katabatic wind and another by a glacial tsunami – learning experiences the hard way. The copy that charter produced in New Zealand led to a firm marketing base in Australasia that continues to this day.

A while back designer Tony Castro and I were recounting some early boyhood adventures for no reason at all. He told how he and his friend borrowed without notice the friend's Dad's 32 footer and sailed it out of Lisbon Harbour down the coast for 30 miles to Sesimbra and anchored, as you would do. They were 14. When the search and rescue airplane flew over the next morning and dipped their wings it was all over but the consequences.

I had one better, age 15, which might explain the original question posed. The details of how this deal was struck escape me now, but I 'chartered' my father's 40-foot cruiser/racer to six high school seniors just graduated. This was a Friday evening sail up and down the Chicago lakefront. Things got out of hand. Fuelled by the booze on board (my Harbor Rat crew of two and me stayed dead sober) they started to climb the mast and make other gymnastic moves trying to impress their terrified girlfriends. Then, to cap things off, while motoring back in at 0100 the engine quit in the harbour entrance in a dead calm. Harbor Rat crew Billy immediately dived over the side and swam the 200 metres to the dock to bring back the dinghy for a tow in. We then managed to get the hysterical 'charter guests' off the boat and into their car, plastered, but luckily never seen again.

The next morning my dad and crew were due to arrive for the Saturday regatta. The Rats and I spent the early hours of the morning giving the boat a pull through, but at short notice the smell of whiskey and cigarettes was difficult to wash out of the upholstery.

My old man didn't say anything that day and I was sure I had gotten away with it. Years later I was reminded of this adventure when reading Mark Twain who said, which I will paraphrase: 'When I was 14 it was amazing how ignorant my father was. He didn't seem to know anything. By the time I was 22 it was incredible how much he had learned.'

MY COVID LOCKDOWN
IN CAPE TOWN

'Being locked down in South Africa can be likened to a long voyage... but with some gardening thrown in'

July 2020

I just made it down from the UK back into Cape Town in March 2020 before all flights in and out of South Africa were cancelled. I thought my two week quarantine would be well spent in Langebaan, a west coast town on a pristine estuary at the end of Saldanha Bay, north of the city, where I keep my Laser and share a Hobie 16. What more would I need than the internet connection in the cottage and a covert trip or two to the supermarket during my incarceration? I had two marvellous days sailing, the only boat on the estuary, and I was happy as. Then the government announced the lockdown with three days' notice. I took the advantage of another day's sail and then bolted back to town.

Once there, I had to race around to get various supplies, although I was not too worried about food and having travelled in the Middle East I was certainly not hoarding toilet paper. Garden supplies were more of a priority and by the time I got to the garden centre all the seed packets where gone, the same for potting soil and compost. With persistence and the clock running down I hit every small outlet in town and managed to load up with everything I needed in that department. Many people obviously had the same idea.

The other priority was the liquor store. As of Thursday night, on the 23rd March, all bottle shops were ordered to close for the duration. Later that afternoon I drove over to my usual in Hout Bay, threw a line ashore and lo and behold I found a few yachting friends who were thinking the same. I managed to score the last case of Windhoek lager light, 12 bottles of red and a bottle of gin. Don't get me wrong here, but this was a three-week lockdown, you understand, most likely to be extended.

While milling around the parking lot, we speculated on what this all meant. Louis said he wasn't worried at all as we were all used to being in a confined space with a few people for weeks and possibly months on end – yes, from a lifetime of moving yachts around the world.

He was dead right of course. While housebound, there will be inconveniences for sure, but when it comes to keeping our own company we are pretty good at it. When we cast off on a long delivery it is a lockdown in the strictest sense (and generally no alcohol allowed!). But while I was hoping for a Transatlantic, it now looks like it will turn into a full circumnavigation.

I always considered it a great privilege to be locked down, out of touch at sea, for weeks on end. The difference with this landlocked lockdown is that I have never been so virtually connected. Not only are there webinars to participate in, but all sorts of online forums to listen to. Skype or Zoom calls to long lost friends to catch up with is a nice thing to do, but will we see each other ever again and press the flesh, if not just shaking hands? And of course, those endless WhatsApp clips of how people are handling the incarceration; some inane, others amusing and others pretty shocking, even for this old sea dog – many of which you just can't help but forward on to so and so. All this fills up one's day.

Unlike being at sea where a good book, some fishing gear and a stock of tinned beans was all that was needed for contentment, while at home we are all more than busy and the days go by alarmingly quickly. In among this endless communication for one thing or another, there is much else to do. I have finally learned how to use that drone that a friend gave me contra for a reduced charter fee. That thing had been sitting on the shelf for three years. The filing cabinet of old slide transparencies of racing and cruising, some going back four decades is being whittled down to scan the 'good ones' when the photo shop re-opens. I found it risky. This can be an exercise in emotional self-control when those old girlfriends smile up at you from the light box. Helping my son repair his surfboard and continually losing to my daughter at chess are needed distractions from all those screens, for all of us.

My runner beans are well trained now and doing great. But they need to be talked to and listened to. Prince Charles was right, you know.

COWES MEMORIES

'A visit to Cowes on the UK south coast provokes a trip down memory lane, although not everything is quite as Skip remembers...'

January 2021

With not much happening on the water for me, it's time for a dose of nostalgia. I recently was invited to do one of Shirley Robertson's podcasts in Cowes on the Isle of Wight. This was a real privilege to be interviewed by an Olympian and to take a place on her weather rail of eclectic racing sailors both very current and those a bit over the hill. I am surely in the latter. Readers under the age of 50 might want to skip this column.

On my way back to meet the Red Jet to Southampton I had time to stroll around Cowes High Street in a light drizzle and many memories were rekindled. This was the place I had started my European, no, global racing career. In the summer of 1976, fresh off my first Transatlantic delivery as a skipper, I joined the Australian Frers 53 *Bumble Bee III* for Cowes Week and stayed with her for the Skagen Race in Scandinavia later in the summer, then the Middle Sea Race beginning in Malta. One thing led to another, possibly for no other reason than being a novelty, of an American sailor having let go his anchor, in the UK of the day.

That autumn, in the Fountain Hotel bar over a pint, I was engaged to navigate *King's Legend* in the 1977 Whitbread Race. It was as simple as that – a ten minute conversation. Consequently, I spent part of the winter of 1976/77 in Cowes based at Groves and Guttridge, then the Dickensian shipyard, which is now the upmarket Cowes Yacht Haven.

All those pubs... They were not visited, they were 'used.' And we used them all. The Spencer's Rigging Company, just above the High Street, smelling of hemp and tar, was a gathering point. There was always rigging to do, and it was always best to check on what month it was on their colourful wall calendar(s). The characters who worked there, many who had been around for decades, were known as the Spencer's Boys. And whichever pub was in favour with the Spencer's Boys was the one the rest of us would frequent.

On my walking tour, I saw that The Union had hardly changed. Further on, the Island Sailing Club was remembered as a Sunday lunch favourite. But I could have sworn the Three Crowns was just down the street on the right. Possibly it had eventually collapsed into itself with all those spongy floorboards upstairs, no doubt full of dry rot. I was informed by the lady in the newsagent on the quay that it had burned down 25 years go. They made a superb cottage pie as I recall.

The Pier View, The Anchor Inn, and at the far end past the cop shop, the Duke of York. For some unexplained reason we never used the Vectis Tavern adjacent to the Fountain Hotel. It is hard to believe it might have been 'too rough' even for us, but possibly. Only years later I would venture south of the high street to realize what a rural paradise the rest of the island in fact was – but that is another story.

On the Red Jet quay I sat on a bench, socially distanced, overlooking the hard at the Yacht Haven with the aroma of chips and vinegar in the air. That hadn't changed, but the proliferation of yachts both big and small was impressive. At the same time of year in 1977 the yard was a shadow of what we have today.

My mate Blowie, a rough spoken Aussie of Finnish extraction, and I were living on board *King's Legend*, and for a time she was up on the poppets for a bottom job and other repairs. I couldn't help thinking back to the time... The two lovelies we had met in the Anchor Inn that evening were from Wolverhampton, down to the island for a few days of a winter holiday. The girls were fascinated having met two sailors and after pub closing were invited on board to 'see the yacht'. One thing led to another and they stayed the night.

That morning we woke up to the roar of the travel lift underway and realized we were in for it; the yard in full swing. Sheepishly we helped our guests in their dresses and high heels down the steep rickety wooden ladder, and while the travel lift throttled down for no other reason than the driver to focus on us, the yard workers also appeared out of their workshops to witness the procession of Blowie and me leading them across the hard, down the alleyway and into the High Street.

If this wasn't straight out of a Benny Hill sketch, it was definitely Pythonesque.

The guys in the yard didn't say much about it, but 'a nod's as good as a wink'... And let's remember before too many letters of condemnation are penned to the editor, it was 1977.

Postscript

This column caused some anguish at Yachting World *and initially the editor said she could not run with it – the boatyard story being too risqué. I sat on it and eventually replied that maybe it was time I called it a day at the column if I could not tell a tale as harmless as that. They came back, having come to their senses, and said it would do, but I insisted it had to stand unedited.*

HOW TO CONJURE UP A COLUMN

'A curious skipper's mind works in mysterious ways, and never more so than in extended lockdown'

June 2021

I'm closing in on seven years writing this monthly column. When asked to climb to the masthead of *Yachting World* I thought to myself that this is a good opportunity to grind a few axes, offer up some opinions to wake people up on various issues (not always welcomed) and so forth. In fact, in the beginning I banked up a reserve of column pieces so I could just press the button and dish them out, well before the end of month deadline.

Things then settled down and evolved into a routine whereby I would come to grips with an idea on the deadline and bang it out. There are always plenty of topics around: racing, cruising, big events, types of craft, safety issues, maritime disasters with lessons learned (or not), to foil or not to foil, etcetera. If I was in extremis I could always reminisce about something interesting that happened to me decades ago. 'Write whatever you like,' I was told.

That was when all things were happening. Now we have void spaces everywhere in our bilges. Cancelled events are legion, with speculation on further cancellations, and uncertainty or downright over optimism about others. Cowes Week without a beer tent is sort of like a football match without the fans in the stadium. Other preposterous ideas have been implemented like limiting the number of crew on board certain boats in certain races for social distancing. Cruising boats are still stuck in the Caribbean, some denied an exit and others with no place to go with the hurricane season coming on. Our sailing world has been reduced to webinars, Zoom Meetings, virtual yacht races, tutorials and unending vicarious experiences displayed in rectangular format.

Meanwhile my charter fleet has been more or less stranded, but we have survived as a business. *Pelagic Australis* managed to make ends meet based from Cape Town with special projects, all needing quarantine. *Pelagic* has been on the hard in Maine and will remain so this summer, with nowhere to go in Arctic waters. Canada has closed its borders to recreational craft until February 2022. Greenland is still waffling about how to 'open up.' Our new build, the Pelagic 77 *Vinson of Antarctica*, has been sea-trialling in Holland without me, while I'm stuck in red-listed South Africa. It is not satisfying at all commenting on gear placements and modifications during a fit-out – by WhatsApp. No fun at all!

With this deadline looming I went to bed contemplating a column subject, but with no ideas. Instead I lost myself in Joyce's *Ulysses*, a tome that needs a lockdown in one form or another to take it on. I am always at two minds whether to look up the meaning of all those obscure words (some learned and forgotten) or just let the narrative flow; the latter always recommended. I eventually drifted off in a mild sense of insane pleasure that Joyce always engenders. Bloom was, apropos to me at that point in time, thought streaming about water.

Early next morning I had a dream about a recurring theme that I have promoted often in this column – simplicity of systems on board. It went like this: I was surprised to see that the engine on *Pelagic* was being turned off with the stop button, which controls a solenoid that shifts a lever on the injection pump that cuts off the fuel. A standard configuration on every diesel engine. Years ago, we eliminated this solenoid, which is prone to failure (read: electricity plus salt water plus movement). This can fail at the most inopportune of moments, not when you need to shut down the engine but when you try to restart, as if the solenoid doesn't retract, no fuel goes to the pump – think man-overboard, or some other critical manoeuvre. Instead we eliminated the solenoid and installed a simple push pull cable operated from the pilot house and it never fails. Ditto on *Pelagic Australis*.

The dream ended with me convincing my crew to reinstate the system and I woke up not in cold sweat. It was more dream than nightmare, but with an epiphany on a topic – not so much about diesel engines and simple systems, but rather on how sometimes the weird and wonderful ways of getting to your subject happen in the first place.

ADVENTURES IN THE SUEZ CANAL

'The blocking of the Suez Canal reminds Skip of an eventful transit of his own'

July 2021

When the story broke about the Suez Canal fiasco I was reminded of my transit in May of 1980 and not least of all of how I got there in the first place.

It all started in Fremantle. I was asked by Peter Wright, the owner of the Swan 65 *Independent Endeavour,* a yacht I skippered on the 1979 Parmelia Race (Plymouth to Cape Town to Fremantle), what we should do with the boat as it had to leave Australia to avoid paying VAT. I suggested a charter season in the Med, which he agreed to. The owner was a fascinating chap who, with this partner Lang Hancock, prospected, discovered and developed the Pilbara iron ore fields in Western Australia, which made their fortunes. The federal government had failed to stump up the finance so Peter tapped into Japanese capital, and consequently led the failed secessionist movement for Western Australia. His weekly tabloid, *The Sunday Independent,* was the movement's mouthpiece, and our apparent sponsor for the race.

Logically the Suez Canal was our route north, and Peter, a sprightly septuagenarian, wanted to sail with us at least to the Seychelles. During one balmy starlit night while he and I were on watch, he admitted that the only reason he bought this expensive yacht was for an escape vehicle for his family – when the Chinese invaded Australia, which he was convinced would happen. At the time I thought this pretty far-fetched and didn't know what to say. Fast forward 40 years and how prescient Peter was. Not a land invasion mind you, but certainly an economic one had happened over time and in many places.

Ten glorious days were spent in the Seychelles, precariously moored to a collection of objects both natural and manmade in Victoria's harbour. This was long before the dreadful Eden Island landfill development that changed that paradise for the worst, as all marina developments do. We met and socialized with the local Seychellois and a few young Brits living rough in beach huts having their last hurrahs before disappearing forever into the City of London. Right out of Graham Greene, we often missed the curfew and diverted into so-and-sos for the night, sleeping on their living room floor, as was routine during the time of the attempts of *coup d'etat* against the one-party socialist regime.

On we went around the Horn of Africa giving Socotra a wide berth and had to stop in Djibouti to re-fuel. I remember feeling distinctly uncomfortable with our shiny yacht while all along the perimeter fence of the post-colonial yacht club hundreds of starving refugees were camped out. It was obvious to cruise in this part of the world, if you had the *cojones* to try, would require a wreck of a floating object in an attempt to blend in and possibly survive. And if you lost the whole shebang, so be it.

At the southern entrance of the Red Sea we like to think we were shot at by pirates while going through the Straits of Bab el-Mandeb, but that popping noise could have been the engine backfiring on that fishing boat barely visible in the heat haze. It was a dreadfully long, hot slog going up the Red Sea, in convoy with shipping and never a shoreline visible to break up the monotony.

Our canal agent, the 'Prince of the Red Sea', had his launch at the ready off Port Suez. The launch driver kindly offloaded our six or so plastic bags of rubbish, thank you very much — and then promptly walked to the back of his boat and threw them into the harbour. This was an impressive bit of recycling in 1980.

With my briefcase full of *greenbacks,* I took a nerve-wracking ride on the back of a scooter to downtown Port Suez and was ushered into the Prince's HQ. Sharing his hubbly bubbly pipe, we exchanged niceties, then got down to negotiating his fees, which of course were somewhat more than published, for all sorts of reasons. He then related the story of a British sailing couple who refused to pay and had been in Port Suez for three months. I gladly shelled out what he asked for. Our pilot was arranged to be on board first thing in the morning.

I have forgotten the pilot's name but not his face. Promising us to guard the boat while we spent the night tied to a barge in Ismailia, I found him fast asleep by 2300 on our saloon floor. All along the canal passage he politely asked for 'presents', which we dished out, i.e. lengths of old rope, which are always useful, a pot from the stove he had his eye on and even some paint we had for his house, which no doubt needed a lick of. As we neared Port Said the requests became demands and the last straw was when he 'had to have' my rigging knife (not yet lost as a sentimental object). I objected strongly. Luckily his launch came alongside in the nick of time – and I argued him into it with shouting and waving of arms on both sides. He fell backwards in his bilge and as his launch pulled away I put our hammer down and the last thing he shouted was, 'I will keel you!!!' Shortly after we were thankfully flushed out into the relative sanity of the eastern Mediterranean, on our way to Monaco, no less.

PELAGIC AUSTRALIS SOLD TO GREENPEACE

'It's the end of an era, as Skip hands over the keys to Pelagic Australis'

August 2021

You read that right. On 17th May 2021 *Pelagic Australis* was handed over to Greenpeace International in Cape Town and is currently on her way to the Netherlands with skipper Chris, mate Sophie and a Greenpeace crew of three. The send-off was a carnival affair for the seller (second happiest day of a boat owner's life) and the buyer (the first...) complete with Zulu dancers cavorting on the foredeck laid on by Greenpeace South Africa. This was a one-on-one transaction with no brokers involved. DIY, just the way I like things.

Greenpeace seldom divulges specific campaign plans going forward but we can say she will be undergoing a refit in the Netherlands, making 'green-tech' modifications and running a competition for a new name. Then she goes into campaign service. So, remember the shape and configuration of *Pelagic Australis* as a likeness may suddenly appear on the horizon or maybe the AIS (or not!). Rest assured she will no doubt pop up in the media at some point soon, decorated in her rainbow colours.

This was of course a major decision, but not a difficult one. The negotiation began over six months ago while I was desperately conjuring up a southern charter season based from Cape Town. When Greenpeace contacted me and said they needed a small vessel with a lifting keel and rudder for 'close quarter campaigning', I had an epiphany. I had no intention of selling *Pelagic Australis*, not least of all as I had a full book of clients from our normal season with nowhere to go that I was in the process of rolling over to 2021/22. This was a dilemma to be solved. But given my age, the vessel's age, and not least of all the ongoing Covid story where uncertainty continues through 2021 and on into 2022, it was the right thing to do, certainly from a financial perspective. In other words, 'the hand writing was firmly visible on the bulkhead.'

After 20 years filled with memories and the casts of characters we have hosted, the timing was right to pass her on to begin a new chapter – and what better home than Greenpeace for this venerable expedition vessel. Many people have asked, 'Was this difficult emotionally to part with *Pelagic Australis*?' And, 'Aren't you sentimentally attached?' You might make a case in this regard for the original *Pelagic,* which launched a dream way back in 1987 and awaits me on the hard in Maine for future Arctic adventures. But for *Pelagic Australis*, not at all. She is metal, wood and fibre (mostly metal). The memories I have well filed. To steal a phrase, she was, for me, a 'taxi to the snowline.'

The good news, though, is I have almost seamlessly gone from one situation to another (the story of my life, various friends remind me). I have just re-joined, after a six month hiatus, the new Tony Castro designed Pelagic 77, *Vinson of Antarctica*. She arrived in my old 'home port' of the Hamble on 15th May. I had not seen her since October 2020 on my last visit to KM Yachts in Holland before retreating to family in Cape Town for another lockdown. In the interim I've have been working on the fit-out and sea trials with KM and our sailing crew on WhatsApp and Zoom – frustrating? For sure. We already have a long list of minor modifications for when she returns to KM Yachts in September, but nothing substantial so far. Safe to say, though, 90% of those could have been dealt with had I been on-site as was planned. In any event she is up and running awaiting her first big gale and a taste of ice which will tell the tale if she is really fit for purpose.

By the time this column piece goes to print we should be in Svalbard on a month long science charter with a German university group of geologists. After a visit to the shipyard in September for warranty and modifications she sails south to Port Stanley for a science charter to South Georgia and the Antarctic Peninsula.

Vinson of Antarctica is a collaboration with my Chilean colleague Nicolas Ibanez and will, to a great extent, take up where *Pelagic Australis* left off. Our charter focus will be more weighted to science, film and educational projects of high value, but we will also be accommodating, when possible, our usual guests wishing to visit places of high latitudes. The fact is professional projects can still jump through hoops and climb ladders, accepting quarantines and spending inordinate amounts of time in the planning with Covid mitigation measures, risk assessments and more just to get their jobs done. For our 'tourist' visitors travel in this fashion is not practical or even possible going forward in the immediate future.

This Covid story ain't over yet.

Postscript

Pelagic Australis *was renamed* Witness *on her launch in the Netherlands after a refit and modifications. She did a campaign in the summer of 2022 against further oil exploration and extraction in the eastern Mediterranean then moved on to the same issues along the Argentine coast in 2023. The abuses of salmon fishing in Chile and climate change ramifications in the Pacific basin are also on their agenda of non-violent direct action campaigns.*

MAKING A DEAL IN THE RITZ

'The expedition charter business has changed over the years, as Skip recalls how deals used to be done'

April 2022

In January 2022 my daughter and I were bussing it on the upper deck along Piccadilly and as we slid by the Ritz Hotel, my memory twigged. There was enough time on the way to Victoria Station to tell her a story, an old favourite, of how I got one of my most interesting charters on *Pelagic* back in 1993. A sort of 'back in the day' tale, noting my current 25 pages of contractual gobbledygook to keep me and my charter clients happy.

At a drinks party in the New Forest I was introduced to a foreign gentleman in his mid to late 60s who was an avid yachtsman. When the conversation came around to the fact I had a 54-foot expedition yacht based in Southern South America, he immediately asked if I could sail him and his friends around Cape Horn and up the west coast to Puerto Montt in Chile. I guess he assumed that the company I was keeping (if truth be known this was via my then girlfriend's company) was enough due diligence on this part.

This was in October and he, a busy man, had to do this trip the following March, which was the end of our Antarctic season. While munching on a canape I explained that a group of scientists had an option on *Pelagic* for that month. He said, 'Come have lunch with me at the Ritz next week and we can talk about it. I stay at the Ritz when in the UK.' It was more of an instruction rather than a request, so I agreed. As the saying goes, 'When you can get a free meal, take it.'

I turned up on the day, unknowing that a jacket and tie was required, so I was ushered into the cloak room to suffer the embarrassment of having to don a jacket too short in the sleeves and put on a well-worn, food-stained tie, dished out by the concierge who was smirking, not smiling. My host was waiting for me at table and we settled into an animated conversation that had nothing to do with sailing.

The sommelier arrived, a diminutive man in tails who was on a first name basis with my host. Both gesticulating with the wine list they settled on a bottle of, let's say for sake of the discussion, a Bâtard-Montrachet for our salmon starter. I was made aware, somehow, that was £200 a bottle. And the red for the main course? The sommelier tried his luck with an £800 bottle, but the gentleman took a pull, exclaiming that was ridiculous, saying, 'Who would pay £800 for a bottle of wine?' They compromised on a £600 bottle of Château Haut-Brion '66 (also a supposition).

As we worked our way through lunch, knowing my excuses about prior options were well and truly drowned, the general charter plan was outlined. He would meet us with four friends in Puerto Williams. We would sail around Cape Horn and then take three weeks to go north through the inside of the archipelago to Puerto Montt, all in about 1,000nm.

Fast forward to March and on the date, they arrived by private plane, laden with the wine supply and a case of Laphroaig whisky. Plus, the host brought on board a sizable box of books, which one by one he devoured during the trip. This was prescient, as although it was a fascinating cruise through that complicated archipelago with a stunning anchorage every night, it was a motor sailing slog against wind and rain most of the time. My girlfriend Julia and I were up at 0600 in pre-dawn darkness to cast off the shore lines and up anchor, always joined by the ex-Chilean admiral, who was to become my friend and fixer for all problems in Chile going forward for many years. We usually tied up just on dark...

The highlight of this voyage was listening to these old friends having lengthy discussions about a variety of topics; economics, global politics and history. I put my foot in the discussion a few times and was corrected with inarguable facts and reasons – a sort of awkward reality check on my admittedly none-too-brilliant education.

Back up to the Ritz. When lunch was winding down, and we were enjoying the Armagnac, my new friend having paid the bill, started fishing around in his jacket pockets and pulled out an envelope with $10,000 and laid it on the table. 'Can we make a deal?' he said. I thought of my scientists with that option... for only two seconds, and replied, 'OK, deal.' And we shook on it.

I slipped the envelope into my pocket, not bothering to count the money at the table – you just don't do that type of thing at the Ritz.

Postscript

Accepting cash for charters in those days (see page 267) was very common and well appreciated as the black market in Argentina, being well established, was the only way to do business. The store that sold toys and fluffy stuffed animals in town was one of the many 'currency exchanges.'

When I look at the old charter agreements I was using back then I have to laugh. We actually had a thing called a 'Herring Clause', which was a Bill Tilman classic; 'every herring should hang by his own tail' was the quote and it was our waiver. Of course, this was a joke of sorts and many clients never bothered to ask exactly what it meant, but signed the document anyway. They certainly wouldn't do that today.

THE EPIPHANY OF NOT HAVING A CAMERA

'Being in the moment in the Antarctic – rather than trying to capture it on camera – proved a rare treat'

May 2022

Last December we were burgled in Cape Town, something everyone who lives in South Africa goes through at some point. My camera gear was passed out the window, among other essentials. I never got around to replacing the cameras for our Antarctic charter with a film crew on the *Vinson of Antarctica* that took place in February.

Nowadays, with the competition between the streaming services, wildlife production companies were down south in force and Port Stanley in the Falklands is now known as 'Little Bristol', a legacy from the BBC days of David Attenborough. When you work for one of these companies everyone has to sign Non-Disclosure Agreements (NDAs) so I can't tell you what we were filming and for whom. So happy snaps were not to be encouraged and a mis-click of the shutter can get you into hot water later. Plus, I thought to myself, after all these years of photographing everything that moves – wildlife a given, icebergs included, and every vista of Antarctic scenery, both in the days of slide transparencies and then in digital – let's do an experiment and just look at all these attractions without a lens in the way.

Granted, I had been there, done that, closing in on 35 years in the high latitude expedition game, so all was 'in the can.' During various Covid quarantines I had whittled down my filing cabinet of transparencies to digitize, that content, now relegated to hard drives and in the cloud, hoping that all of it doesn't evaporate one day back into the upper atmosphere.

Well, being in Antarctica without a camera was an epiphany. Although I had spent enormous amounts of time over the years photographing penguins and seals, I also did spend time just watching them – as they don't run away. Not so with whales, dolphins and birds on the wing. We all know what it's like when someone shouts 'Whale!' Chaos ensues as people fight to get out of the companionway, getting stuck two at a time like something out of a Benny Hill sketch. Cameras are flying around loose from necks and everyone rushing up to the bow tripping over running rigging, then back to the stern, then the port side, then the starboard, as these clever leviathans continually seem to outsmart us, loving to play this game of hide and seek. The problem is the lens is always in the way of the action.

We had humpbacks alongside on several occasions and without the pre-occupation of the camera I noticed things I had never seen before. Things I could really focus on like details of scratches and scars on dorsal fins, the number and size of barnacles on flippers and tail fins and having the time to go eyeball to eyeball as they spy-hopped right up to the top of the lifelines. Also savouring the fishy smell of a whale's breath (not everyone's cup of tea) rather than agonizing over the oil on the lens that ensues.

And, no matter how many times you have been in ice-covered waters you can never be tired of seeing icebergs. Although the temptation is to shoot every novel shape and texture, without a camera I was more enthralled and contemplative instead of just recording. Ice avalanches, calving icefronts and bergs capsizing are also things to capture if you are quick enough on the shutter, but by the time you hear the cannon fire and then grab the camera, focus and shoot, most of the high drama is over. What joy just to watch!

Recording a life at sea, by whatever means, is a given, but I am fascinated in the proliferation of videos and blog posts from cruisers, which by my observation and discussion with others (and not by my volition!) has become almost addictive to a large part of the cruising public; an addiction akin to other forums of online material. These clips in the public domain, the most popular made by cruising couples, range from the evocative to the mundane, from the instructive to the frivolous; revenue is generated by advertising algorithms. What a clever way for people to finance a world cruise!

Formerly, people who were not self-financed got a sewing machine and fixed other cruiser's sails and boat covers along the way, or if you have a mechanical bent, engines, electrics and plumbing on other boats always needed mending to earn a crust. You might even have to graft ashore for months to make the boodle to carry on. It seems with the advent of communications on board, and internet in every gunkhole, this classic wandering with little structure is rapidly going by the board in lieu of recording and posting your every adventure on a regular basis and not far off real time.

And here is the rub for me, and it might not be realized by the followers of these influencers. These folks are doing a job, not a cruise in the sense we might think. I can imagine and sympathize with them. Consider the time taken by the more professionally minded to decide on a topic, film the sequences, make the edit and rush to get to an internet connection in time for the weekly feed. Cruising? The hell you say!

And now, I must get back on Amazon for that new set of camera equipment I need to buy.

Postscript

This phenomenon of what I call 'sailing porn' creates the addiction. The best example I have seen is from one of the more successful couples. An instructional video they shot was how to fillet a lionfish, which no doubt is difficult. The camera focuses low down on the table and the girl is in a scant bikini bottom, just off to the side of the table, her position clearly stage-managed. As she explains how to fillet the lionfish, you dart back to the bikini bottom, then remember the lionfish, but in no time you are back to the bikini bottom. At the end of the clip you have no clue whatsoever about how to fillet a lionfish...

THE FAZISI STORY AND ITS RELEVANCE TODAY

'Current events lead to reflection on Soviet Russia's famous *Fazisi* project'

August 2022

I would be remiss, given the current conflict in the Ukraine, not to re-tell in the nutshell of this column a few anecdotes of my experience skippering *Fazisi* in the 1989/90 Whitbread Race.

When people bring up the story in conversation they more often than not will start out with something like, 'How was it with the Russians?' Lest we forget, this project started out pre-Perestroika and was truly a Soviet affair both in organization and in the composition of the crew. In the team we had Russians, Ukrainians, Georgians, a Moldavian and a Latvian. One of the Russians was from the Far East and looked Asian, so was considered yet another nationality thrown into the mix. Although Russians and Ukrainians for the most part dominated the team, the chairman of the project was Georgian, the designer was Russian, and the skipper elect was Ukrainian. When I joined the team properly in Poti in Georgia where the hull was built, the mood was collegiate and Soviet.

I knew enough history and current affairs to see how this could all work. The Soviet Union was at that point still cohesive but on the edge of disintegration. The project had no financial backing from the State, but neither did the State stand in their way of raising sponsorship money (some from very obscure origins) in hope of competing in an international event without some form of Soviet 'supervision' (read: no commissar along for the ride). Perhaps the Soviet system was at that point tired of control freakery, or some footlights were beginning to show through the Iron Curtain before the first act of Glasnost.

Everyone in the team knew the deal. Whatever differences of opinion there were on nationality issues, they had to get along for everyone's benefit. But it was clear the common tongue was Russian. On a personal level there was a lot at stake. Passports were finally issued to the crew as we waited at Sheremetyevo Airport with *Fazisi* in the belly of the Antonov 124 aircraft, scheduled to fly to London. This was the crew's ticket out of the Soviet system, probably for good, and they knew it.

During our eight months of getting *Fazisi* around the world, with all its dramas including the suicide of the Ukrainian co-skipper after Leg 1 in Uruguay and the ever-present threat of having to throw in the towel due to lack of campaign funds, I could honestly say that national politics and identities were never that much of an issue. Arguments on deck were a feature, some light-hearted, others not so, and seldom were they explained to this non-Russian speaker. Only one incidence of physical violence occurred, a Georgian knocked the Moldavian to the bottom of the cockpit, but that luckily turned out to be over a woman in the last port.

On a darker note, when the Russian cook told me in confidence what word he used to describe the Georgians (it began with N, and I'll leave the rest to your imagination), I realized that this kind of racism was boiling under the surface. On a lesser note, almost everywhere we went the media pronounced that 'The Russians are coming!' (in Australia, New Zealand, Uruguay and Florida), not having done their homework and leaving the non-Russians in the crew out of the party. But in fairness, by the time we were halfway around, the Soviet Union did not exist. So how to describe this crew other than Russian? It turned out to be as confusing for the public and press as it was for the crew. We had three communist party members when we started, and they had no party to return to.

With many changes along the way, only a small core of the crew finished the race, and with a few exceptions most did not return to their homes, sadly having left their wives and families to stay in the West. Tough decisions, but in their eyes an obvious one. Even more tragic was that two more crew, one a Russian, another a Georgian, took their own lives within a few years of the finish.

I believe most of the Russian *Fazisi* crew that went global, and without exception became successful, probably would not be recognized as Russians today. They would be under the radar for current events back home. I hope they are never obliged to explain or defend themselves for being Russian.

Fast forward to my visit to my Russian agent in Moscow in 2014, shortly after Russia invaded the Crimea. My previous experience of this great city was as its empty shell in 1989 and it was now unrecognizable in its Western-style renovation. We had been hosting many Russian charter clients through the 90s and the 2000s on my *Pelagics* in the far south. So much so, we were developing a Russian-language version of our website and document set. While there I was hosted in a former client's dacha outside Moscow and one evening invited to a dinner with her friends in the city – all young professionals living what appeared to be a very pro-Western, affluent lifestyle.

During the dinner I put my foot in it big time by commenting on the dreadful state of affairs in Crimea – and was left in no uncertain terms where they stood, firmly behind the invasion, firmly behind Putin. If the current news is anything to go by, it sounds all too familiar.

SEARCHING THE FAR NORTH FOR SOLITUDE

'True high-latitude wilderness is becoming increasing difficult to find... unless you know where to go'

October 2022

Rather than pontificating about another aspect of maritime minutiae (think: split pins) or rehashing anecdotes of decades ago, I actually went sailing recently. I just signed off *Pelagic* at Iqaluit, Baffin Island, after a delightful three week friends' cruise that began in Ilulissat, Greenland, in mid-July.

One of my original partners in the *Pelagic* project, Chuck Gates, my oldest sailing friend from Chicago going back 60 years (OK, there is some background to rehash here) collaborated in getting the boat up and running after two years on the hard in Maine during the Covid crisis. While I was tending to *Vinson of Antarctica* (my day job) in Cape Town, starting the three month annual down time and service from our southern theatre, Chuck and Tor, a young South African, relaunched and prepped the *Pelagic* for an Arctic summer so he and friends could sail up to Greenland. This is an accolade to a partnership that worked in 1986 and lives on. Most boat partnerships do not.

Pelagic has been the tool for high latitude passions (and some obsessions) for 36 years. I like to describe her as a boat with a history. Every dent, abrasion and ad hoc modification has a back story, all within the fabric of this homebuilt 54 footer. Yes, folks, I am planning to write the book one day... Having said all this, I must pay homage to Jerome Poncet (*Damien, Damien II, Golden Fleece*) who celebrated 50 years in the south this year. We who came after Jerome always say we are beginners, still. He was the inspiration. He is still the guru.

Sorry, one more anecdote needs telling. When *Pelagic* was on her first Antarctic expedition in 1988, I was so enamoured with the region I vowed never to return up north. While incarcerated during a prolonged storm on the Peninsula, as a statement of intent, I cut up all of our Admiralty charts from Europe and hand stitched them into a book (wooden binding, Treadmaster cover) with the flip side pages for the entries – a guestbook cum diary. The only rules for contributions were no narrative of thanks allowed; only original prose, poetry, ballads and artwork. It is a coveted record of the many insanities we perpetrated and risks we took at least by today's standards of due diligence and safety. Eating the wildlife, now protected by law, was one of them.

Changing from south to north with *Pelagic* recently was only for the simple reason that I need to go there to cover some new ground and gain some space. Read on. During my three weeks after we sailed north from Disco Bay having waved goodbye to the few yachts in the harbour, we did not see another yacht nor a cruise ship, nor even a fishing boat for that matter until we arrived in the upper reaches of Frobisher Bay, Baffin. It was a revelation.

There is a conclusion to be drawn here. With my hand on my heart I cannot now deliver a truly Antarctic experience for my charter guests, as we knew it, due to the incredible proliferation of expedition tour ships on the Peninsula, to some extent also on South Georgia. It has turned into a different world, not a wilderness, but a managed park. The number of tourist visitors projected this coming season are staggering and certainly depressing. Sadly, this same crush of 'visitors' has also arrived in Svalbard. It seems, though, you can still lose yourself to a great extent on the Greenland coasts and in the Arctic Canada environs.

We had a spectacular sail north to Upernavik under poled out yankee and reefed main, threading our way through the bergs. Upernavik was our ultima Thule at 73 degrees north. For those of us always seeking some originality this Greenland community was a great place to stop – no wifi, no café, not even a postcard to send. I felt incredibly relieved of all responsibility to 'stay in touch' and this was 'enhanced' by our antiquated Iridium system which was so slow to connect we didn't bother to communicate. After three days cruising in the archipelago there we headed back south.

Completing our loop along and into the Baffin Bay ice edge south to Frobisher Bay was a long haul and challenging in mainly fog bound conditions, but we managed some great sailing in the 1/10th pack ice.

A polar bear with a cub was spotted on a floeberg 80 miles offshore. This would be a long swim for a cub. I would say their only hope was for an east wind to compressed the pack so they could walk off on to the shore. A pod of orcas stayed with us on another day. Compared to the south, the wildlife up north is few and far between. And so are other ships and people.

In Iqaluit, provincial capital of Nunavut, *Pelagic* was dried out on the 12m tide in the inner boat harbour and I flew out while Chris and Tor started to prep the boat for a British/American climbing expedition to the big walls at the mouth of the bay.

It was very satisfying being back on board this little steel boat, realizing once again how capable *Pelagic* is in this polar environment. Another example of less is more.

Postscript

In the 2023 season we returned to the Arctic and sailed with friends from Maine to Cape Farvel, the southern tip of Greenland, and cruised the entire length of west Greenland to just below 78 degrees north. Then we continued across to Baffin Island and down to St Johns. In two and a half months in the field we saw only a handful of yachts.

For high latitude sailing there are fundamental differences between the Arctic waters and the far south which includes South Georgia. The former has enormous geographic scope, meaning many miles between points of interest; less traffic (so far) and more problems with ice navigation generally. In the southern context it is now terribly crowded with ships and yachts, but still, the amount of wildlife on tap is more than prolific. In the far north it is very slim pickings and you have to be lucky to see many of the celebrated big animals. Furthermore, cruising in the north is a cultural experience with indigenous peoples; in the south you only come across transient folk on science stations.

NAUTICAL GENDER GYMNASTIC SEMANTICS

'Delving into nautical linguistics – why yachts will always be "she", and "man overboard" can't be meddled with'

November 2022

I enjoy skating on thin ice. Editor Helen's opener in the September 2022 issue of *Yachting World* raised the topic of gender sensitive nautical terminology, which to some might be ripe for discussion. In fact, it has already generated plenty of feedback. Here is how I started out thinking about it. I always consider first principles if at all possible. The word 'man' in many contexts, at least for me, doesn't mean a male but rather the species – the one that walks on two legs, wears clothing and is a sentient being, willing to readily engage in measured, civilized arguments. And here it seems we have one that looks to be a long running-debate.

My premise was that when Darwin wrote *The Descent of Man* I don't think, even in Victorian times, he was referring to only the male of the species. *Rights of Man* by Thomas Paine is another example that immediately came to mind, although Joyce's *Portrait of an Artist as a Young Man*, and most other titles in the 'Best 100 Books with Man in the Title' on the web do sink this theory upon close inspection. That is how a conversation began with my 20-year-old daughter, fresh out of her Day Skipper's Practical course in the Solent. She then proceeded to tie me up in a macrame of historical facts and logic – a metaphorical *Ashley Book of Knots*. I admit I was blown out of the water and a full retraction of the first premise should be noted by all readers.

It is true, though, that 'man' found its way into the nautical lexicon because the male of the species did the sailing, right back to the time of Ulysses. If we can accept that 'man' now in modern and enlightened times is gender neutral at least in this nautical context it solves the problem, if in fact there is one.

Having said all this, I admit it might be useful to distinguish a 'yachtsman' from a 'yachtswoman' in some, but not necessarily in all, circumstances and certainly not by those females who do not want to be considered anything other than just sailors or crew. The all-encompassing solution of 'yachtsperson' sounds awkward to my ear and just does not cut it. But any distinction between male and female should end there when actually on board lest we engage in verbal gymnastics that can actually impact safety, if not operational issues.

The most obvious one is indeed the man-overboard scenario. I can't see how that one can be squared and changed. It is an international standard. And how would you change 'manning?' Not sure. Let's imagine some attempts at a change of phrase: 'We need more "person power", Jane or Tom, give us a hand!', 'Tell the bow person to come aft!', 'We need to get a body aloft to sort out that jammed halyard!' Question is can we really get around to achieving this fundamental change of semantics and the variations of same that will come to the fore, superseding a system that is well-entrenched and must have some traditional value if you believe in tradition at all. If we have to have a change, what will it look like? Who will decide this? It can't be left to an evolution; rather it has to be standardized as it is now and fit for purpose. There cannot be a bow person, a bow body or just a bow as a possible menu of choice. Even my daughter has admitted that it is just not worth the effort to change any of the terms. More to the point what matters are the social dynamics on board between all of us, of all genders.

And now it is time to take one more step off the ice edge possibly into open water. If man has historically done the sailing that has landed us in this lexicon, what about the women? Well, historically they are the object of our male desires, at least for this old sailor, and that is why ships, yachts and just about any floating thing that can move in a steady direction is referred to in the feminine – motor or sail. Of course, history is history and women are now certainly in the mainstream of all things in yachting and no one would gainsay that.

This issue is simply one of semantics that is easy on the ear. To wit 'She has fine classic lines', 'She sails well off the wind', 'She was flying along!', 'We drove her under with the Code Zero!', 'She's the most powerful tug on the Mississippi', 'We love *Pelagic*, we just love her!' OK, I can think of some examples less flattering but let's not go there.

Can this kind of description evolve into the gender neutral, destroying what can only be described as, more often than not, complimentary, if not thought provoking? For all of the examples above, 'they' would not work. And 'it' would just not sound right, nor inspiring as a beautiful yacht should be. The impersonal pronoun 'it' might even be an insult to the vessel itself.

Postscript

Unexpectedly, this column did not generate a flood of letters to the editor, or at least none were published. Possibly I made sense out of the issue and we might realize there was no problem at all, so why invent one? Or possibly the proponents of this discussion have stowed it all in the 'too difficult box', for now.

However, another old shipmate (and ex Pelagic partner) was contacted by a female superyacht captain absolutely livid with the article. Through simple association with me, she gave him 'what for,' when he tried to stand by me. The conclusion is that I might have to be ready for a good all-out argument still, down the line. Stand by this article? I certainly will.

A FILM ABOUT THE 1983 AMERICA'S CUP

'Having watched a behind-the-scenes look at the Australian victory in the 1983 America's Cup, could the latest chapter possibly rival it?'

January 2023

Flicking through the Netflix menu I came across *The Race of the Century*, the story of the Australian victory in the 1983 America's Cup. For me this was a must watch, not necessarily because it was about sailing, but rather it was a film about the boats and the era I could immediately relate to – yachting back in the day on the east coast of America.

I never participated in the America's Cup as in those days American racing sailors at top level international competitions were divided into one of three disciplines – the America's Cup, Olympic/Championship classes and the Whitbread Around the World Race, and in 1983 there were only a handful of Americans who had ever done the latter. There was some crossover between dinghy champs who were past the gymnastic stage taking the helm and doing the tactics of the Cup boats, but that was about it. Today, the professional sailors are seamless between all three. They step off a circumnavigation and start another Olympic campaign with no holiday in between, while negotiating their contracts for the next America's Cup.

Historically, that 1983 win of *Australia II* skippered by John Bertrand against the incumbent New York Yacht Club's *Liberty*, skippered by Dennis Conner, was a game changer as it broke the 132-year deadlock that was considered to be unassailable due to the financial might and influence of the New York Yacht Club.

In the film, I immediately recognized the faces of the Australian crew. I had met most of them before or after that event. In fact, Skip Lissiman, the port trimmer on *Australia II* who is interviewed in the film, crewed for me on *Independent Endeavour* in the 1979 Parmelia Race from Plymouth, with a stop in Cape Town and down to his hometown of Fremantle. He was 22 at the time. He, John Longley, Grant Simmer, John Bertrand and others recounted in interview how the Aussies were winging things with Alan Bond's cheque book, and of course Ben Lexcen's winged keel was the key, which when revealed upset the men in straw hats from the New York Yacht Club to no end. They contested it legally and luckily for the sport, lost. This was a classic underdog story.

The sailing footage was fascinating and a nail-biter right up to the final deciding race. Of course, it is unimaginable today for an inshore yacht race, now commercially dependent on spectators and TV slots, to have an event where there is a five hour time limit to finish, dependent on something so fickle as the wind. Nevertheless, if you were on the water or watching what TV coverage there was and knew something about the sport, watching 'grass grow', as it's been described at times, was not a problem. In the film, the manoeuvres were riveting, with tacking duels and all kinds of activity on deck: sheets flailing around, gybing spinnakers, then massive wind shifts and gear failures – all sorts of variables that kept me on the edge of my couch.

A large part of this documentary dipped into the archive coverage of previous Cups and I recognized faces in the melee along the docks and marching up and down Newport's Thames Street. There was the mouthpiece of American sailing Gary Jobson, tactician for Ted Turner on *Courageous* in the 1977 Cup, who would sail with me twice on *Pelagic* in the 90s making ESPN specials. I knew Ted Turner. In fact, after an Annapolis Newport Race during a food fight in a restaurant between the *Aura* crew and Ted's rogues on *Tenacious* I managed to plant a bread roll in his face. He answered with more fire, as he was that kind of guy. We were a bunch of amateur sailors back then, and so was Ted Turner.

When yacht racing began to cater for a non-sailing audience this signalled the end of the era with its complications, intricacies, subtleties and challenges understood only by the cognoscenti, which were few, like me. Attenuated attention spans in general also work for the current iteration of the Cup that is now essentially a 'drag race' that can even be appreciated by gearheads in American. On these incredibly exciting foiling monohulls we are now down to 20-minute heats with only two

SKIP NOVAK ON SAILING

key celebrity players on board. The grunt that goes in to power these flying machines of today is by a bank of faceless athletes, slaves to their emperors in the cockpit. Indeed, everyone is unrecognizable with helmets, body armour and headset microphones in the way.

I now understand that big money is going in to produce a documentary series on the next America's Cup due to take place in Barcelona in October of 2024. A collaboration of the directors of the Oscar-winning film *Free Solo* and David Ellison's production company promise an 'all access, behind-the-scenes' extravaganza of both on and off the water action and no doubt intrigue. I wonder, though, knowing how tight-lipped the teams now are, how much security they work under and how strict crew and staff contracts will be, just what exactly will be revealed. Will we get to know the human side of these teams, or only their avatars, pre-programmed?

Needless to say I prefer the old movies on Netflix, not the modern blockbusters. And, in this proposed documentary series for 2024, I suspect we won't see any food fights between the teams in Barcelona restaurants.

STEPPING ASIDE AND FAREWELL

'When things run their natural course it's eventually time to let someone else take the helm'

Skip's final column, February 2023

I have reached 100, folks. Not in age, as that is still three decades away, but 100 columns written for this esteemed organ, *Yachting World*. Leading up to this magical, purely arbitrary number I had a think and decided this might be a good time to quiver my pen.

When the editor asked me to take over the column from Robin Knox-Johnston for the October 2014 issue, I readily agreed. Not only do I enjoy writing down my thoughts, but I had some axes to grind, scores to settle from previous civilized discussions, points to make with particular orthodoxies in the marine industry, and observations about some worrying trends in boating in general. What a great soapbox to climb up on to!

The editor said I could write whatever I like, including looking back anecdotally to yacht races, cruises and adventures that in my case go back a staggering 50 years plus, right to my roots in Belmont Harbour on the Chicago lakefront. I certainly have had a few stories to tell, and I told many in this column, but many of the more risqué ones are left untold with deference to some of our sensitive readers. I took the low hanging fruit first on controversial topics as diverse as an over pre-occupation with safety, rescues at sea and why they were not necessary in the first place, how to learn how to sail (start in a Laser), automation on marine systems and navigation systems in particular and the resulting loss of first principles. You get the idea.

Never seen in print, but I know for sure that it happens in conversations, I have been accused of Luddism, retro thinking and looking back in time too often, but I was always secure in the knowledge that unless one pushes back every now and again on the relentless march of progress in technologies that breed conveniences, there is a downside, not least of all loss of simple pleasures.

I have always made a point to be thought-provoking, have tried to be balanced in my narrative, at times ironic, and with a sense of humour.

After all, yachting is a pastime that should be enjoyed so the idea is not to take oneself too seriously for fear of really going overboard, with or without wearing a lifejacket.

As the years went on, though, I had to be careful in not repeating myself, but I do admit to writing three articles, more or less along the same lines about the proliferation of abandonments of yachts for no apparent reason other than discomfort. And, there is no doubt over time you begin to struggle for ideas and this pressure makes your enthusiasm wane. It's similar in mustering the will when getting up for that 0400 watch in a gale on a yacht with a flush deck.

This column can be considered a big ask if done well – it needs to comment on yacht racing in all its forms, on cruising both local and worldwide as well as dipping into the extremes of expedition sailing that is trending. If the truth be known it is decades since I did my last ocean race and I feel out of touch with the flying machines of today other than as an armchair onlooker, foiling vicariously. And the cruising genre is more than well covered by the surfeit of YouTubers that deal in instruction, provide cookbook travel logs or go online just for fun. They could teach this old cruiser plenty.

That leaves me with my expertise, passion and profession of expedition sailing and it must be admitted that habitually sailing in freezing cold with snow on deck and ice in the rigging is not everyone's cup of tea, all of the time. In this regard, you will hear from me about my *Pelagic* adventures from time to time in the features section, rest assured.

So, it is time, friends, to turn this over to hopefully a much younger person, possibly of a different gender, of which there are today many, and someone with more 'skin in the game.' I wish them luck.

This column began over eight years ago with a look back to some shenanigans on the Hamble River, my spiritual home since I came to this country of warm beer and baths rather than showers way back in 1976. I loved it all.

This column ends as I stand on the public jetty of that same river, that artery that leads to the Solent – the heart of all things yachting in this country, if not the world. Now it's time to stroll up to the King and Queen for a pint of heavy. Cheers!

EPILOGUE

I am very aware that many consider me a sea-going dinosaur of sorts. 'He is retro,' they will say, 'working with old solutions, although tried and tested, where modern ones would make his life easier.' True, but it is an exaggeration for anyone to think, in spite of my somewhat inexhaustible supply of yarns of yesteryear, that I am living in the past (but yes, we did enjoy ourselves back then!), because I continually have new projects planned for at least the next two years, always looking forward, strapped to the mast, totally ignoring the siren's song to call it a day and put my feet up in between gigs on a lecture tour about past accomplishments, as many 'adventurists' often do. For me, never! Some friends often ask, when will you stop? Answer: at the bitter end of what has been a long rope.

While aboard *Vinson of Antarctica* on a wandering albatross survey for the South Georgia government in January 2024, I read for the first time *The Odyssey*, and then followed that reading Adam Nicolson's magisterial book *The Mighty Dead – Why Homer Matters*, for the second time to better understand what Homer was all about. And here is the metaphor clearly explained by Nicolson in Chapter One:

'To live well in the world, nostalgia must be resisted: you must stay with your ship, stay tied to the present, remain mobile, keep adjusting the rig, work with the swells, watch for a wind-shift, watch as the boom swings over, engage, in other words, with the muddle and duplicity and difficulty of life. Don't be tempted into the lovely simplicities that the heroic past seems to offer.'

Coal Harbour
South Georgia
January 2024